The Structural Determinants of Unemployment

VULNERABILITY AND POWER IN MARKET RELATIONS

QUANTITATIVE STUDIES IN SOCIAL RELATIONS

Consulting Editor: Peter H. Rossi

UNIVERSITY OF MASSACHUSETTS
AMHERST, MASSACHUSETTS

In Preparation

Peter H. Rossi, James D. Wright, and Andy B. Anderson (Eds.), HAND-BOOK OF SURVEY RESEARCH
Toby L. Parcel and Charles W. Mueller, ASCRIPTION AND LABOR MARKETS: *Race and Sex Differences in Earnings*

Published

Paul G. Schervish, THE STRUCTURAL DETERMINANTS OF UNEM-PLOYMENT: *Vulnerability and Power in Market Relations*
Irving Tallman, Ramona Marotz-Baden, and Pablo Pindas, ADOLESCENT SOCIALIZATION IN CROSS-CULTURAL PERSPECTIVE: *Planning for Social Change*
Robert F. Boruch and Joe S. Cecil (Eds.), SOLUTIONS TO ETHICAL AND LEGAL PROBLEMS IN SOCIAL RESEARCH
J. Ronald Milavsky, Ronald C. Kessler, Horst H. Stipp, and William S. Rubens, TELEVISION AND AGGRESSION: *A Panel Study*
Ronald S. Burt, TOWARD A STRUCTURAL THEORY OF ACTION: *Network Models of Social Structure, Perception, and Action*
Peter H. Rossi, James D. Wright, and Eleanor Weber-Burdin, NATURAL HAZARDS AND PUBLIC CHOICE: *The Indifferent State and Local Politics of Hazard Mitigation*
Neil Fligstein, GOING NORTH: *Migration of Blacks and Whites from the South, 1900−1950*
Howard Schuman and Stanley Presser, QUESTIONS AND ANSWERS IN ATTITUDE SURVEYS: *Experiments on Question Form, Wording, and Context*
Michael E. Sobel, LIFESTYLE AND SOCIAL STRUCTURE: *Concepts, Definitions, Analyses*
William Spangar Peirce, BUREAUCRATIC FAILURE AND PUBLIC EX-PENDITURE
Bruce Jacobs, THE POLITICAL ECONOMY OF ORGANIZATIONAL CHANGE: *Urban Institutional Response to the War on Poverty*

The list of titles in this series continues on the last page of this volume

The Structural Determinants of Unemployment

VULNERABILITY AND POWER IN MARKET RELATIONS

Paul G. Schervish

Department of Sociology
Boston College
Chestnut Hill, Massachusetts

ACADEMIC PRESS

A Subsidiary of Harcourt Brace Jovanovich, Publishers

New York   London
Paris   San Diego   San Francisco   São Paulo   Sydney   Tokyo   Toronto

ACADEMIC PRESS, INC.
111 Fifth Avenue, New York, New York 10003

United Kingdom Edition published by
ACADEMIC PRESS, INC. (LONDON) LTD.
24/28 Oval Road, London NW1 7DX

LIBRARY OF CONGRESS CATALOG CARD NUMBER: 83-07819

ISBN 0-12-623950-9

PRINTED IN THE UNITED STATES OF AMERICA

83 84 85 86   9 8 7 6 5 4 3 2 1

To my father, George,
and in memory of my mother, Margaret

Contents

Introduction

1

The Logic of Analysis of Segmentation Research

2

Segmentation of Market Relations
and Segmentation of Unemployment

3

Data, Measurement of Variables,
and Techniques of Analysis

4

Class Segments and the Structure of
Unemployment

5

Economic Sectors and the Distribution
of the Unemployed

6

Business Cycle, Economic Sector, and Unemployment

Conclusions

Appendix A: Technical Considerations: Relation of Theory and Data, Model Determination, and Odds Ratios   197

Appendix B: Census Occupation Categories Composing Class Segments   209

Appendix C: Census Industry Categories Composing Economic Sectors   217

References   223

Preface

This book is at once an ambitious and a limited undertaking. It is ambitious in that it joins a growing body of sociological research striving to link Marxist theory, contemporary economic analysis, and empirical methodology. It attempts to make these linkages by studying unemployment—a subject area only now gaining appropriate recognition by sociologists. At the same time, the book is a limited work. Despite its sweeping theoretical constructs, large data base, and somewhat cumbersome methodology, the volume remains largely an exploratory investigation. It suggests a terrain of research and a line of argument that require cautious scrutiny and further development. As such, the book is more a successful documentation of the existence and direction of relationships than it is an adequate estimation of them.

Most Americans believe that individuals achieve their maximum economic attainments by developing personal capacities and then investing them in the marketplace. This perspective shapes American social and economic institutions. It also has influenced theory and research on the process of economic attainment by defining an individualistic rather than a structural analytic paradigm. The distribution of ability and motivation rather than the distribution of opportunity serve to explain the distribution of economic outcomes.

The book enters into the long-standing and recently revised debate about whether the economic fate of individuals resides in their own hands or is, at

least in part, a function of the structure of the economy. Is it the case that as Cassius counsels Brutus in *Julius Caesar*, the fault that we are underlings lies not in our stars, but in ourselves? Or is it, to reverse Shakespeare, that the fault is not in ourselves, but in our stars?

It is neither unreasonable nor novel to argue that both our selves and our stars merit consideration in a market economy where forces of supply and demand remain (despite significant restrictions) interdependent. In the present research, I emphasize the demand side, not so much because the individualistic perspective necessarily or theoretically excludes attention to the structure of demand, but rather because the research taken from that perspective has nonetheless neglected to investigate the demand side with the same astute care as it has lavished on exploring supply-side factors.

I argue that more than personal characteristics matter in the determination of employment resulting from job separation. Individuals are located in class positions, economic sectors, and periods of the business cycle, all of which vary in their capacity to insulate persons—across a range of personal characteristics—from negative aspects of job separation. Together, class, sector, and aggregate business conditions constitute what I call the *structural determinants* of unemployment. Over and above personal characteristics, these structural determinants help shape both the national and individual pattern of unemployment. They do so by providing individuals with various resources of bargaining power that reduce their vulnerability to unfavorable economic outcomes. Depending on the location of their employment position in the class structure, the location of their firm in the industrial structure, and the period of the business cycle, individuals either become endowed with resources of power to enhance or protect their standing in the labor market or become subject to sources of vulnerability which weaken their standing.

Every stage of capitalistic economic development creates a particular array of class and firm divisions that define the conditions of vulnerability and power during that period. This research seeks to uncover some of the especially complex and varied contours of the structural conditions of vulnerability and power in advanced capitalism. In this stage, such structural conditions are distributed unevenly not only between classes but within classes and economic sectors. Just as classes and sectors are internally differentiated or "segmented," so, too, are the economic outcomes (e.g., unemployment) associated with them. Consequently, by examining the relation between the segmented nature of the economy and the segmented nature of unemployment, I hope to shed light on both as well as on the relationship between them.

Chapter 1 elaborates a conceptual framework for studying segmentation research and reviews developments in this research over the past dozen years from the perspective of this framework. Chapter 2 gives an overview of the theoretical and conceptual considerations that undergird the analysis presented in Chapters 4–6. Drawing on the conceptual framework developed in the previous chapter, the first section of Chapter 2 discusses the three structural variables—class, sector, and business cycle—as sources of vulnerability and power and formulates the three fundamental propositions explored in the empirical analysis. The second section reviews current trends in research on the dependent variable, unemployment. The third section suggests how studying the relation between segmented employment and unemployment sheds light on both. The chapter concludes with a detailed conceptualization of modes of job separation.

Chapter 3 details the methodological and statistical techniques used in the research, points out various divergences between CPS data and the research question, and discusses the development of the general log-linear model. Chapter 4 elaborates and tests the relationship of class fractions to unemployment. Chapter 5 does the same for economic sectors. It also studies an aspect of internal labor markets by investigating how the effect of age on employment status varies by sector. Chapter 6 examines the averaged effect of the business cycle on the levels of unemployment and type of unemployment. It also examines the interaction effect of business cycle, sector, and unemployment.

Acknowledgments

Many people have contributed to this book from its inception during my doctoral work at the University of Wisconsin, Madison, to its completion at Boston College where I serve on the Faculty of Sociology. Most especially, I wish to thank my fellow graduate students at the University of Wisconsin for their challenging yet noncompetitive colleagueship, for readily sharing their ideas, and for offering their assistance. In this regard, I am most grateful to Catherine McLaughlin, my patient tutor in labor economics, and to Robert Kaufman, who so graciously and competently advised me through every stage of this research. Members of the faculty, too, were completely helpful at every juncture. I am grateful for the hours of help provided by Glen Cain, Sheldon Danziger, Charles Halliby, Lee Hansen, Robert Hauser, Robert Mare, and Leonard Weiss. A special thanks is extended to Hal Winsborough and Erik Wright who helped me plough through many difficult twists and turns in the unfolding of the theory and methodology. But the fullest dept is owed Aage Sørensen, under whose guidance the intellectual foundations of this book were laid and who prodded me through their many permutations with insight and encouragement.

Many other friends and colleagues also extended the courtesy of providing useful comments on all or part of the text: Barry Bluestone, Tom Daymont, Randy Hodson, Larry Griffin, Arne Kalleberg, Sy Spilerman, and various

anonymous reviewers, especially one who made suggestions for the final revision.

For their generous assistance in the day-to-day execution of the research I thank Pearl Alberts, Barb Aldrich, Jeanne Chisholm, Anne Cooper, Gordon Caldwell, David Dickens, Peter Dickinson, Michael Dunham, Patricia Fleming, Robert Kaufman, Virginia Rogers, Ruth Sandor, Al Schubert, Julie Wakstein, and Nancy Williamson. For their careful attention to the preparation of the manuscript I am grateful to Karen Price, Mary Regan, Many Ann Sveum, and Julie Zappia. For financial support I wish to thank Gene Summers, Aage Sørensen, and Irwin Garfinkel. The latter provided assistance through the Institute for Research on Poverty funded by the Department of Health, Education, and Welfare pursuant to the provisions of the Economic Opportunity Act of 1964. At Boston College the book was supported generously by the Summer Research Grant Committee and by the resources of the Social Welfare Research Institute. Finally, for seeing me through the various strains and anxieties of this project I thank Maureen Hallinan, Dayton Haskin, Barry Bluestone, and my wife, Terry Chipman, who means more to me than any book.

The Structural Determinants of Unemployment

VULNERABILITY AND POWER IN MARKET RELATIONS

Introduction

In 1969 the official unemployment rate dipped to 3.5%, its lowest level since 1953. Henry Luce's boast in 1941 that the United States was entering the "American Century" appeared prophetic for the economy. As it turned out, however, guns for Vietnam and butter for the American people had so heated (some would say distorted) the American economy that in just 2 short years the picture had changed considerably. If the 12 years following the 1958 recession had been a period of new employment, the next 12 years beginning in 1970 were to constitute a period of new unemployment.

By 1972, unemployment had risen to 5.6% and the process had set in by which joblessness inched continually upward, with post-recession levels never quite returning to their prerecession lows. In May 1975, unemployment shot up to 9.7%, the highest level since World War II. After a brief and shallow respite, it was on the rise again as the recession of 1980 approached. And during the 1981–1982 recession the unemployment rate surpassed even that of May 1975. In November 1982, as the deepest and most enduring economic crisis since the Great Depression continued its relentless course, 12 million workers were without jobs, and another 1.6 million workers wanted jobs but had simply stopped looking for employment in the face of such bleak job prospects. Although one of out every nine workers was out of work during the November survey week, unemployment had become an unwelcome intruder into even more lives over the course of the

year. According to the Department of Labor, 21.4 million people experienced some unemployment in 1980; in 1981 the number climbed to 23.4 million; and, with the recession deepening through to the end of 1982, it may well happen that nearly one out of every four members of the labor force will have been without work sometimes during the year.

As stark as these figures are, they elude any simple interpretation because of a variety of anomalies in the composition of the labor force and the nature of unemployment:

- The traditional inverse relation between unemployment and inflation represented by the Philips Curve disappeared in favor of the now familiar problem of stagflation.
- Sectoral differences in rates of growth and decline resulted, until most recently, in the simultaneous growth of employment and unemployment.
- Many unemployed, especially those on temporary layoff, engaged in no job search, returning in time to their former jobs.
- For many of the unemployed, particularly those in families with second earners, joblessness seemed to impose less grave economic hardships than generally imagined.
- Workers left and reentered the labor force as a regular part of their work histories.
- The labor force participation rate of women increased while that of men decreased, raising the question of how demographic trends affected the upward creep of the unemployment rate.
- Black teenage and youth employment skyrocketed despite the raft of employment and training programs targeted for these groups.

Just what these fluctuations and anomalies represent for the overall health of the economy or for personal hardship is a topic of much theoretical and technical debate. In large part, this debate arises from the growing appreciation by researchers of the simple fact that unemployment is not a unidimensional reality. There is a vast difference in the causes and consequences of unemployment for various members of the labor force. Thus, the following cases, although weighted equally in the official monthly unemployment rate, nonetheless differ radically: the steel worker with 20 years of tenure on temporary layoff and with supplemental unemployment benefits; the 60-year-old Polaroid chemist who is forced into early retirement but still wants to work; a 22-year-old engineering graduate who is searching for her first job; a black teenager with a 10th-grade education and no formal skills who is fired from his loading dock job at Sears; the computer systems analyst who quits his position at a university to seek out a higher-paying job

in industry; and the Portuguese-American mother of four who begins looking for work in textile mills when her husband loses his automobile-assembly job.

SEGMENTATION OF UNEMPLOYMENT AND EMPLOYMENT

The upshot of the realization that, when it comes to unemployment, things are not as simple as they seem has been a spate of research attempting to unravel the many complexities characterizing the nature of contemporary unemployment. No single volume, of course, could cover the intricate terrain of all the current controversies. This book cuts into the debate in two ways. First, focusing on unemployment that results from job separation, it argues for the importance of distinguishing types of unemployment that researchers and commentators continue to lump together in a single category of joblessness. In particular four types of unemployment are studied: temporary layoffs, indefinite layoffs, firings, and quits that do not eventuate immediately in a new job. The second way in which the book cuts into the discussion on unemployment is its argument that the shape of unemployment is a function of the shape of employment: The likelihood that someone will become separated from a job, and the form such job separation will assume, depends in part on the type of employment position from which the person becomes separated. As will be seen, neither of these two arguments is completely novel. But when joined together, they provide the basis for a sociological theory of the structural determinants of job separation, specifying how segmentation in employment affects the segmentation in unemployment and complementing the vast array of literature on the personal determinants of unemployment.

The research strategy of exploring the linkages between segmented employment and segmented unemployment is built on the foundation of much previous work. Labor market research has emphasized the segmented character of the American economy both in regard to outcomes or rewards and in regard to the sources of these outcomes. Rather than examine how a continuous distribution of outcomes is determined by a set of continuous personal or even organizational characteristics, this research has examined how qualitatively different outcomes are determined by qualitatively different labor market forces.

Two aspects of the recent emphasis on structural segmentation in particular have influenced the present research. The first is the discussion concerning the segmented nature of unemployment. Hall (1970a, 1970b,

1972) and Feldstein (1975, 1976), among others, have stressed that the aggregate unemployment rate needs to be decomposed into its constituent parts in order to assess properly the distribution of hardships entailed in unemployment for various groups, the job search behavior of the unemployed, and the changing nature of unemployment itself. The second aspect of segmentation research that has been drawn on is the analysis in economic, sociological, and Marxist literature of discontinuities in the employment structure. This segmentation research differentiates characteristics of persons, jobs, economic sectors of firms, and labor market processes. It examines the theoretical and empirical relevance of such segmentation for explaining patterns of outcomes in the labor market (cf. Averitt, 1968; Beck, 1980; Beck, Horan, and Tolbert, 1978; Bluestone, 1970; Doeringer and Piore, 1971; Edwards, 1979; Edwards, Reich, and Gordon, 1975; Gordon, 1972; Gordon, Edwards, and Reich, 1982; Hodson, 1978; O'Connor, 1973; Piore, 1970, 1971; Shepherd, 1970; Wachter, 1974; Wright, 1978, 1979). Although some research in this tradition studies unemployment (Buchele, 1976; Cornfield, 1981; Doeringer and Piore, 1975; Feinberg, 1979; Mueller, 1972; Norris, 1978; Schervish, 1981), the research reported in this volume differs by distinguishing types of unemployment and focusing explicitly on class and business cycle rather than just on industrial sectors or primary and secondary positions.

RESEARCH OBJECTIVES

Baron and Beilby (1980) argue that structural analyses of labor market outcomes must empirically specify the organizational characteristics of work that are internal to a firm because models of economic segmentation are theoretically specified at such an organization level. The research reported here concurs with this view, analyzing the organizational characteristics of class position and firm sector that contribute to unemployment outcomes.

   The book studies the *structural determinants* of unemployment by setting forth and testing a theory of the sociology of unemployment in the United States from 1969 to 1978, a period that spans the lowest and (until July 1982) the highest unemployment rates in the past 30 years. The approach taken here emphasizes that research must focus on, not only unemployed persons, but also the nature of unemployment itself. It also emphasizes that unemployment must be studied in its relation to the way workers are employed. The structural determinants of unemployment are defined as the institutional aspects of employment relationships that affect unemployment outcomes. Here, three structural determinants are investigated: the class

position in which a person is employed, the product market characteristics of the firm in which the job is located, and the period in the business cycle.

Together, these structural determinants affect economic outcomes for individuals by the way they contribute to the *vulnerability and power* of individuals in their labor market transactions. Members of the labor force obtain more or less favorable employment outcomes depending upon the combination of personal and structural resources they are able to draw on in initiating, maintaining, and terminating their relationship to an employer. Power in market relations is defined as the possession of personal and structural resources that enhance the individual's ability to obtain favorable labor market outcomes. Vulnerability in market relations is simply the obverse, namely, the personal and structural conditions that reduce or constrain the attainment of favorable employment outcomes.

The key question of the book, then, is how the structural determinants of vulnerability and power embedded in class, firm, and the business cycle systematically relate to fluctuations in the level of unemployment types. By exploring this question, I hope to shed light on some previously unexplored aspects of unemployment as well as on the complex workings of the segmented U.S. economy.

Empirically, this research first tests a series of hypotheses from the theoretical arguments about the structural determination of unemployment; it then investigates a number of further relationships that are indeterminate according to theory, especially aspects of the relationship of quits to the structural location of an employment position; and, finally, it estimates the relative incidence of unemployment and unemployment types by class, sector, and business cycle period.

Conceptually, the task is (*a*) to decompose unemployment into four types of job separation: temporary layoffs, indefinite layoffs, firings, and quits; and (*b*) to differentiate employment positions by their class and firm resources of bargaining power.

Theoretically, the task is to examine the structural determinants of unemployment due to job separation. The thesis is that the measured distribution of persons in the various forms of job separation is a function not only of their personal characteristics but also of the underlying social processes of vulnerability and power derived from class fraction, economic sector, and period in the business cycle in which the separation occurred. Depending on their employment position and stage in the business cycle, workers will experience different levels of unemployment and will tend to receive one type of unemployment over another.

The vulnerability of employment positions to market relations depends on the position's location along two dimensions of segmentation of the

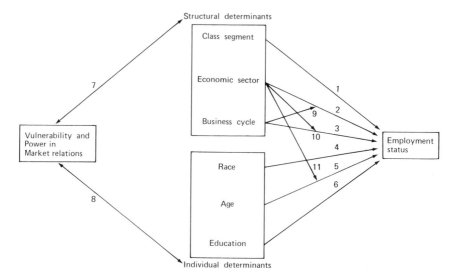

FIGURE I.1. Relationships among employment status and independent variables.

employment structure. The first is the class segment of a job and the second is the economic sector of the firm in which the job is located. The class segment (operationalized by occupation) of the position provides the worker with varying types of bargaining power for deflecting negative outcomes and obtaining positive ones in relation to unemployment. The economic sector (operationalized by industry) determines the types and degree of a position's vulnerability to a decline in the demand for labor.

THEORETICAL ARGUMENT

Figure I.1 diagrams the theoretical arguments that I analyze. The dependent variable is employment status, a five-category nominal variable measuring the relative distribution of workers to four types of unemployment and to the comparative category of employed.[1] The figure indicates that the

---

[1]The comparative category of the employed is included in order to estimate properly the log-linear parameters calculated for the analysis (see Chapter 3). The concern is to measure the relative frequency of unemployment and types of unemployment for independent variables whose categories vary in their marginal distributions. By including the category of employed in the dependent variable the tau-parameters reflect the comparative frequency of unemployment types across categories of an independent variable relative to the number of cases in each category.

propensity of workers to be in a particular category of employment status is a function not only of personal characteristics, but of class position, economic sector, and stage in the business cycle. Arrows 1 to 6 signify that class position, economic sector, business cycle, race, age, and education exert a direct effect on employment status as a result of the vulnerability and power they afford members of the labor force. That is, the structural characteristics of positions, business conditions, and personal characteristics determine the pool of unemployed and their types of unemployment. The double-headed arrows, 7 and 8, signify that the impact of the structural and individual determinants results from the capacities that accrue to positions, firms, and individuals in their market relations. They also signify that these structural and individual determinants, in turn, provide resources for altering the distribution of vulnerability and power. Arrows 9 and 10 indicate the interaction between sector and business cycle analyzed in Chapter 6. I interpret arrow 9 to mean that the structural effect of sector on employment status varies across periods of the business cycle. Arrow 10 indicates that the impact of the business cycle on employment status is mediated by differences in sectoral market power that extend recessions and exacerbate unemployment. Finally, arrow 11 indicates that the effect of age on employment status varies by sector.

1

The Logic of Analysis
of Segmentation Research

The thesis of the research reported in subsequent chapters is that different class positions and different industrial sectors are associated with different levels and types of unemployment. This thesis is located within the theoretical framework of segmentation research. The purpose of this chapter is to structure systematically the array of understandings of segmentation in the existing literature. The next chapter employs this conceptualization to demarcate the theoretical argument used in the subsequent analysis.

SEGMENTATION LITERATURE: FUNDAMENTAL PROPOSITIONS AND A REFORMULATION

Throughout this chapter, the term "segmentation research" is defined broadly to include (a) the so-called "dual" or segmented labor market literature; and (b) the explicitly Marxist class and sectoral literature. The central task in clarifying the concepts underlying theories of segmentation is to construct a common framework within which the often divergent arguments of the existing theories can be understood. The hope is to go beyond building a simple descriptive taxonomy that neatly categorizes theories of segmentation according to the types of variables they employ or

according to their findings. Although such categorization is important, my aim is to explicate how the actual logic of argument varies among theories of segmentation. To expose this variation in logic requires a systematic statement of the range of relationships that constitute the essence of economic analysis in general. With such a framework in hand it becomes possible to locate the various approaches to segmentation research, including my own, according to the kinds of economic relationships singled out for analysis and the structure of the arguments concerning these economic relationships. As will be seen, although much of the segmentation literature is conducted under the rubric of "dual" or "segmented labor markets" this term is sometimes a misnomer.

The Theory of Segmentation

The first task in explicating the general framework is to review the underlying argument common to studies in this tradition. The fundamental proposition of segmentation research is that qualitatively different economic processes govern different realms of the economy. It is not simply that various persons, employment positions, or firms vary in the degree to which a common relationship or outcome obtains. Rather, the economic rules of the game determining relations and outcomes are themselves structurally demarcated.

In its most rudimentary form, such an argument is not the product only of the last decade or so. It can be traced back at least to to the middle of the nineteenth century to Marx's contrast between competitive and monopoly organization of the economy. The institutional economists of the early decades of the present century (e.g., Commons, 1918–1935; Perlman 1928) argued that social arrangements varied so much across economic units such as firms that classical and neoclassical theory at best only partially explains the real forces differentiating characteristics and outcomes in the economy. In the 1950s, Kerr (1950, 1954) formulated various structural or institutional aspects of matching labor supply and demand, which he termed the "balkanization of labor markets." Then in the late 1960s and early 1970s, a series of dissertations written at Harvard (Edwards, 1972; Gordon, 1971; Reich, 1973) renewed the debate with the neoclassical school. These writers, along with Bluestone, Doeringer, and Piore, offered an alternative to the supply-side, human-capital-deficiency explanation for poverty and low wages among sectors of the population prominently analyzed in anecdotal and sociological case studies of ghetto and urban poverty (see Liebow, 1967). This radical–Marxist critique of the standard analysis of labor

markets and income attainment instituted the "dual" or segmented perspective:

> Toward the end of the last decade [1960s], some economists began to argue that a dual labor market theory could best explain the phenomena of urban poverty and underemployment. The theory suggested that a dichotomization of the American labor market had occurred over time, forging two separate labor markets—in which workers and employers operate by fundamentally different behavioral rules [Gordon, 1972:43].

Elaborating the nature and consequences of these "fundamentally different behavioral rules" has constituted the major task of writers in this perspective. Common to segmentation analysis is the proposition that these different behavioral patterns are not distributed randomly. Rather the behavioral rules are distributed systematically such that locating where one set of rules leaves off and another takes up actually defines a segment. Along some relevant dimension of socioeconomic relations groupings may be constructed such that variation in that dimension across groups is greater than variation within.[1]

Thus, although sharing the consensus that real boundaries exist between economic units, segmentation research differs on (a) the fundamental economic relationship that differs qualitatively from segment to segment; and (b) the number of these relationships that converge within segments. First, there is no single dimension of segmentation agreed on by all researchers in this tradition. Areas investigated include segmentation of occupations or jobs, classes, industries or firms, persons by race or gender, and labor market mechanisms—both external (Thurow, 1975) and internal (Doeringer and Piore, 1971). Second, there is no agreement on just how segmentation in one arena intersects with segmentation in another. Bluestone speaks of the tripartite economy in which characteristics of primary, secondary, and irregular industrial sectors correspond to a tripartite structure of jobs and persons. And Edwards (1979) shows how modes of control of the labor process vary by job segment and industrial sector. More will be said in the following on how various theories differ in their focus and line of argument. But this elaboration will be carried out more profitably in view of the general framework of socioeconomic analysis to which I now turn.

---

[1]For instance, determining just what the relevant dimensions are and what constitutes greater between- than within-group variation is at the heart of the debates concerning the existence and nature of the class structure. Marxist theory argues that the relevant dimension is one's own or one's family head's location in the relations of production; class theory in the Weberian tradition argues that the relevant dimension is one's income level, life-style, or degree of authority. Much other economic and sociological theory, however, argues that no relevant boundaries separate an essentially continuous class structure.

The Logic of Analysis

How the logic of analysis of segmentation research differs among its various versions becomes clarified by relating each current to a common framework. The framework is adapted from the circular flow diagram of the economy developed by the Multi-Regional Policy Impact Simulation (MRPIS) staff (1981) of which I am a member. This framework simultaneously situates in a larger scheme the variables employed in segmentation studies and indicates the general lines of relationship among these variables.

THE UNITS OF ANALYSIS

The actors in the economy as shown by Figure 1.1 are persons, firms, and the government. These actors participate in economic behavior according to their relation to two sectors and two markets. The two sectors are the household and business sectors; the two markets are the product and labor markets. The household sector consists of families and individuals and can be classified according to demographic and other personal characteristics such as race, gender, age, education, training, labor force experience, propensity to save, and consumption patterns. The establishments in the business sector are characterized by a host of attributes including location, size, market share, conglomeration, vertical and horizontal integration, technological arrangements, capital–labor ratios, and cross-national ties (for a fuller list of such characteristics, see Kaufman, Hodson, and Fligstein, 1981). The government sector, as will be discussed, is part of the business sector to the extent that it employs labor and sells services. But, as Figure 1.1 also shows, the government is a legal and economic environment for the two sectors and two markets through its regulatory and income-transfer activities.

MARKETS

Connecting each of these two sectors of actors are the product and labor markets. In common parlance, a market is an arena of exchange regulated by a set of rules. But since the notion of market is a central concept of segmentation research it is necessary to be more precise. A *market* is the arena of exchange in which buyers and sellers of commodities come together to match a supply to a demand. One of the earliest definitions of the notion of economic markets was formulated by Walras in terms of an auction. In the Walrasian view, general (economy-wide) equilibrium is reached in all markets between supply and demand. Markets embody an invisible (though

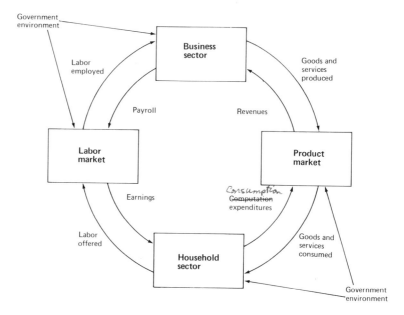

FIGURE 1.1. The basic circular flow of the economy.

functional) auctioneer directing the contracting and recontracting of suppliers and demanders for whom both prices and quantities are flexible. Keynesian Non-Walrasian or market models, also argue that a general equilibrium is reached but one in which purchases equal sales rather than one in which supply equals demand (see MRPIS: 1981). This is because rigid prices force quantities to adjust such that shortages and surpluses of quantities occur. Distinguished from either the Walrasian or Keynesian arguments that markets provide general economic equilibria is the Marshallian perspective. For Marshall and contemporary neoclassical theoreticians, markets provide only partial equilibria. That is, a particular, market may equate supply and demand for a particular good since quantity decisions depend only on the price of the good in question.

Be this as it may, the point is that the defining characteristic of a market is the presence of a systematic relationship of matching or exchange of supply and demand, and not the specific mechanisms of matching and exchange. Whether markets entail equal or unequal power, provide for general or partial equilibria, involve flexible or inflexible prices, or ensure full or partial clearing are not matters of definition but theoretical and empirical issues that motivate the diversity of labor and product market research. In fact it was precisely the accumulation of evidence that labor and product markets work

differently depending on the characteristics of individuals and firms participating in them that stimulated much of the segmentation research in the first
place.

PRODUCT MARKET

The *product market* is the arena of exchange between two firms or
between a firm and an individual or household. From the point of view of a
producing firm, a supply of goods and services are exchanged for revenue,
which is a function also of the price and quantity of goods and services
demanded. From the point of view of the consuming household or firm (in the
case of demand for intermediate commodities), a demand for goods and
services expressed through consumption expenditures is exchanged for a
supply of these goods and services.

Characterizing the product market in this fashion sheds light on further
dynamics or relational characteristics of households and firms. For the
household, as a demander of goods and services, it highlights such factors as
its pattern of consumption, its ratio of consumption to savings, its elasticities
of demand for certain commodities, and its level of disposable income. Firm
relations that are emphasized by the production and sale (or realization) of
commodities in the product market include: the firm's utilization of
technology and capital; its pricing decisions; its product market share; its
linkages to other firms as a buyer and seller of intermediate goods and as a
price leader or price follower; its investment and disinvestment decisions;
and, again, the range of factors already cited such as its position as a
conglomerate, or as a vertically or horizontally integrated corporation.

LABOR MARKET

Just as the product market links firms to households in the economic
activities of production and consumption, the *labor market* links firms to
households in the arenas of employment and earnings. The labor market can
be viewed as the set of allocation mechanisms by which the supply and
demand for labor are matched. From the supply side, this matching
mechanism transforms a labor force or a labor supply into labor supplied by
exchanging employment for earnings. Or in Marxist terms, the labor market
is the social relationship that transforms the labor power of persons into the
commodity of labor by the establishment of a wage contract. But whether
understood in traditional economic or Marxist terms, the essence of the labor
market from the supply side (see Figure 1.1) is that persons with a range of
background and demographic characteristics either (*a*) offer themselves for a

range of employment positions in exchange for earnings or (b) remove themselves from such employment. From the demand side, this same relationship can be expressed as firms either (a) filling job vacancies with incumbents through payroll expenditures or (b) separating workers from jobs through involuntary unemployment.

Examination of the labor market relationship between the business and household sector also accentuates particular characteristics of firms and households. *Firms* are viewed as employers with an existing but evolving distribution of positions. Such positions most often are described as occupations but may be categorized as segments (for example, primary and secondary jobs), as earnings levels, as manual versus mental positions, as productive versus unproductive positions, or as classes defined at the level of relations of production. The other major function of the business sector in view of its labor market activity is the determination of wages and working conditions. Such determination is viewed traditionally as part of the labor market negotiation on a micro- or macro-level. But to the extent that wages and work conditions are set and attached to positions independent of labor-supply decisions by workers (the extreme instance being the case of a monopsonist employer), such determinations become located conceptually in the business sector.

In view of their role in the labor market, relevant aspects of household or individual activity include the wage level required to induce labor force participation (reservation wage), labor migration, investment in education and training, type and hours of employment sought or obtained, and decisions concerning the relative distribution of leisure, paid work, and home work. Another aspect, one that also serves to distinguish the labor from the product market, is that labor is not an inert or totally passive commodity. Just as under certain conditions the determination of wages and work conditions may become removed from market negotiation and located in the business sector, the opposite tendency also may occur. Labor organization, legislation, custom, and the level of occupation-specific labor supply all serve to enhance the bargaining power of the agents of labor and return wage and work-condition decisions to the labor market or, in the extreme instance, to the household sector. Sellers of commodities in the product market shape or endure more or less favorable conditions of exchange—conditions that likewise serve as bases for segmentation. But in labor market, the commodity exchanged is capable of entering into a struggle to determine its conditions and rate of exchange. To the extent labor resists being a passive object of exchange and actively shapes its fortunes, it becomes decommodified.

MARKETS AS UNEQUAL EXCHANGE

To phrase the relationship between households and firms as a matter of exchange or as a matching mechanism does not imply that the classical assumptions necessarily hold. Nothing in this definition requires that the matching between supply and demand be either (*a*) free and competitive or (*b*) isomorphic (i.e., complete). This lack of perfect functioning of markets has been recognized, of course, by all but a few intellectual diehards and those who employ the imagery of free and perfectly competitive markets for political ends.

First, to note that markets are *not* free and competitive exchanges between actors does not deny the existence of markets. Inequality of power is consequential precisely because of the continued exchange relationship that exists between actors who meet in the market. Unless transactions continued to occur in both labor and product markets inequalities of bargaining power would not be played out: Surplus value would not be extracted and expanded reproduction would falter. In the product market, trusts, monopolies, oligopolies, cartels, and conglomerates engage in noncompetitive trans-actions that nonetheless remain market exchanges. Similarly, in the labor market, the existence of unions, labor and safety standards, business associations, and employer resistance to unions all attest to the persistence of noncompetitive struggles to rectify or expand inequalities of bargaining power. In fact, a central Marxist tenet, in contrast to traditional economic presuppositions, is that within a capitalist society, the exchange relations between firms and firms, firms and consumers, firms and workers, and firms and the government are all relationships of unequal rather than equal exchange in which capital dominates. To rephrase this proposition in terms of Figure 1.1, since capital in the business sector enjoys a legally and ideologically protected control over society's productive capacity (i.e., control over investment and labor process decisions), it likewise dominates the exchange relationships in the product and labor markets.

Second, to demonstrate that markets do *not* perfectly equilibrate does not nullify the social fact that markets may imperfectly match supply and demand. Marxist, as well as mainstream, analyses accord much attention to imbalances in this matching. As will be argued more fully in the next chapter, the notion of the reserve army is fundamentally a thesis about the relative ability of capital to benefit from the persistent nonmatching and mismatching of workers and positions in a capitalist economy. In traditional analyses, incomplete labor-market matching takes the form of labor shortages,

demand-deficiency (cyclical) unemployment, or a combination of the two in sectoral unemployment. Likewise, in the product market incomplete matches are expressed in gluts (overproduction and excess capacity) and shortages along with their respective distributional mechanisms of "dumping" and rationing.

INTERNAL LABOR MARKETS

To complete the conceptual overview, two other components of the circular flow of the economy need to be discussed: internal labor markets and the government sector. *Internal labor markets* are allocation mechanisms by which persons and jobs within a particular establishment or occupation (see Doeringer and Piore, 1971:3–4) are matched. Like labor markets in general, the major feature is the matching relationship of a supply of workers with a structure of vacant positions.[2] But unlike "external" labor markets, the pool or supply of labor for filling positions is internal to the firm or occupation. In practice, of course, the functioning of internal labor markets is not hermetically sealed from the functioning of external labor markets. The likelihood that a vacancy will become filled by internal promotion can be expressed as a probability (usually less than one). In the case of enterprise internal labor markets, the size of this probability is a function of the degree of firm-specific skill requisites, custom or firm policy, union or other binding contracts, and the size of the external pool of workers with appropriate supply characteristics. In the case of occupational internal labor markets, the probability is a function of the extent to which job ladders bridge more than one establishment. This is the case for some managerial or craft markets that span across plants in a corporation or even across corporations (see Althauser and Kalleberg, 1981).

THE GOVERNMENT SECTOR

Finally, it is important to explicate the place of the government sector in the analytical framework because of the increasing importance accorded the state in socioeconomic analysis from every theoretical vantage point. As O'Connor (1973) and others in the segmentation tradition attest, the importance and distinctiveness of government employment, production, and regulation warrant that special attention be paid to how the underlying behavioral rules in this sector differ from those operative in segments of the private sector. Two major roles of government in economic activity are its

---

[2] See H. White (1970) and A. Sørensen (1979) for a discussion of a theory of vacancy chains within a firm.

functioning (*a*) as a part of the business sector and (*b*) as an environment both for the business and household sectors and for the product and labor markets.

As an economic actor in the business sector, the government employs labor and produces goods and services. As such it acts like a firm or, better, like a series of firms over a range of industries. Government bodies exist at the federal, state, county, and local levels and participate in the labor and product markets ranging from education and medical care to construction and provision of recreational facilities. In the labor market, the government exchanges wages for employment in this full range of types of economic activity. In the product market, the government as a demander of goods and services exchanges revenue for such commodities as research contracts and military equipment. In this regard the government is similar to firms purchasing raw materials and intermediate goods. At the same time the government functions in the product market as a producer of commodities. It provides employment and legal, educational, and medical services; it operates sanitation and water utilities; it runs urban transport networks and recreational facilities; and it sells food, agricultural products, and licenses.

The second function of government in relation to the circular flow of the economy is as an environment for private firms and households and for their relationship in the product and labor markets. It is not necessary to catalogue the vast array of money and in-kind transfer programs, tax structures, regulations, subsidies, labor legislation, and monetary and banking policies to recognize the scope and depth of government intervention in the private economy. In fact much popular commentary and social science research is devoted to the debate over what the impact of this interaction is and should be.

VULNERABILITY AND POWER IN MARKET RELATIONS

The previous section outlined the circular flow of the economy and described its components. The final set of considerations needed to complete the conceptual framework specifies a fundamental aspect of advanced capitalist economies, namely that of relative vulnerability and power in market relations. I have noted that the relationships between the household and business sectors in a capitalist society take the form of markets. But in contrast to the prevailing neocloassical view, the segmentation perspective assigns a centrality to the argument that the behavioral rules of markets systematically vary for different segments of firms and households. At a high

level of abstraction—one that ignores for the moment the range of concrete variation embodied in particular theories of segmentation—the fundamental distinction is between markets in which the behavioral rules dictate relatively equal exchange relations and markets in which institutional constraints provide for unequal exchange relations.

Relationships of equal exchange may be typified as free competitive markets in which buyers and sellers of commodities conduct their exchanges in an environment of equal power and full information. Such markets are idealized in formal neoclassical theory. Relationships of unequal exchange may be characterized as markets in which buyers and sellers of commodities participate with relative inequality of power and knowledge. Taking such arrangements of domination as the essence of the social economy, the segmentation perspective elaborates both the pattern of structural sources of inequality in the household, business, and government sectors and the consequences of these unequal structural conditions for transactions in the product and labor markets. In this perspective, markets in capitalist society are only seldom truly competitive, and then only fleetingly.

Although a tendency toward actual competition in product and labor markets may have marked the era of petty commodity production, the history of capitalism since the initiation of wage labor has been marked by relations of superordination and subordination not only between employers and workers at the point of production but between firms and members of the labor force, firms and firms, firms and consumers, and firms and the state apparatus at the point of exchange in the labor and product markets. This, of course, was Marx's point all along as he attempted to dispel the "economic fiction" (1967 I:628) of some political economists who ignored the social and political forces of domination that shaped the seemingly benign and inexorable workings of supply and demand. For instance, Marx's assessment of the labor market at once refutes the mystification of the classical laws of supply and demand and firmly plants the social and political element: "Relative surplus-population is therefore the pivot upon which the law of demand and supply of labour works. It confines the field of action of this law within the limits absolutely convenient to the activity of exploitation and to the domination of capital."

In this way, the issue of *vulnerability and power* is accorded a primary rather than a residual role in the workings of the circular flow of the economy. Power or domination is the ability of economic actors in the household, business, and government sectors to make use of resources to reconstruct or circumvent market relations of equal exchange replacing them with market transactions structured to produce outcomes favoring their interests. Vulnerability is the obverse of power; it is the type and degree of susceptibility of a person, position, or firm to market relationships.

SEGMENTATION RESEARCH

This section draws on the conceptual framework just outlined as the basis for reviewing the theoretical logic of various stains of segmentation research. I begin by reviewing the work of Piore (1970) and Bluestone (1970) since their seminal formulations of segmentation theory are among the most comprehensive in linking the elements diagramed in Figure 1.1. Both authors claim a correspondence between (*a*) types of persons in the household sector; (*b*) types of jobs in firms; (*c*) types of firms or industries in the business sector; and (*d*) types of product market behavior. Such correspondence, though rejected in later research for being too rigid, served the purpose of setting off segmentation perspectives from its neoclassical alternative.

Piore's (1970) leading question was to explain the employment and earnings problems specific to the poor:

> The central tenet of the analysis is that the role of employment and the disposition of manpower in perpetuating poverty can be best understood in terms of a dual labor market. One sector of that market . . . offers jobs which possess several of the following traits: high wages, good working conditions, employment stability and job security, equity and due process in the administration of work rules, and chances for advancement. The secondary sector has jobs that are decidedly less attractive, compared with those in the primary sector. They tend to involve low wages, poor working conditions, considerable variability in employment, harsh and often arbitrary discipline, and little opportunity to advance. The poor are confined to the secondary labor market. Eliminating poverty requires that they gain access to primary employment [p. 55].

The implications of Piore's analysis and his recommendations for manpower policy need not be discussed here. It is more important to uncover the logic of dualist analysis embedded in his argument. The following summarizes Piore's five propositions which explain how the dual market structure is generated and how it confines the poor and the secondary sector.

1. Certain worker traits such as lateness, absenteeism, and lower skill levels are tolerated more by secondary than primary employers.
2. Discrimination traps some workers with traits required for primary employment in secondary jobs.
3. The distinction between primary and secondary jobs is not "technologically determinate," that is, some primary jobs could in fact be adequately accomplished by secondary workers. Nor is the distinction necessarily parallel to a clean distinction between enterprises; many enterprises, while generally associated with one type of jobs, also contain jobs from the other segment.

4. Employment in secondary jobs reinforces and may even create traits of secondary workers.

5. There is a compatibility between secondary employment and the ability to obtain extra-employment income through such sources as public assistance and illicit economic activity [1970:55–58.].

Considering Piore's formulation in view of the model of economic relations outlined here, the most striking fact is that Piore actually does not analyze labor market dualism. Little attention is given to how the nature and process of matching a supply of labor and a demand of jobs differs between two labor markets. Instead, Piore defines two types of jobs in the business sector and two types of workers in the household sector. The differing processes of mapping secondary workers into secondary jobs and primary workers into primary jobs are not explicitly examined. Such differential allocation, of course, is assumed. But neglecting this important component, as I shall argue, resulted in an overly rigid formulation of the allocation mechanisms in the form of empirical propositions about barriers to mobility between markets for primary and secondary workers.

The equally innovative and seminal work of Bluestone (1970) moves closer to a genuine labor market analysis but again stops short of a full exposition of market dynamics. In contrast to Piore's emphasis on the implications of dualism for developing demand-side manpower policies, Bluestone focuses on the problem of low wages and poverty by linking three segments of workers on the supply side to three sectors of jobs on the demand side: "A revised labor market model is needed which pays proper attention to both sides of the wage nexus. ... The model must posit 'segmentation' on both sides of the market, for labor is not fully mobile between sectors of the economy, and industries vary greatly in terms of their ability to pay high wages [p. 21]."

Bluestone (1970) constructs a model of a "tripartite economy" in which three distinct patterns of bilateral segmentation structure economic attainment for workers. Following Averitt (1968) the core economy is characterized by "high productivity, high profits, intensive utilization of capital, high incidence of monopoly elements, and a high degree of unionization [p. 24]." Workers in this "economy" share in the employment and earnings benefits that accrue to their firm based on its production and product market strengths. In contrast the peripheral economy is composed of firms characterized by "small firm size, labor intensity, low profits, low productivity, intensive product market competition, lack of unionization, and consequently low wages [p. 24]." Finally, the irregular economy is composed of employers generally outside of the national accounting mechanisms. The irregular economy is generally ghetto employment and

requires occupational skills and criteria not operative within the conventional economy. The logic of Bluestone's analysis is more complex than Piore's. Characteristics of firms and their derivative product-market relationships determine distinctive labor-market patterns and hence distinctive patterns of earnings for members of households. In the core economy, the traditional competitive restraints are overcome in the product market thereby providing greater benefits in the labor market. In contrast, the peripheral economy is constrained by the "repressive economic environment" of competitive product markets, thereby limiting the range of labor market benefits. Finally, the inconsistency of product demand in the irregular economy creates a corresponding unevenness in employment and earnings streams.

On these rudimentary foundations a decade of research was built. This subsequent research specified these original formulations in three ways. First it developed and tested the thesis of what Bluestone (1970) termed "chronic immobility" across sectors, an immobility deemed so central to the argument that Bluestone, for instance, refers to each segment as an "economy." Second, it sophisticated the conceptual categories of segmentation, especially in regard to the dualisms of primary and secondary jobs and primary and secondary industries. The third direction of subsequent research was to formulate and test empirically the structural segmentation hypothesis, especially in the area of income generation.

Chronic Immobility

The hypothesis of chronic immobility is the most rigid formulation of the segmentation hypotheses; however, it has been subject to rough critical appraisal. It is fundamentally a theory about (a) structural isomorphism and (b) tracking. The proposition of structural isomorphism argues—with some leeway—for a correspondence among segments of households or persons, job types, and industry types. Secondary workers (generally blacks, unskilled white males, and women) are employed in secondary jobs in secondary or peripheral industries. In contrast, primary workers are employed in primary jobs in core industries. The proposition about tracking then argues that there are boundaries to mobility for secondary workers such that the empirical correspondence of secondary workers in secondary jobs and industries reflects real social processes. Secondary workers are "tracked" to corresponding secondary employment. Not only is there a dual character to the demand side, but over and above this, certain households on the supply side are linked only to this demand of secondary employment.

In this sense, then, there are virtually two economies. They interlock to the

extent that low wages in one sector reduces costs of intermediate goods to firms and final goods to consumers. In the labor market, however, they form separate streams. Given this logic of tracking, that is, since the major allocation of workers to jobs and earnings is accomplished separately in these two (or even three) economies, it follows that little attention is devoted to the explication of labor market mechanisms themselves despite the label of "dual labor market" research. Instead, an appeal to direct or statistical discrimination often serves to explain the pattern of worker–job matches.

Efforts to establish the dual labor market hypothesis by empirically testing the "strong" proposition of chronic immobility include the work of Andrisani (1973) and Rosenberg (1975, 1980). Central to each of their investigations is (a) a description of occupational categories into primary and secondary jobs and (b) a measure of immobility. Andrisani's test of dualism challenges the validity of the immobility proposition but confirms other aspects of the theory, especially the importance of structural segmentation in wage determination processes (to be discussed later). Based on the National Longitudinal Study (Parnes data) sample of males 14 to 24 years of age in 1966 who were interviewed in 1966, 1967, and 1968, Andrisani investigated the mobility patterns of these youths from their first job to their 1968 job. He concluded:

> The empirical results make it rather difficult to accept an extreme hypothesis of labor market segmentation. In other words, there do not appear to be impenetrable boundaries separating two broadly defined market sectors, since the secondary sector hardly appears to be an economic prison from which there is no escape. . . . [However,] it is equally at odds with the facts to suggest that equivalent levels of human capital, motivation, and demand render opportunities equal [for either white or black youths beginning in secondary employment, p. 86].

Although Andrisani's findings struck a telling blow to the theory and imagery of chronic immobility, he continued to defend a less rigid formulation of segmentation.

Rosenberg (1975) dissects the tracking hypothesis into two components: (a) the personal and background characteristics distributing workers to first and current jobs in primary and secondary positions; and (b) the impact of this first employment on subsequent employment, that is, the extent of cross-sector mobility. Rosenberg distinguishes primary from secondary jobs by a multidimensional method and constructs a series of models to measure the impact of a worker's first full-time job on subsequent labor market outcomes, controlling for human capital variables. In terms of the economic model the issue is whether tracking is the labor market mechanism that distributes certain workers to primary jobs and others to secondary jobs, and, once in a sector, whether there are barriers to mobility across sectors. Analyzing the

1970 Census Employment Survey (CES), Rosenberg concluded that the evidence does not support the proposition of "two sectors between which mobility is impossible": "A more accurate picture of the secondary sector is as a reserve labor force to the primary market. In times of tight labor markets, some secondary workers get pulled up into primary jobs. . . . When labor markets loosen, many of these people return to the secondary market. Thus, their connection with the primary market is not a permanent one. [p. 170]"

This negative assessment of the "barriers to mobility" proposition is repeated also by researchers less favorably disposed to the segmentation perspective. Wachter (1974) for instance, cites research by Alexander (1974), Andrisani (1973), Lowell (1973), and Okun (1973) to argue that "evidence on the mobility issue clearly refutes a literal interpretation of the dualist model [p. 659]." Also Leigh (1978), testing the immobility hypothesis formulated by Wachtel and Betsey (1972), rejects the hypothesis that "industry and location of employment have important independent effects on occupational mobility, particularly for black workers [151]."

Conceptualizing Segmentation

The second line of development of segmentation research was to sophisticate the conceptualization of dualism. The simple dualism in which primary and secondary workers (households) were aligned isomorphically to primary and secondary jobs in primary and secondary industries of the business sector was replaced by a more complex formulation.

The most prominent conceptual innovation was proposed by Piore (1972/ 1975) and embodied in almost all subsequent theories of segmentation (e.g., Edwards, 1979, Edwards, Reich, and Gordon 1975; Reich, Gordon, and Edwards, 1973). On the one hand, the primary sector was subdivided into primary independent and primary subordinate jobs. On the other hand, the strict alignment of job segments to industrial sectors was eliminated. The first innovation incorporated the notion that "there are distinctions between primary jobs which are in many ways as important as the distinction between the primary and secondary sectors [Piore, 1972: 3]." Jobs distributed within the business sector warrant a more complex set of categories since earlier formulations of the dual hypothesis were "really characteristic of the lower tier [of the primary sector] alone [p. 3]." That is, the set of "work rules and formal administrative procedures" such as those organized around unions, that distinguished primary from secondary sector jobs, were not in fact characteristics that set off professional and managerial jobs from the secondary sector. Aspects of these upper-tier or primary independent

positions include higher pay and status, greater promotion opportunities, turnover patterns associated with advancement along a career ladder, internalized codes of behavior, formal educational requisites, greater room for individual creativity, and greater job security. The job structure suggested by separating protected working class positions from professional and managerial jobs is one reflecting, says Piore (1972), "the distinctions made in the sociological literature between the lower, working, and middle class subcultures [p. 4]."

Along with this more adequate formulation of job segmentation, researchers began to distinguish the segmentation of jobs within firms from the segmentation of firms in the business sector. While suggesting that there is an empirical correspondence between types of positions and firms distinguished by modes of control (simple, technical, and bureaucratic), Edwards (1979) indicates that such correspondence is not absolute. For instance, a firm organizing production under technical control may well exercise bureaucratic control over primary independent employees such as engineers and executives.

Modeling Structural Variables

The third line of development in segmentation research, explicitly modeling structural variables in the attainment process, proved to be both the most sustained and most critically received avenue of empirical research. Although early empirical tests of the immobility thesis by Rosenberg (1975) and Andrisani (1973) challenged its validity, these same studies demonstrated that structural variables associated with job positions make independent and significant contributions to explaining the distribution of economic outcomes. Human capital theory in economics and status attainment research in sociology explained economic outcomes as a function of current and background personal characteristics on the supply side. But the segmentation researchers insisted that characteristics of employment positions or the demand side also mattered in explaining labor market outcomes, especially earnings and income.

In terms of the circular flow of the economy, the argument is that the labor market connecting persons in the household sector to positions in the business sector is not unidimensional. The matching of persons to jobs and the corresponding level of earnings is not a single process that varies along a continuum of personal attributes. Rather the nature of the labor market process itself (and thus earnings attainment) varies according to the actual employment position being matched to the person. Earliest attempts to

model and measure this explanation of earnings attainment failed to differentiate systematically between job and firm aspects of labor market segmentation and failed to explicate sufficiently actual labor market dynamics. Nevetheless, their argument with traditional approaches was clear enough: Labor market segmentation means that the degree and type of nonmarket or institutional characteristics of employment positions structure the matching and, hence, the earnings attainment processes linking the household and business sectors.

Andrisani (1973) specifies a model to test labor market variation between primary and secondary jobs. He predicts that human capital and movitivation are related to wage attainment in the primary sector whereas, in the secondary sector, employers fail to differentiate and reward workers on the basis of productivity. Andrisani tests this proposition by modeling four wage equations—one each for blacks and whites in the primary and secondary sectors—using four sets of independent variables: family background, human capital, attitudes, and social environment. His results, although not overwhelmingly conclusive, demonstrated that labor market relations in the primary sector (and especially for whites) tended to evidence the impact of human capital variables more than labor market relations in the secondary sector: "while it is not entirely true that all secondary workers are hired as though they constituted a homogeneous pool of manpower, there is considerable evidence to support the contention that 'all blacks look alike' to secondary sector employers [pp. 78–79]."

Similarly, Osterman (1975) investigated whether earnings functions vary for the secondary, lower-tier primary, and upper-tier primary sectors in accord with the prediction that personal characteristics such as education and experience would count for more in determining earnings as one moves to higher sectors. Earnings equations were run for the three sectors on a sample of urban males in the labor force from the 1967 Survey of Economic Opportunity. Personal characteristics included years of school completed, age, age squared, race, weeks unemployed the previous year, hours worked the previous week, and 14 industry categories (excluding durable manufacturing). On the basis of this research, Osterman concluded that regression results "strongly support the dual labor market theory [p. 520]." The wage-setting process differs among sectors. In the secondary sector, wages depend on time worked rather than on experience (age) or even race. The two primary sectors evidence a greater impact of human capital variables. This is especially true for the upper tier whereas in the lower tier the significant racial coefficient indicates "that institutional constraints and long-established practices permit racial discrimination to continue [p. 519]."

The defense of segmentation theory and the challenge to neoclassical

orthodoxy embodied in the empirical strategy of Andrisani and Osterman has set the course, as will be seen, of much subsequent research. While elaborating the underlying theory of labor market segmentation and specifying more fully the structural variables included in wage equations, the fundamental thesis has endured. The labor market dynamics described by neoclassical theory as applying to the economy as a whole actually hold only for the upper-tier or primary-independent segment of the economy.

One line of criticism of such research is that it is plagued by a serious methodological flaw, "that of fitting the regression to a sample that is truncated on the values of the dependent variable [Cain, 1976: 1246]." If sectors are divided in the first place on the basis of income level, then estimated coefficients of the impact, say, of education on earnings are biased. Such truncated regression models, says Cain (1976), mar the work of Doeringer, Piore, Feldman, Gordon, and Reich (1972), Osterman (1975), Bluestone, Murphy, and Stevenson (1973), Wachtel and Betsey (1972), and Harrison (1972a, 1972b). Counterarguments emphasize that truncation is not problematic since actual boundaries exist between labor markets. Still, Cain (1976) argues that even "more troublesome" than the biased estimation of the human capital variables in the wage equations, "is the persistent finding that industry characteristics have significant effects in earnings regressions that include human capital variables [1976:1246]." Instead of reflecting structural or institutional effects of wages, such variables may in fact capture transitory demand factors, nonpecuniary reward systems, or unmeasured human capital effects.

Despite these and other misgivings, the modeling of segmented labor-market dynamics continued by developing, as already noted, a more elaborate theory of actual labor-market mechanisms implied by the wage equations and by specifying the meaning and measurement of the structural variables seen as determining the segmentation.

One of the earliest such attempts was Hodson's (1978) analysis of the contribution of capital sectors. Following O'Connor's (1973) division of the economy into monopoly, competitive, and state sectors, and various dualists' division of job positions into primary and secondary slots, Hodson evaluates a series of hypotheses generated from the segmentation literature. The major innovation of the study was to classify industries into the three productive sectors on a range of empirical criteria. The aspect of his analysis most relevant to the present discussion is his test of the contribution of structural factors in explaining economic returns. Analyses were run with annual earnings regressed on human capital and structural variables. Hodson finds that controlling for the impact of human capital variables of race, sex, age, and education, both productive sector (monopoly, competitive, state,

construction, agriculture) and employment position (primary and secondary jobs) contribute significantly to explain earnings. Such results, says Hodson, demonstrate that "sector differences in earnings cannot be explained away as artifacts [p. 43]" of either individual characteristics or dual employment positions. Although Hodson's research is noteworthy for its careful delineation of productive sectors defined according to industry categories and for its distinction between sectoral (industrial) characteristics and job characteristics, subsequent research continued this analysis but with more explicit attention to theoretical arguments about the labor market dynamics underlying the findings on structural forces (e.g., Beck, Horan, and Tolbert, 1978) and more elaborate differentiation of aspects of firms, persons, jobs, and markets (e.g., Althauser and Kalleberg, 1981; Edwards, 1979; Kalleberg, Wallace, and Althauser, 1981; Schervish, 1981; Wallace and Kalleberg, 1981).

FURTHER LINES OF DEVELOPMENT

A number of existing publications review the major developments in theory and research in the segmentation tradition (e.g., Althauser and Kalleberg, 1981; Baron and Bielby, 1980; Granovetter, 1981; Leigh, 1978; Sørensen and Kalleberg, 1979; Wallace and Kalleberg, 1981; Wright, 1979). This literature attests to the fact that segmentation research has matured sufficiently to assume a respectable place in sociological research and a provocative—though generally less respected—place in economic research. This maturation over the past decade has been manifested in four developments: (a) the clarification of realms of analysis and a corresponding sophistication in the elaboration of the level of analysis and the variables appropriate to the fundamental demand-side analysis; (b) the incorporation of Marxist class categories; (c) the explication of labor market mechanisms linking persons to jobs; and (d) the extension of segmentation research to nonincome issues of employment and unemployment.

Clarification of Theory and Variables

Early segmentation research, as I have said, often confused segmentation in supply-side characteristics of households or persons, demand-side characteristics of jobs and firms, and processes of labor market matching between the two. Moreover, in view of the circular flow model of the economy, it is possible to clarify a further aspect of the theoretical logic of

work such as Hodson (1978) and Beck, Horan, and Tolbert (1978). Implicit in both of these papers concerning the contribution of business sector variation to income determination processes and in the later debate over the empirical validity of methods for defining sectors is actually a proposition about the impact of product market characteristics on labor market processes. Although current research (e.g., Althauser and Kalleberg, 1981; Kalleberg and Griffin, 1980; Kalleberg, Wallace, and Althauser, 1981; Kaufman, Hodson, and Fligstein, 1981) has come to define production sectors by firm characteristics as well as product market characteristics, never made explicit is the fact that designation of monopoly and competitive sectors is a function of product market power whereas aspects such as size of the establishment, presence of government contracts, multinational structure, and level of technology are more directly characteristics of firms themselves. The upshot is that segmentation research fails to explicate the linkages between product market behavior of a firm or industry and labor market outcomes.

In contrast, segmentation research did become more exacting in demarcating variables and constructing theories about their relations. Human capital variables are viewed as characteristics of the household sectors whereas structural variables are viewed as characteristics of jobs and firms in the business sector, and the labor market is viewed as the process of matching the two sectors. For instance, Granovetter (1981) distinguishes three factors that contribute to earned income: "(a) the characteristics of the job and employer; (b) the characteristics of the individual who occupies the job; and (c) how a and b get linked together—what I will call *matching processes* [p. 12]."

Incorporation of Marxist Class Categories

The second current development in segmentation research has been to define job positions in terms of Marxist class categories rather than in terms of primary and secondary slots. Whereas the two approaches focus on the impact of variation in job characteristics on employment outcomes, Marxist research divides employment positions according to their decision-making control at the point of production. Wright (1979) and Wright and Perrone (1977) define classes at the level of relations of production according to decision-making capacities over investments, the labor process, and other employees. Wright (1979) concludes from extended regression analysis that class position (employer, manager and supervisor, petty bourgeois, and worker) "consistently and significantly mediates the income determination

process [p. 161–162]." Both the level and process of income determination differ by class. That is, controlling for a range of personal and job characteristics (a) class position is associated with different levels of income and (b) different processes of attainment measured by returns to education:

> People occupying different class positions but with the same level of education and occupational status, the same age and seniority on the job, the same general social background, and working the same number of hours per year, will still differ substantially in their expected incomes. And people in different class positions can expect to receive different amounts of additional income per increment in educational credentials, even if they do not differ on a variety of other characteristics [p. 162].

Managers and supervisors have higher incomes than workers controlling for relevant factors; they also enjoy higher returns on educational credentials. These and other findings confirm that, for a complex set of reasons associated with the nature of class relations in a capitalist society, the class position in which one is employed structures the level and process of income attainment. In terms of Figure 1.1, the class position in the business sector to which a person is matched constrains the labor market mechanisms determining outcomes—meaning income here. Over and above personal and other structural characteristics, class makes an independent contribution to the determination of wages and salary.

Elaboration of Labor Market Dynamics

Along with the more exact specification of theory and models of segmentation and the introduction of Marxist class categories, a third development is the elaboration of the actual social processes that underly the segmented relationships between the household and business sector in the labor market. The fruit of a decade of research in the segmentation perspective confirms the existence of different levels and processes of income attainment by job segment, class, or business sector. But not until Thurow (1975) formulated the distinction between wage and job-competition labor markets, were the differences in underlying matching mechanisms systematically detailed.

Thurow calls the traditional neoclassical model of the labor market "wage competition." Workers come to the labor market with differing marginal productivity. Wage rates determined simultaneously by the supply of human capital and the demand for labor clear the labor market in the short run.

Workers with differential investment in human capital compete for positions, therefore, on the basis of the wage level that they are willing to accept. In contrast to this market process, but coexisting with it, is the job-competition mechanism. "In the job competition model, instead of competing against one another based on the wages that they are willing to accept, individuals compete against one another for job opportunities based on their relative costs of being trained to fill whatever job is being considered [1975:75]." What attaches wages to jobs rather than to market negotiation? And what form of labor market mechanism then supplant wage-competition in matching workers and jobs?

The basis for job competition is the fact that wages are removed from labor market negotiation. Firms with dynamic efficiency frontiers both require and are able to pay for a labor force that is stable and willing to engage in on-the-job training of fellow workers and consent to organizational and techno-logical innovation without the fear of job or wage loss. As a result, workers obtain various benefits including the removal of wages from market competition. In turn, the labor market functions to match individuals to jobs with predetermined wage rates. Consequently, market mechanisms different from traditional wage-competition are required. The job-competition labor market "is not primarily a bidding market for selling existing skills but a training market where training slots must be allocated to different workers [Thurow, 1975:76]." This allocation is accomplished by matching members of the household sector arrayed in a labor queue to jobs in the business sector arrayed in a job queue. The labor market then functions to hire workers into the job queue on the basis of their rank on a labor queue determined by the a worker's trainability: "supplies of trainable labor are matched with training opportunities [p. 79]."

Although Thurow takes an important first step in formulating the theory of segmented labor markets, it requires elaboration because of two inter-connected limitations. First, Thurow neglects sources of job control other than on-the-job training that take wages out of competition. Accordingly, Thurow unnecessarily limits job-competition relations to the technologically dynamic sector and wage-competition relations to the static sector. Sørensen and Kalleberg (1981) argue that in addition to training requirements the following factors constrain neoclassical labor markets: "(a) the degree of interdependence among jobs, and the existence of job ladders; (b) the measureability of the output from jobs and autonomy; and (c) the existence of collective action by employees [pp. 59–60]." Accounting for all these factors produces what they term the "vacancy-competition" labor market where "employees have control over access to the job . . . [so that] others can only get access to the job when incumbents leave [p. 65]." Whereas in wage

competition wages can be adjusted according to the marginal productivity of workers, in vacancy competition there are barriers both to measuring marginal productivity and to enforcing such estimates since wages are not tied to productivity. Thus employers rely on preemployment indicators of productivity that result in potential employees being ranked in a labor queue. Similarly, there is a queue or rank order of available jobs established by the earnings, career trajectories, status, and other extrinsic and intrinsic characteristics of a vacant job. The labor market, then, matches the queue of persons and the queue of vacant jobs. But again, like the less elaborated job-competition model of Thurow, there is no single labor-market mechanism matching persons and jobs with wage rates. Rather, the wage-competition labor market functions to determine wages by simultaneously matching the supply-side labor characteristics with demand-side job opportunities and requirements. In contrast, the vacancy-competition market, firmly emphasizing the demand-side opportunity structure, matches workers to jobs with set wages.

One important implication for the application of job- and vacancy-competition models to the study of labor markets is the tendency to reverse the theoretical logic of earlier segmentation research. That is, Osterman (1975) and others in the first generation of empirical research focused on the inapplicability of traditional labor-market theory to secondary sector matchings in the labor market. Models explaining earned income with a theory of returns to human capital investment were deemed most applicable to the primary–independent sector. Just the opposite imagery, however, imbues the later theories of Thurow (1975) and of Sørensen and Kalleberg (1981). In their formulations, the factors contributing to "closed employment relationships" exist in the primary–subordinate and primary–independent segments. Thus the questions: If real demarcations exist in institutional arrangements by jobs and/or by industry (or firm) and if traditional competitive relations characterize some markets but not others, which jobs or production sectors are associated with which pattern of market dynamics? Is the competitive sector generally engaged in job-competition labor markets?[3] Are secondary sector jobs defined by their vulnerability to wage-competition labor markets with their corresponding returns to human capital or are they to be characterized by the absence of such neoclassical mechanisms? Is the primary sector the realm of "closed employment relationships" described by

---

[3]Thurow seems to imply that it is to the extent that the competitive sector is defined as technologically static—a questionable assumption in the case of the high-tech computer and aircraft-supply corporations. Sørensen and Kalleberg seem to argue that the alignment of labor-market dynamics is not by sector but by institutional characteristics of employment positions.

vacancy-competition labor markets or the realm of open employment relationships described by neoclassical wage-competition labor markets? Such questions do not pose insuperable problems, but they do point to some fundamental inconsistencies in imagery and logic in the exposition of the labor market dynamics associated with various jobs or industry segments. One way through this debate, of course, is to argue that certain aspects of neoclassical markets obtain under vacancy competition, particularly the return to human capital endowments, but that the process by which these returns are made is not that described by the theory of marginal productivity. Persons with high educational attainment receive high wages *not* because they are inherently more productive but because they have obtained a high-wage job on the basis of their ranking on the labor queue—a ranking derived largely on the basis of educational attainment.

A second approach in explaining the high returns to education in certain jobs without resorting to neoclassical labor-market theory is Wright's (1979) argument that returns to education differ by class position due to the different meaning and role of education across the class structure. Each class position in the business sector defined by its type and relative degree of control at the level of production is associated with different earnings-generating labor market processes. In this view, the level of earnings and the labor market process by which they are obtained results more from variation in the type of decision-making control associated with each class position than from the institutional or organizational constraints summarized by Sørenson and Kalleberg's vacancy-competition model.[4]

For instance, a close scrutiny of the job requisites differentiating working-class and managerial-class positions indicates that in the labor market distributing income to individuals in the working-class education functions as a human capital attribute indicating skill or competence. In the labor market distributing income to individuals in managerial positions, however, education serves two further purposes: First, it imbues individuals with initiative and responsibility; second, it legitimates inequalities "in terms of meritocratic myths of equal opportunities, success through achievement, etc. [Wright, 1979:90]." Consequently, because education serves all three functions in the labor market matching workers to managerial positions whereas it serves primarily the first function in the labor market of the working class, both the level of earnings and the returns to education are greater in the managerial class than in the working class. In short, the

---

[4]One consequence of Wright's focus on relations of control within the firm as the basis for class-specific labor market dynamics is that, with the exception of the managerial class, no internal differentiation of classes—for example, of the working class into unionized and nonunionized positions—is specified in the models.

demand side of segmented class positions in the business sector structures a comparably segmented system of labor markets that, in turn, produces class-based differences in employment outcomes for individuals.

Extension of Segmentation Research to Unemployment

A final development in segmentation research has been to extend applications beyond the determination of earned income to unemployment. Although implications of segmentation for employment stability were part and parcel of the earliest formulations of the perspective, little systematic research ensued. Secondary labor markets, secondary jobs, and the secondary productive sector were said to entail greater frequency of unemployment. For instance, Doeringer and Piore (1975) argue that the secondary sector is "marked by low-paying, unstable, and dead-end employment, with frequent lay-offs and discharges [p. 71]." Secondary sector jobs tend to be self-terminating and grant few incentives for voluntary attachment. Hence, both voluntary and involuntary turnover are higher in this sector. Moreover, as Osterman (1980) adds, minority teenagers differ from their mainstream counterparts in that although both groups experience frequent voluntary turnover in employment, the pattern continues for the latter group only until education is completed, whereas for the former, it becomes a permanent aspect of their employment history. Now this imagery of the distribution of frequency and type of unemployment remained unquestioned despite the anomalous findings of both Hodson (1978) and Beck, Horan, and Tolbert (1978) that unemployment levels in the so-called monopoly and competitive sectors were not in the expected direction. Hodson, using durable manufacturing as a proxy for the monopoly sector and wholesale and retail trade as a proxy for the competitive sector, finds that unemployment is greater in the former sector during recessions but greater in the competitive sector during nonrecessionary periods. Beck, Horan, and Tolbert (1978) find that in a cross-sectional comparison, the core and peripheral sectors do not significantly differ in the proportion currently unemployed or in the proportion unemployed at least once in the past 10 years.

In contrast to these research findings on the aggregate level of unemployment across segments, the work of Buchele (1976), Cornfield (1981), and Schervish (1981) sought to untangle the complex relationship between segment and unemployment. The strategy for doing so was to specify the relation between the employment segment and the level of unemployment disaggregated by type. Each of these studies argued that to understand the relation of segment to unemployment requires an investigation of how the

sources and meaning of unemployment varies by production sector or job segment. Whereas Buchele focused on unemployment differences for mangerial, professional, and working-class positions, Schervish and Cornfield studied the differences by both job segment and industrial sector. Buchele found that risks of unemployment are greater for primary–subordinate than for secondary workers because the former workers are more vulnerable to unemployment in business downturns.[5] Unemployment is lowest for supervisory positions in the independent primary segment. In contrast, professional and craft positions in this segment experience levels of unemployment comparable to secondary jobs. Although job switching in the secondary sector does not result in career advancement, job switching among professional and craft workers does. Cornfield, investigating the impact of various institutional constraints on the utilization of layoffs as a means of labor force adjustment in downturns, found that the layoff rate is largely a function of the type of intrafirm employment structure (a centralized authority structure and a high proportion of production jobs and the existence of a layoff–recall system (measured by the expectation of recall) explain three-quarters of the variance in layoff rates across 94 industries. Schervish found that controlling for race and sector (e.g., monopoly and competitive) primary jobs are associated with short layoffs and voluntary job separation (quits) whereas secondary jobs are associated with firings and long layoffs.

THE LOGIC OF THE CURRENT STUDY

The research reported in this volume draws on the material previously outlined. But it does so with much effort devoted to setting forth the theoretical logic and social processes by which the various sectors and markets of the economy are linked. Recalling Figure I.1 (p. 6), the fundamental thesis is that the type and degree of vulnerability and power in labor- and product-market transactions determines a person's employment status. Such vulnerability and power is a function of personal characteristics as well as of the structural environment of work. This structural environment, in turn, is composed of forces of vulnerability and power attached to labor market resources associated with class position, product market resources associated with the industry within which the job is located, and business

---

[5]Edwards (1979) points out, however, that when Buchele's data "are corrected for employment by core versus periphery firm (as should have been done in *defining* market segments), the secondary-market peripheral firm worker has a substantially higher overall unemployment rate, frequency of unemployment, and probability having been laid off than subordinate primary-market core-firm workers [p. 238, footnote 18]."

cycle conditions within which the labor and product market resources are played out. Employment status, the multicategory dependent variable, indicates whether a person is employed or unemployed, and if unemployed, whether the person is on temporary layoff, indefinite layoff, was fired, or quit. The specific theoretical arguments about the relation of various structural determinants to employment status are detailed in Chapters 4, 5, and 6. The next chapter casts the general argument underlying these analyses in terms of the economic flow diagram explicated in the first section of this chapter.

2

Segmentation of Market Relations and Segmentation of Unemployment

This chapter provides an overview of the theoretical and conceptual considerations that undergird the analysis presented in Chapters 4–6. The underlying argument in these chapters is that the economic organization of advanced capitalism is characterized by a particular arrangement of class fractions and economic sectors. This segmentation in the employment structure reflects the different processes of adjustment available to establishments in the face of changing business conditions. In turn, this segmentation mediates the impact of the conditions on individuals by producing distinct patterns of job separation.

In a modern market economy four sources of vulnerability and power determine transactions in the labor market and hence economic outcomes for members of the labor force: (a) personal characteristics of members of the household sector; (b) the class location of an employment position in a firm; (c) the sector location of a firm in the business sector; and (d) the business cycle.

The first section of this chapter sets forth a theory óf the structural determinants of unemployment in terms of the economic flow diagram elaborated in Chapter 1. It elaborates the specific structural forms of vulnerability and power considered in this research and formulates the three fundamental propositions explored in empirical analysis. The second section reviews current trends in unemployment research in order to identify the

specific contribution of my study to research on unemployment. I conclude that even though current research sets the stage for a segmentation analysis by presenting unemployment as a variety of underlying types, this literature fails to examine how these varying types are associated with structural divisions in the economy. The third section draws together the themes from the first two sections. It argues that studying the relation between the segmented structure of employment and the segmented structure of unemployment uncovers aspects of economic segmentation not revealed by the study of earnings attainment. The final section elaborates a conceptual framework of modes of job separation based on how adjustments in the employment structure intersects with adjustments by individual employees.

THE STRUCTURAL DETERMINANTS
OF UNEMPLOYMENT

The structural determinants of unemployment examined in Chapters 4–6 are class position, economic sector, and the business cycle. Many other structural factors could be studied but since, to my knowledge, this is the first attempt to construct and test propositions systematically on the relation between segmentation in employment and segmentation in unemployment, a simpler model has been retained. The economic flow diagram presented in Chapter 1 indicates that outcomes of the matching process, such as earnings or the number of unemployed, result from the way characteristics of a supply of workers (from the household sector) intersect with characteristics of the demand side (the business sector). The fundamental argument examined in detail in subsequent chapters is that unemployment outcomes (in number and type) result not only from personal characteristics of age, race, and education[1] but also from the structural or institutional factors embodied in the segmentation of employment positions (class) and firms (economic sectors). These two aspects of the business sector or demand side, then, are expected to make significant and independent contributions to explaining the distribution of the unemployed. The business cycle, the third structural variable, is interpreted as capturing how the impact of class and economic sector on unemployment changes with the level of aggregate economic conditions. In short, not only personal but structural factors contribute to producing unemployment outcomes. Further, the structural factors are themselves segmented such that the outcomes differ by class position, economic sector, and stage in the business cycle.

---

[1] Gender of a worker is, of course, another supply-side characteristic of workers that should be included in this list. However, for reasons discussed in Footnote 2 of Chapter 3, women were not included in this study.

Structural Sources of Vulnerability and Power

Underlying the specific analyses in Chapters 4–6 is the assumption that within a market economy, various factors make an individual, group, or economic unit subject to or sheltered from the relations of domination in the labor and product markets. This, I have said, is the issue of vulnerability and power.

In the case of individuals, traditional economic analysis argues that personal endowments of ability, experience, motivation, and training primarily determine economic attainments. Other sources of vulnerability and power, especially the class and sector location of an individual's job in the business sector also contribute to the individual's economic prospects. This is especially important in advanced capitalism where the significance of the state sector, oligopoly market power, managerial hierarchies, and professional–technical positions have increased. As a consequence, structural inequality between capital and labor is complemented by segmentation within capital and within labor.

Two general propositions provide insight into the importance of class and sector sources of vulnerability and power. The first is an abstract proposition concerning the nature of markets and vulnerability in capitalism. The second is historical, arguing that the transition from competitive to advanced capitalism is based on and reflects a new arrangement of structural differentiation in market power.

First, structural differences among class fractions and economic sectors both reflect and become manifested in market transactions. This does not mean that the underlying score of social relations of domination is market relations. It does mean, however, that one way such domination becomes socially consequential is through its impact on market relations. In the classical model, transactions among and between firms, workers, and consumers occur among actors with equal vulnerability and power. In contrast, Marx stressed that as the transitory petty-commodity phase of capitalism becomes superseded by competitive and centralized (monopoly) capitalism, an imbalance of vulnerability and power arises both between workers and capitalists, and, increasingly, among capitalists as well. Neoclassical analysis, too, recognized variation in vulnerability and power among individuals and firms. It incorporated into theory differences in marginal productivity or human capital of workers and differences between competitive firms and concentrated ones in both factor and product markets. With some exceptions, however, economic outcomes continued generally to be viewed as a function of individual variation in facing markets rather than of the structural variation in those markets themselves.

The second proposition is that the transition from competitive–centralized to advanced capitalism is based on and reflects new forms of structural differentiation in market power. These new forms provide certain workers, class positions, and firms with new resources of bargaining power both to insulate themselves from competitive market relations and to shape economic exchanges to their benefit. Many critics of neoclassical and of the related sociological status-attainment research emphasize that free competitive markets no longer constitute the sole or even primary linkages in the determination of economic outcomes. This point is made by Kalecki (1943), Robinson (1969), Thurow (1975), Lindblom (1977), Galbraith (1967), Sørenson (1977), and Granovetter (1981). A similar argument is made by those who espouse the segmentation perspective such as Averitt (1968), and Edwards, Reich, and Gordon (1975). Likewise, Marxists such as Wright (1978, 1979), Edwards (1979), Burawoy (1979), and Braverman (1974) argue that variation in vulnerability and power among classes and firms dictates that no one particular economic process determines all labor market outcomes.

Common to all these alternative views is the assumption that neoclassical notions of markets are inadequate. Historical developments in industrialized capitalism systematically produce enclaves. Markets are in fact arenas of exchange between classes and sectors with structural inequalities of vulnerability and power. Even where individuals are equally endowed with human capital, structural sources of inequality confronting these individuals independently contribute to unequal outcomes for them. In such a differentiated economy, struggles among capital and between capital and labor result in shelters from vulnerability for certain workers, positions, and economic units. Consequently, research should incorporate such sources of inequality into its theoretical model.

Class Fractions and Economic Sectors in Advanced Capitalism

The previous section argued that structural capacities are relevant for determining economic outcomes. This section details the particular shape of class fractions and economic sectors that define the structural sources of vulnerability and power in advanced capitalism. Even though these two aspects of segmentation are discussed in turn, it is important to keep in mind that the emergence of class fractions and economic sectors occurred simultaneously and were mutually determinative.

CLASS FRACTIONS

Poulantzas (1975), Wright (1978), Edwards (1979) and other researchers of segmented labor markets have traced the changes of the class structure from slightly different but related theoretical motivations. Poulantzas emphasizes the growth of what Braverman (1974) calls the "middle layers" of professional, technical, managerial, clerical, and sales positions. He examines how the traditional dichotomous class structure of bourgeoisie and proletariat has become more complex as these middle layers expand. He goes on to argue that these positions are theoretically difficult to categorize according to criteria based on relations of production. He suggests that political and ideological criteria derived from the relations of production must be added to determine the class location of these middle layers. Wright (1978) criticizes Poulantzas's approach for its inconsistency and an absence of theoretical rationale.

Following Przeworski (1977), Wright (1978) defines classes as sets of positions or "empty places" within the relations of production. He argues that the middle layers of small employers as well as semi-autonomous and managerial employees occupy contradictory locations between classes whereas sales and clerical positions and contradictory locations.

Edwards (1979) combining class analysis and segmentation perspectives stresses the historical development of these middle layers. He argues that transformations in the accumulation process created new needs and opportunities for social control of work relations. The divisions in the working class as well as the elaboration of professional and managerial positions, which result from new forms of social control, contribute to the segmentation of job positions into upper- and lower-tier primary positions and secondary positions. In this formulation, the basis for segmentation becomes the rewards or outcomes connected to positions rather than simply their location within the relations of production. Although this last point is problematic because it too readily collapses diverse classes into the same segments, it also enables Edwards to stress segmentation of working class positions.

In reference to our discussion of class variation in vulnerability or resources of bargaining power, the point is that the development of class fractions is simultaneously the development of vulnerability and power in relation to the labor market. Across and within classes, labor market relations dictated by the principles of supply and demand have for some class segments remained consequential whereas for other segments they have become less imposing or even superseded. As I argue in Chapter 4, just as resources of bargaining power have become unevenly distributed among class segments, outcomes in the labor market—especially for levels and

types of unemployment—have become segmented as well. The fundamental source of this variation, as we shall see, is the qualitative variation of class fractions in remaining vulnerable to or in becoming sheltered from the market mechanisms that generate unemployment.

ECONOMIC SECTORS

Along with the transformation of class structure, the historical development of capitalism has entailed the transformation of the accumulation process. Concentration, centralization, and state participation in the accumulation process have produced a division among sectors based on their relative vulnerability and power in factor and product markets.

The economic sector in which a firm is located is determined by the type and degree of vulnerability and power evidenced by the firm in confronting the product market, the arena of exchange that produces revenue and realizes profits. Traditional economic research as well as institutional and Marxist literature focuses on designating three sectors; oligopoly, competitive, and state. Although Marxist literature generally distinguishes between monopoly and competitive rather than between oligopoly and competitive sectors, I shall employ the latter distinction in order to emphasize the empirical fact that few firms are so concentrated in their product markets as to be considered pure monopolies.[2]

In early phases of capitalism the segmentation of capital into functional sectors was more relevant than it is today. Industrial, commercial, financial, and agricultural sectors represented differing arrangements of productive and unproductive labor (labor producing value and labor involved in its realization). In the monopoly phase of capitalism the horizontal and vertical integration of capital made such functional distinctions outmoded. Instead, capital became segmented into oligopoly and competitive sectors.

An important aspect of this attempt to tease out analytical distinction between oligopoly and competitive sectors entails distinguishing old and new competitive capital. An exposition of the debate is beyond the scope of this book (see Edwards, 1979:72–89). But its fruit is that competitive capital should not be defined simply as the remnant of petty-bourgeois production or commercial activity. Rather, according to Averitt (1968) and Poulantzas

---

[2]It should be noted, however, that Marx's use of the term "monopoly" or "monopoly capitalism" does not refer to the technical notion of being the sole seller in a product market. Rather, for Marx, monopoly refers to absolute size or centralization of capital as well as to relative concentration in the product market. Thus, a diversified congolmerate like General Motors is clearly a monopoly sector firm in Marxist terms but not according to the technical definition in traditional economics texts.

(1975), competitive capital is best understood in the advanced stages of capitalism as subordinated yet articulated to oligopoly capital. On the one hand, this satellite competitive capital is distinguished from petty-bourgeois production and commercial activity. On the other hand, it is distinguished from "loyal opposition" firms that provide moderate competition for oligopoly firms in an industry and from "free agent" firms that are free from affiliation with center firms.

According to Averitt (1968) and Poulantzas (1975), such nonoligopoly or satellite competitive firms are characterized by their functions for oligopoly capital:

1. Competitive firms shoulder a disproportionate amount of the business risk associated with pioneering new investments and with downturns in the business cycle.
2. Competitive firms engage in less profitable but necessary sectors and thereby free oligopoly capital for investments with higher profitability.
3. Competitive firms also engage in secondary and nonintegrated lines of production.
4. Competitive capital has high commodity prices, legitimizing the comparably higher pricing of oligopoly firms whose costs do not warrant such price levels.
5. Competitive capital utilizes a disproportionate degree of labor-intensive production and thereby functions as a staging post for the general subjection of labor by removing some labor–organization conflict from oligopoly capital.

As a result of the historical process of segmentation among economic sectors, it is possible to distinguish for these sectors differing relationships in the labor and product market. Such distinctions are most often made on the basis of product market concentration. Although nonentrepreneurial, nonprofit, or state sectors sometimes are distinguished (e.g., Hall, 1975; O'Connor, 1973; Weisbrod, 1977); Weisbrod and Long, 1977), the reliance on the criterion of product market concentration results in most research focusing on the difference between oligopoly and competitive sectors. Even then, the causal links between concentrated markets, administered pricing, economies of scale, higher profits, higher wage rates, and other labor outcomes, are the subjects of much debate (cf. Scherer, 1980:267–295). Despite problems of quality and comparability of data, Scherer (1980:294–295) concludes that there is "considerable statistical support for industrial

organization theory's predictions of a relationship among profitability, seller concentration, and barriers to entry."

Thus, I argue that the existence of economic sectors, like those of classes and class fractions, reflects an underlying differentiation among groups of firms in their vulnerability and power. These differences are examined in more detail in Chapter 5. There I argue how firms vary in their fundamental capacity to maintain revenue and how, in reference to unemployment, the relation of a firm to external and internal labor markets and to product markets determines the level and type of unemployment associated with that firm. Just as firms relate to these markets with differing capacities according to their economic sector, so too do they vary by sector in their levels and types of unemployment.[3]

THE BUSINESS CYCLE

The final structural variable affecting the vulnerability and power of individual actors in obtaining labor-market outcomes is the business cycle. In the present research, the business cycle refers to the short-term rise and fall of aggregate demand rather than the long-run, secular business cycles or long waves analyzed by Kondratieff (1935), Gordon (1978, 1980), or Wiesskopf (1981). The official demarcation of a business cycle is determined retrospectively by the National Bureau of Economic Research. It is defined as a periodic fluctuation in aggregate business conditions. The importance of the business cycle in the analysis is twofold. First, it is, in its own right, a structural variable that affects both the overall number of unemployed and the level of types of unemployed at any one time. Second, it interacts with the vulnerability and power provided by the structure of class positions and economic sectors. At different stages in the business cycle, the vulnerability

---

[3]A further point in discussing the evolution of class fractions and economic sectors is that the qualitatively different ways segments relate to markets is not merely an inevitable outcome of structural forces. Although the tendency to reduce the contingencies of markets is dictated in part by the expansionary imperative of capitalism, the relation of classes and firms to the market is not merely a given. Granting the structural motivation of classes and firms to enhance their market power, the particular way in which markets are shaped and reconstructed and the transitions in economic relations of vulnerability and power they entail are themselves objects of struggle through power. Although this research is not a study of the forces that have shaped markets over the last 100 years, it does assume the fruit of such historical analysis in arguing how differentiated classes and economic sectors exercise independent structural effects on unemployment.

and power of class position and economic sector work differently in creating the pool of unemployed persons.

Major Propositions

In view of the analytical framework of the economic flow diagram and the consideration reviewed thus far in this chapter, the three fundamental propositions examined in Chapters 4–6 can be formulated.

RELATION OF CLASS POSITION
AND UNEMPLOYMENT

Chapter 4 examines the structural impact of class position on unemployment, controlling for the modeled impacts of economic sector, business cycle, race, age, and education. The goal is to discern the independent contribution of the type of resources of power associated with employment in a certain class position on the distribution of persons to types of unemployment. The argument is that characteristics of the demand side embodied in the class or class fraction of employment in the business sector affect the distribution of unemployed. Independent of other structural and personal sources, the type of vulnerability and power associated with a position of employment in the class structure shapes the distribution of unemployed to types of unemployment. For instance, over and above the insulation provided by their personal characteristics, type of firm, and stage in the business cycle, employment in a managerial position, shelters workers from a high probability of unemployment due to the position's importance in the relations of authority.

RELATION OF ECONOMIC SECTOR
AND UNEMPLOYMENT

Chapter 5 turns to the relation between economic sector and unemployment. Over and above the impact of class position, a second source of structural, demand-side factors affecting labor market outcomes for members of the household sector is the sector in which the employment position is located. Chapter 5 details the linkages between various economic sectors and unemployment outcomes, controlling for the modeled effects of personal and other structural variables. In terms of the economic flow diagram, the type and degree of control of a firm in the product market (i.e., the manner and

degree to which a firm is able to maintain the generation of revenue) affects the manner and degree to which a firm makes unemployment adjustments in the product market power serve both to distinguish the competitive, oligopoly, and state sectors (among others) and to influence their labor market behavior in terms of levels of types of unemployment. Although most recent research in the segmentation tradition has emphasized actual characteristics of firms (such as size, international structure, capital intensity, and size of assets; see Kaufman, 1981, Hodson, 1980; Wallace and Kalleberg, 1981), the analysis reported in Chapter 5 focuses on the impact of firm characteristics determined by and reflecting product market power. For instance, oligopoly firms, those with a high degree of product market concentration, are conceived as price administrators and output adjusters in the labor market.

BUSINESS CYCLE AND UNEMPLOYMENT

Chapter 6 examines the relation between stage in the business cycle and unemployment. In terms of the economic flow diagram, the argument is, first, that the business cycle has a direct effect on the labor market by determining the level of economic activity in the product market. In business downturns, for instance, the level of aggregate economic activity in the product market constricts such that, given the distribution of personal and structural forces, certain labor market adjustments of unemployment occur due to the level of economic activity. Second, the business cycle serves as the environment within which the the impact of economic sector changes. Thus, Chapter 6 also analyzes the interaction effect between business cycle and economic sector. In effect, this significant interaction argues that the effect of sector on the labor market changes according to stages in the business cycle. For instance, the findings indicate that not only do the relatively equal levels of overall unemployment in the oligopoly and competitive sectors obscure the differences in types of unemployment (Chapter 5) but that examining aggregate levels also obscures the greater fluctuation of unemployment (especially through layoffs) in the oligopoly sector over the cycle.

In brief, the labor market relation between persons in the household sector and type of firm in the business sector is segmented not only according to firm type but over and above that by the differentiated impact of stages in the business cycle on the different firm types. By examining the differences in unemployment among firm types over the business cycle, it is possible to decompose the averaged or general relation between firm and unemployment into the stage-specific variations that constitute the averaged relation.

CURRENT RESEARCH ON UNEMPLOYMENT

This section outlines some major trends in recent research on unemployment as a prelude to developing a framework for studying types of unemployment. It simultaneously reviews the varied meanings of unemployment in terms of the economic flow diagram of Chapter 1 and argues that this recent research has advanced the understanding of unemployment only in a limited way. That is, it stresses the variety of types and processes of unemployment that comprise the aggregate level but continues to focus only on the variation of these components of unemployment by demographic groups or by individual differences in human-capital endowments. Neglected is the relation between types of unemployment and structural variables.

Unemployment Theory

With the exception of some very recent work (e.g., Berg, Bibb, Finegan, and Swafford, 1981; Cornfield, 1980, 1981; Schervish, 1981) sociological literature offers little guidance for research on the social–structural sources of types of unemployment since it has focused almost exclusively on the social–psychological causes and consequences of unemployment (cf. Aiken, Ferman, and Sheppard, 1968; Brenner, 1976; Cohn, 1977; Ferman, 1964; Jacobs, 1965; Komarovsky, 1940; Tiffany, Cowan, and Tiffany, 1970; Wilcock and Granke, 1963). Neoclassical economic literature, on the one hand, and institutional and Marxist literature, on the other, are more helpful.

Studies on the sources of unemployment can be classified according to their level of analysis and according to the kinds of variables they consider. Although few researchers or specific studies adhere mechanically to a particular approach, there are general schools of thought that determine the level of analysis and the variables deemed appropriate for explaining the sources of unemployment. These schools of thought are portrayed in textbook accounts of unemployment as frictional, structural, and demand-deficient unemployment.[4] Which of these models is pursued in explaining

---

[4]*Frictional unemployment:* The notion of frictional unemployment is derived from the assumptions of the microeconomic, neoclassical tradition espoused by Marshall. It is simultaneously a thesis about the source and level of unemployment. Unemployment results from the normal, short-run adjustments between supply and demand of labor. But as a theory of unemployment, the frictional hypothesis stresses the nature of worker supply: It maintains that during periods of growth, workers voluntarily leave present jobs or enter the labor market in search of new employment; in periods of decline workers become unemployed because they

(continued)

unemployment (or at least that level of unemployment that exceeds "full-employment") derives largely from the researcher's adherence to (*a*) a Marshallian, or (*b*) a Keynesian economic perspective.

The Marshallian world of neoclassical economics emphasizes the decision-making capacities of individuals, firms, and industries within free markets of supply and demand cleared by prices. In accord with Say's law, supply in the labor market creates its own demand. Thus, unemployment is a short-run abberation due to voluntary worker decisions to persist in wage demands above the market price. In contrast, Keynesian economics emphasizes the aggregate conditions of economic and labor-force disequilibria that emerge from the inability of market forces to reestablish a full employment equilibrium. Some unemployment, Keynes recognized, resulted from the voluntary flows of workers from one job to another. Nevertheless, in the wake of the Great Depression, Keynes (1936) formulated his theory of involuntary unemployment in which workers are unable to locate jobs even when offering to work at the wage-level paid to other workers with the same

---

choose not to work in jobs at the lower equilibrium wage. It argues that a certain level of unemployment can be considered normal because it reflects an expected level of labor turnover as market mechanisms shift the match of workers and jobs at the equilibrium wage. Frictional unemployment is eased by achieving a more efficient matching of workers and jobs through increased information and by removing barriers to mobility.

Demand deficiency unemployment: Demand deficiency or cyclical unemployment is involuntary joblessness due to an insufficient number of job opportunities. Even when workers are willing to work at the equilibrium wage for their skill level, employment is unavailable. When demand decreases over the business cycle, workers are fired or laid off and new job seekers cannot find work. To mitigate unemployment, then, targeted fiscal and monetary policies are needed to revise aggregate demand.

Structural unemployment: The structural hypothesis proposes that unemployment derives from the mismatching of the supply of workers having particular skills with the demand of job opportunities requiring different labor capacities. This mismatch results from both demographic changes in the number and characteristics of labor and changes in the composition of employment positions. Frictional unemployment occurs because workers have not yet located the existing job that fits their skills. Structural unemployment, however, occurs when jobs exist but workers are either over- or under-trained for them. Quantitatively, structural unemployment hypotheses suggest that unemployment rates have come to exceed what can be accounted for by normal frictional flows. Proposals for lowering structural unemployment invariably include policies for retraining workers and offering employer incentives to provide on-the-job training.

Recent research on unemployment continues to employ the distinctions among frictional, structural, and demand-deficiency unemployment. However, this research has elaborated these models and sophisticated the debate among them. Three developments have occurred: (*a*) conceptualizing and measuring unemployment as a differentiated dependent variable; (*b*) fuller consideration of institutional economic factors and government activity as independent and intervening variables in explaining characteristics of unemployment; and (*c*) separating the effects and sources of unemployment according to demographic groups and labor market segments.

skill. Put simply, labor supply outstrips demand. Demand for labor lags because the demand for goods and services tends to lag behind the capacity of the economy to produce them. Due to saving, income obtained by workers and firms fails to translate into an equal level of demand.

Macrolevel Theories

DEMAND DEFICIENCY

During the 1950s and 1960s, theories of unemployment tended to reflect the Keynesian emphasis on deficient demand. The unemployed were presumed to have lost their jobs and, in Feldstein's words, were pictured "as an inactive pool of job losers who had to wait for a general business upturn before they could find new jobs [1975:725]." Okun (1962) quantified this relationship between GNP growth and the level of unemployment exceeding normal "full-employment" unemployment. Okun's law proposes that on the average, a percentage point increase unemployment above 4% is associated with about a 3% decrease in real GNP.

In terms of the economic flow diagram of Chapter 1, demand deficiency unemployment exists when the number of household members seeking employment exceeds the number of employment positions available. That is, downturns in aggregate economic activity result in job loss for members of the labor force already matched to jobs and in the decreased probability of nonworking persons to find employment. Thus demand deficiency unemployment is the circumstance in which either or (usually) both of the following two situations occur:

1. Existing matches between persons and jobs are broken.
2. The incidence of new matches is curtailed.

This demand-deficiency view received criticism from two directions as a number of changes in the labor force became recognized. These included the increasing number of secondary workers, especially the dramatic increment in female (especially married) labor-force participation rates; the acceleration of technological disemployment due to automation; the stable disparity between black and white unemployment rates; and the provision of poverty level incomes by full-time employment (Levitan and Taggart, 1974: 8–10).

STRUCTURAL UNEMPLOYMENT

The first line of criticism was an elaboration of the argument concerning structure unemployment. Structural unemployment may be defined as the

simultaneous occurrence of both an excess of persons seeking jobs and an excess of empty employment positions; regardless, the persons seeking employment remain unmatched to vacant jobs. This happens because the persons and jobs are geographically separated or because the persons seeking employment lack the personal characteristics deemed necessary for employment in the vacant jobs. In this sense, structural unemployment is a group- and sector-specific *inability* to match persons and jobs. In the long run it is possible to train workers and transform job requisites. When this occurs, structural unemployment or the inability to match workers and jobs becomes transformed into frictional unemployment or, simply, the *failure* to link potentially matchable workers and jobs. In the short run, however, the inability of the labor market to match the current supply of workers and demand of jobs is the fundamental source of structural unemployment.

Among those emphasizing this targeted or group-specific nature of unemployment are Killingsworth (1974) and Killingsworth and King (1977). They attacked the conventional wisdom of the 1960s that "sufficiently strong application of fiscal and monetary policy, *without anything else*, is capable of reducing unemployment to the 3.5 percent level. Any unemployment rate higher than that is clear evidence of an insufficiency of aggregate demand and nothing else [1974:97]." Rather, the drop in the national unemployment rate from 5.7 to 3.5% between 1963 and 1969 was largely an artifact of changes in the official definition of unemployment, the expansion of manpower training programs and the Armed Forces, and changes in draft deferment policies. Therefore, the confirmation of Okun's law by the conjunction of tax cuts and decrease in measured unemployment was only apparent. These decreases also obscured the persistence of high rates of structural employment for black men and black youth. These two groups not only experience unemployment rates more than twice those for whites, they also tend to leave the labor force in greater numbers during recessions. They swell the ranks of the "hidden unemployed" while making it appear that the black unemployment rate is growing at a lower pace than the white rate (see also Clark and Summers, 1979). Killingsworth thus argues that the major problem of unemployment is the structural imbalance between job opportunities and the level of training of potential incumbents, especially black youth. Policy must become targeted directly toward the retraining of these workers and supplying public service employment.

SEGMENTATION PERSPECTIVE

A second critique of demand deficiency analysis is provided by advocates of dual or segmented labor markets, including those proposing various forms of queue theory. These theorists, like Killingsworth and King, offer a view of

the sources of unemployment that is simultaneously an alternative view of the nature of the labor market. Although diverse in their emphasis, these theorists concur that neither Keynesian nor neoclassical theory can explain unemployment because the labor market itself is structurally differentiated. Demand in the labor market is discontinuous. Therefore, some sectors of jobs or industries, even in recessions, continue to enjoy low unemployment whereas other sectors are immune from fiscal stimulus and suffer high unemployment whereas other sectors are immune from fiscal stimulus and suffer high unemployment even during expansionary periods (cf. Bluestone, 1970; Doeringer and Piore, 1971, 1975; Edwards, Reich, and Gordon, 1975; Gordon, 1972). In a similar vein, queue theory (cf. Thurow, 1975, 1978, 1980) holds that macroeconomic stimulation as well as upturns in demand over the business cycle affect demand precisely in those sectors of the economy with the tightest labor markets. Sectors of low-paying jobs, where the bulk of the "hard-core" unemployed move in and out of employment, remain generally unaffected by accelerated demand. Consequently high unemployment is structurally determined, irremediable by macropolicies, and congruent with inflation. Unemployment occurs among those particular groups of workers whose race, sex, training, and trainability places them at the bottom of the labor queue and excludes them from employment in the sectors of the economy where demand is strongest and most susceptible to general expansion.

Marxist Perspective

Marxist analysis of unemployment, like the Keynesian approach, is at the aggregate level. For Keynesian theorists, unemployment results from a correctable deficiency of effective demand; in the Marxist tradition, however, unemployment derives from the general and normal anarchism of the market economy in which what proves beneficial for an individual firm is dysfunctional for the system as a whole (cf. Weisskopf, 1978). Individual firms maximize profits and enjoy their most efficient production at levels of employment that fail to provide employment for the labor force as a whole. This, suggest Robinson and Eatwell (1974:117), means that the Marxist theory of the reserve army of labor is more correctly conceptualized in terms of nonemployment rather than unemployment, and, it should be added immediately, conceptualized in terms of fluctuating and uneven levels of nonemployment.

Within the framework of Figure 1.1, this means that the Marxist perspective focuses less on the particular forms of inadequate labor market

matching between the household and business sectors than on how the labor market itself is an arena of unequal exchange dominated by capital and, therefore, malleable in accord with the changing needs of capital. The focus is on how the secular and cyclical levels of unemployment (no matter what the form) function (a) to enhance the bargaining power of capital in the labor market and thereby (b) to ensure that fluctuations in wage and employment levels parallel fluctuations in general and firm-specific conditions for profitability.

Marx (1967 I:641–644 distinguish among the floating, latent, and stagnant surplus population.[5] Subsequent Marxist research, however, tended

---

[5]The classical statement on the growth and role of unemployment and the unemployed in capitalist, market economies is Marx's treatment of surplus population and industrial reserve army. Marx argues that it is not accidental that capitalism first molds a free industrial working class from precapitalistic agriculture, craft production, and the petty bourgeoisie and then disemploys and pauperizes these workers. This process systematically manifests the essence of capitalist evolution through its cycles of expansion and contraction. The ongoing increase of concentration of capital results in the long run in a reduction of employment positions as the ratio of constant to variable capital increases. Marx proposes, therefore, that the development of capitalism, manifested in accumulation, concentration, centralized and technological innovation, is directly related to the creation of relative surplus population or industrial reserve army.

Since for Marx the basis of capitalism is expansion of profit or surplus value and since this derives at first from "growth of its variable constituent or of the part invested in labour power," then "The demand for labour and the subsistence-fund of the labourers clearly increase in the same proportion as the capital, and then more rapidly, the more rapidly capital increases [1967 I:613]." Through concentration and centralization of capital, however, accumulation "passes from the circular to the spiral form [I:627]" so that "whilst concentration thus intensifies and accelerates the effects of accumulation, it simultaneously extends and speeds composition of capital which raise its constant portion at the expense of its variable portion, thus diminishing the relative demand for labour [I:628]."

Coupled with the capitalization of agriculture and its "freeing of labor" (cf. Marx I:642) the relative decline in necessary laboring population for various industrial firms provides a "disposable industrial reserve army . . . a mass of human material always ready for exploitation [632]." Such flexibility and mobility of labor, both from agriculture to industry and across industries serves well the requirements of capital expansion. As Marx says, over population, in the sense just described, creates a mass of workers able to be thrown "suddenly on the decisive point [of new production] without injury to the scale of production in other spheres [p. 632]." "Periods of average activity, production at high pressure, crisis and stagnation" depend on and in turn determine "the constant transformation of a part of the labouring population into unemployed or half-employed hands [I:632–633]."

The relative surplus population or industrial reserve army takes on three forms, according to Marx. None of these is to be confused with the so-called lumpenproletariat comprised of "vagabonds, criminals, prostitutes, in a word, the 'dangerous' classes [I:643]." The *floating* surplus population is in the centers of modern industry such as factories and mines. As an aggregate, it endures periodic shifts in and out of employment in accord with the growth of capital into new areas and the relative decline in need for labor in established production due to

(continued)

to argue that the leading question is neither empirical investigation of rates, types, and frequencies; nor is it specifically policy oriented. Rather, the question is what unemployment reveals about the workings of the capitalist political economy. Unemployment and its relation to aggregate demand are viewed as telling characteristics of the inherent crises that befall market economies (see Castello, 1980; NACLA, 1975; Sherman, 1976). As such, unemployment or nonemployment is both the condition for and the result of the employment relationship. On the one hand, because profitability requires paying labor a wage lower than the value produced by labor, firms benefit from the existence of surplus population in the form of a malleable reserve army. This reserve army fortifies the employment relationship by disciplining labor turnover and labor demands and by containing wages. On the other hand, the competitive drive for profitability leads to the introduction of capital-intensive technology with a dual consequence for unemployment. In the short run, lowered demand for labor causes disemployment. In the long

---

technological innovation and a rising organic composition of capital. In relation to the labor market, floating laborers "are sometimes repelled, sometimes attracted again in greater masses, the number of those employed increasing on the whole, although in a constantly decreasing proportion to the scale of production [1967 I:641]."

The *latent* surplus population is composed of agricultural labor and, although not mentioned directly by Marx, by those remaining artisans and petty bourgeoisie whose relation to production or commerce is tenuated under capitalist competition and expansion. This group thus stands "with one foot already in the swamp of pauperism" and is "constantly on the point of passing over into an urban or manufacturing proletariat, and on the lookout for circumstances favourable to this transformation [p. 642]." In the case of the agricultural worker, and analogously for the craftworker and petty bourgeoisie, the constant flow into the urban industrial labor force presupposes in the country or noncapitalist spheres of production, the destruction of viable ways to earn subsistence. Thus, the latent surplus population waits in the wings for their call to the stage of capitalist production in the role of wage-labor.

The *stagnant* part of the active labor army, Marx characterizes as an already created and ready reservoir and disposable labor-power. It suffers extremely irregular employment and endures conditions of life that "sink below the average normal level of the working class." It is the most easily exploited branch of labor, forced to a "maximum of working-time and a minimum of wages." It is recruited from the surplus forces of capitalized agriculture and modern industry, "specifically from those decaying branches of industry where handicraft is yielding to manufacture, manufacture to machinery [1967 I:643]."

Finally, Marx describes a fourth group of workers, those most dramatically disposed over by capitalist production. These *paupers*, "the lowest sediment of the relative surplus population," are first, those able to work but employed only at the heights of the business cycle; second, orphans and pauper children likewise employed in periods of boom but otherwise doomed to become the next generation of poor; and third, the demoralized, ragged, sick, and mutilated offspring of industrial machinery and relations of production. These laborers, then, rest in poverty and unproductivity until a spurt of productive growth calls them forth for temporary employment: "Pauperism is the hospital of the active labour-army and the dead weight of the industrial reserve army [1967 I:644]."

run, this creates a crisis of investment and of underconsumption both of which lead to further unemployment (cf. Boddy and Crotty, 1975; Glyn and Sutcliffe, 1972).

Microlevel Theories

In the 1970s many theorists reemphasized the voluntary, frictional nature of unemployment. Inspired by neoclassical assumptions as well as by empirical research confirming the high degree of turnovers and of layoffs in particular (cf. Feldstein, 1973, 1975, 1976; Hall, 1972), this research pursued a sophisticated critique of both demand-deficiency and structural approaches to unemployment. In its extreme form, this approach argues that virtually all unemployment results from worker decisions (cf. Feldstein, 1976). Buttressed by generous minimum wage laws, multiple-income households, welfare, and unemployment insurance "subsidies," workers are able to leave one job before obtaining another, to enter the labor force in search of jobs with high benefits, and to extend durations of unemployment. All this contributes to the view that "the majority of the unemployed do not become unemployed by losing their previous jobs; they quit voluntarily or are new entrants or reentrants into the labor force. Moreover, the typical duration of unemployment is very short; more than half of unemployment spells end in four weeks or less [Feldstein, 1975:725–726]." Also this approach argues that layoffs, which might be considered clear examples of involuntary unemployment, are actually voluntary in the sense that workers help formulate and agree to the rules by which they exchange high wages, unionization, and other benefits for expected patterns of layoffs of short duration with a guarantee of recall (cf. Feldstein, 1976:938, 955).

Three strands of research, all focusing on the supply side of unemployment, share this more sophisticated model of frictional unemployment: (a) empirical turnover models with their foundations in search theory; (b) the theory of specific human capital; and (c) the treatment of abnormally high unemployment rates for blacks as special cases of frictional unemployment.

Common to each of these strands is the notion, as stated previously, that the major source of unemployment is the *lack* of matching between the supply of labor and the demand of jobs. It is not that there is a structural *impossibility* of linking workers to jobs. Rather there are flows in the labor market in and out of jobs, which reflect the voluntary decisions of members of the household sector to enhance the correspondence of personal preferences to job characteristics.

SEARCH THEORY AND TURNOVER MODELS

Search theory, built upon Stigler's (1961, 1962) general theory of information and search, and on empirical data on turnover, argues that workers leave employment or enter the labor force and become technically unemployed in order to invest more time in looking for a job. The theory presumes that such investment is more or less costly depending on the worker's propensity to consume leisure and the changing expectation that continued search will improve job quality. Search theorists differ in their technical assumptions about perfectly functioning demand, the number of searches per day a worker undertakes, and whether skills of searchers are appropriately matched to available job vacancies.

The contribution of search theory is its explanation of duration of unemployment as a function of how aggregate demand, employment policies, and unemployment insurance affect the behavior and decisions of unemployed workers. These decisions entail whether to leave the labor force, to extend one's duration of unemployment, to accept a certain wage, to remain in one's present employment, to leave that job and search for a new one, or to search while still employed.

Turnover models are based on the empirical findings derived from decomposing unemployment rates into layoffs (temporary and indefinite), quits, new entrants, and reentrants to the labor force. Without denying the presence of some involuntary unemployment, turnover research concludes that the vast majority of measured unemployment is accounted for by workers on layoff and waiting to be recalled, new entrants and reentrants to the labor force, and workers who quit their jobs voluntarily in search of new ones. Although all this research—generally based on data and definitions in employment and earnings reports—incorrectly collapses job firings into the category of layoffs, the general argument persists. Two processes are highlighted: flows out of employment and flows into employment. Perry (1972:247) describes this process by a lottery model: "In the process of job search, each unemployed person can be conceived of as having a lottery ticket. If his number comes up, he gets a job. If not, and if he does not quit the lottery and leave the labor force, he continues unemployed another week."

Marston (1975), Stigler (1961, 1962), Rees (1966), Lippman and McCall (1976), among others, analyze these flows of turnover within search theory. The pool of workers in this lottery is constituted also of persons about to enter the labor force and by workers about to leave one job and search for another, either by quitting or by being laid off or fired. Perry finds that flows into unemployment are higher for secondary (largely black youths) than for primary workers because secondary workers are unemployed more frequently, not because they suffer longer durations of unemployment. But this higher frequency is not due to normal transitions resulting from such factors

as school enrollment, having babies, or job changes for building a career. Moreover, when secondary workers leave the labor force it is because they are discouraged by their chances to obtain work. Thus, the measured short duration of unemployment is not due to easy and frequent access to jobs, albeit secondary ones (as Hall, 1970b, seems to imply). Because they move in and out of the labor force during periods of job separation, secondary workers have lower hiring probabilities than primary workers even though these two groups appear to have comparable durations of unemployment (Perry, 1972:278). A similar point is made by Clark and Summers (1979:14). They challenge the turnover perspective by arguing that when the total pool of unemployment weeks is examined, it becomes clear that unemployment "is characterized by relatively few persons who are out of work a large part of the time."

THEORY OF SPECIFIC HUMAN CAPITAL

A second strand focusing on the supply side of unemployment examines the flow of workers from employment to unemployment as a function of the firm-specific human capital of workers. Becker (1962) distinguishes general from specific human capital of workers, and within specific human capital between employer- and employee-financed on-the-job training. Specific training increases a worker's marginal productivity. This becomes embodied in higher wages and results in an incentive for employers to keep workers attached to the firm and for workers to remain in the firm. Most broadly this theory predicts that where the fixed costs of employment, due to on-the-job training, are greatest, unemployment is lowest (Rees, 1973:118–120). Mincer (1962:69–71) finds that black–white differentials in unemployment are related to differences in on-the-job training. Parsons (1972) decomposes unemployment into worker-initiated (quits) and employer-initiated (layoffs) types. He finds that worker-financed specific human capital is negatively related to quits whereas firm-financed human capital is negatively related to layoffs.

ABNORMAL FRICTIONAL UNEMPLOYMENT

A third approach is suggested by Hall's (1970b) notion of abnormal frictional unemployment. This approach begins with the empirical findings that for groups such as black youths and women their higher than expected rates of unemployment at full employment are due not to long durations of chronic unemployment but to abnormally frequent spells of unemployment. This hypothesis runs counter to both the cyclical and structural views, which

concur that even in full employment residual unemployment can be remedied by increasing job opportunities or by training workers. Hall (1970b) maintains that his approach differs from turnover and search models which imply "that every person who reports himself as out of work is spending a few weeks between jobs in the normal advancement of his career [p. 389]." In contrast, he argues that positions are available for workers at their present skill levels. But these positions do not encourage stable employment since they are not integrated into a structure of advancement. This form of unemployment is frictional because jobs are available. It is frictional in an abnormal sense, however, because the low quality of the jobs and their inability to contribute to career advancement induces extreme frequency of turnover.

Evaluation of the Theories

The value of the Keynesian approach lies in its contribution to a general understanding of the causes of and remedies for unemployment. It fails, however to consider how different levels of types of unemployment result from the different degree of vulnerability of sectors of the economy to economic downturns, and within these sectors, from the different degrees of bargaining power attached to employment positions.

Related critiques apply to other strands of research. For instance, the value of the Marxist approach is that it details the sources of lowered demand and the function of unemployment as reflections of the economy as a whole. It also takes into account the importance of employment relationships such as those between workers and unions and other forms of worker organization that grant workers bargaining power and deflect the consequences of crises away from particular workers. Nevertheless, it fails to treat the reserve army as a varied reality comprising workers associated with positions entailing differing types of vulnerability and therefore differing rates and types of unemployment.

The various strains of neoclassical research on the supply side of unemployment have begun to distinguish types and processes of unemployment. But these approaches continue to neglect the aspects of the political economy that interact with worker characteristics to curtail or extend the workings of supply and demand in the labor market.

The present research draws on the findings and insights of the previous research but constructs a theoretical argument that is more encompassing and more focused on the structure of employment. This research takes into account the empirical and theoretical work that decomposes unemployment into its component types. It attempts to bridge the gap between neoclassical theories, emphasizing the relation of personal characteristics (including race,

age, and education) and the institutional and Marxist macrolevel theories emphasizing the segmentation of economic sectors and class positions. These institutional factors include unions, internal labor markets, on-the-job training, and other aspects of positions that affect worker property rights over jobs and worker bargaining power. They also include aspects of technology, degree of market concentration, and elasticity of demand over the business cycle—all of which enhance or diminish the vulnerability of industries and thus of employment positions within firms to economic fluctuations.

UNEMPLOYMENT AS AN INDICATOR OF THE EMPLOYMENT STRUCTURE

Besides providing insight into the nature of unemployment itself, using levels and types of job separation as the dependent variable is an index of the segmented structure of vulnerability and power. Much previous research on class fractions and capital sectors has focused on how the income determination process varies by either class or economic segment (cf. especially Beck, 1980; Beck et al., 1978; Hodson, 1980; Wright, 1979). The approach taken here is different in that it explores the main lines of segmentation by analyzing class and sector variation in unemployment. Unemployment is a particularly fruitful dependent variable for two reasons. First, job-separation unemployment is amenable to exploring qualitative differences among class fractions and economic sectors. It has both quantitative and qualitative components as it varies by both incidence and type. As such, unemployment provides a basis for discussing the qualitatively different ways in which classes and sectors perform in the market place. As this dependent variable entails not only a range but a type of variation in job separation, qualitative and not just quantitative structural differences in classes and sectors can be investigated. This is especially important in light of the empirical requisite that theoretically postulated differences among segments prove amenable to measurement.

Along with being a dependent variable capable of measuring qualitative differences among categories of the independent variable, the second reason why unemployment is useful is that it is an index of aspects of adjustments the economic structure not captured so directly by outcomes such as income.[6] Like power, unemployment is a relational outcome. Job separation

[6]Moreover, such decomposition is necessary in order to target social policy so as to ease unemployment for particular groups, such as inner-city youth, without creating an elaborate jobs program or an inflationary package of economic stimulation. Thus the case is made for distinguishing unemployment due to permanent job loss as opposed to temporary layoffs, unemployment due to voluntary quits, and unemployment due to the entry or reentry of workers into the labor force.

reflects the relations of vulnerability and power surrounding the employment structure. This is true even though unemployment does not represent the entire range of employment outcomes any more than income represents the entire range of financial or in-kind benefits derived from employment relations. For instance, the duration of employment, hours of work, overtime, and job tenure are aspects of employment relations not measured by studying the relative frequency of unemployment across sectors and classes. Nevertheless, as I argue in detail in Chapters 4–6, levels of job separation do reflect the degree to which enterprises are vulnerable to declines in demand in their product markets and the way in which they adjust their wage bills in the face of such downturns. Also the occurrence of, say, turnover types of unemployment such as firings and quits when coupled with high levels of unemployment in a particular sector indicates that these sectors are more subject to competitive market relations in their product and labor markets than are their counterparts with a stronger propensity to induce layoffs. Similarly, unemployment patterns help to distinguish and test resources of bargaining power that accrue to class positions. Where unemployment is high, class positions are, of course, less powerful in their labor market resources. But by taking into account types of unemployment as well, we are able further to discern the relative degree and type of bargaining power even when aggregate unemployment levels are similar. For instance, despite their similarity in overall levels of unemployment, it becomes possible to distinguish among the relative bargaining power of the various working-class fractions by analyzing their relative differences in types of unemployment.

CONCEPTUAL FRAMEWORK OF MODES
OF JOB SEPARATION

This section elaborates a conceptual framework of modes of job separation based on how adjustments in the employment structure intersect with adjustments by individual employees. This framework makes explicit the linkage between personal outcomes of job separation and adjustments in positions.

Unemployment is a particular form of the separation of a worker from a job. A job separation results from the dissociation of a job incumbent from active work in a particular position. Types of separation can be classified according to the particular combination of outcomes for positions and outcomes for workers in relation to their present or most recent job. Variation in these two dimensions determine the particular forms of job separation and unemployment.

First, variations in the number and types of positions represent changes in the opportunity structure or the demand side of the labor market. This variation in demand can occur for any number of reasons: national recession or expansion; structural changes in the types of products and services required by the economy; intensification of national or international competition, which induces firms to curtail or transfer operations; or the creation of vacancies as a result of decisions by incumbents to leave jobs in order to take on new jobs, to retire, to leave the labor force, or to quit and look for different jobs.

The variation in demand can result in any or all of the following changes in the structure of employment, all of which have consequences for job loss:

1. Positions may remain unchanged but become vacancies through the severance of a worker from the position (a) because of employer decisions such as transfers, suspensions, or firings or, (b) because of worker decisions, such as quitting.
2. Positions may be ended temporarily. Downturns in the economy lead employers to end or decrease the number of employment positions for a specific period or until product demand increases again. Workers often are not severed from a temporarily ended position and retain priority for reemployment when the position is reestablished.
3. Positions may be ended permanently, either individually, in sets within a division, or completely when a firm ceases operations. Positions that are ended permanently may in fact be terminated or may be moved to a geographical location where workers who once held them are unlikely to follow.
4. Positions may be reclassified by being upgraded or downgraded. In this case individual workers workers may or may not be severed.

The second dimension that characterizes job separation is outcomes for incumbents. Incumbents may be severed from positions voluntarily by their own decision or involuntarily by employer decision. Variations in outcomes for incumbents of positions that are involuntary include the following cases:

1. Incumbents do not lose employment even though employer decisions result in workers being permanently or temporarily severed from their current positions or in positions being reclassified.
2. Incumbents may sometimes lose their jobs only temporarily. That is, incumbents are severed from positions by employer decision for a limited period and then later enabled to return to their positions.
3. Incumbents may lose their jobs by being permanently severed from their positions by employer decision.

4. Incumbents may voluntarily sever their relation to a particular position in order to take up another position, to leave the labor force for a time, or to leave the labor force permanently.

Combinations of outcomes for positions and outcomes for incumbents of these positions provide a classification of job loss and the subtype of job loss known as unemployment. Such a classification, it should be cautioned, is not an effort to construct a catchy typology or laundry list. Rather it derives from the theoretical stance that position changes assume their fullest consequences for unemployment by their association with outcomes for incumbents.

Transfers, demotions, promotions, and voluntary retirement are modes of job loss that are not simultaneously forms of unemployment and do not necessarily entail the separation of the worker from employment; however, they do involve the loss of a specific job. In transfers, incumbents remain tied to specific positions, which are not ended but are moved; the incumbent moves along with the position. The transfer of a job to another location or subdivision of a firm may, of course, create a vacancy in the original employment structure if the firm wishes to duplicate the transferred position. Transfers of jobs may be temporary as in the case of a short-term movement of a managerial position to the site of a new or struggling operation.

Demotions and promotions are also types of job loss that are not considered forms of unemployment. Promotions and demotions represent the situation where a worker is promoted or demoted, but the status of the worker's former position remains the same. Promotions and demotions represent the situation where the position and incumbent both are reclassified. In reassignment, a position is ended; the worker does not lose employment, but becomes employed in another position. Voluntary retirement is another type of job loss that is not considered a form of unemployment. But voluntary retirements and quits result in the creation of a vacancy and the severance of a worker from employment, but the former implies at least temporary abandonment of the search for reemployment. Quits may coincide with the temporary or permanent ending of positions or with their reclassification. In fact, voluntary departure from a position may provoke its ending or reclassification.

The remaining forms of job loss are concomitantly modes of unemployment. Some cautions should be observed. First, many, but not all, of the forms of unemployment defined here are coterminous with official Department of Labor definitions of unemployment. Second, some distinctions made in official data collection and reports on unemployment, which we will incorporate in later theoretical discussions, are not made here—for instance, the distinction between layoffs of a short duration (less than 30 days) and

indefinite layoffs (30 days or longer). Third, some of the forms of job separation designated here are not immediately relevant for this research. Others would be relevant, but remained unmeasured in national surveys. Finally, other important types of unemployment, such as that experienced by so-called discouraged workers, those entering the labor force for the first time, and those reentering the labor force after having voluntarily left it, are not described here.

A *suspension* occurs when a worker is severed from a position temporarily although the position remains unchanged. A suspension thereby creates a temporary vacancy that may or may not be filled for the duration of the suspension. A *layoff* is the form of unemployment that results from the coincidence of the temporary ending of a position of employment and the temporary severance of the worker from employment. A layoff is distinguished from a firing by the continued connection of worker and position during the period of unemployment. When the position is reopened, the worker retains priority for reentry.

A *firing* occurs when a worker is separated involuntarily from employment regardless of what happens to the position. A firing, as commonly understood, occurs when a position remains open but its incumbent is severed from employment and replaced by another worker: it may also happen, however, when a position is ended temporarily (during a recession, for instance) and the worker becomes unemployed, with little or no priority for reemployment in the temporarily ended position. A final form of firing occurs when individual or sets of positions are ended and workers lose employment permanently. In the case of individual positions, this firing is sometimes called a dismissal or "letting a worker go"; when a whole set of positions is systematically eliminated the firings are called *terminations* or *cutbacks*.

In the analysis presented in Chapters 4–6, only layoffs, firings, and quits are examined—and then only as defined in a rather restricted sense. As shall be discussed in the next chapter, this is because of the limited information about types of unemployment provided in available data sources. Since this results in some ambiguities in the operationalization of unemployment types, it will be important to keep in mind the conceptual framework just developed to remain clear about the actual measurement of the dependent variable.

3
Data, Measurement of Variables, and Techniques of Analysis

This chapter discusses three aspects of the research methodology. The first section describes the data source, sample, and weighting procedures. The second section discusses the operationalization of the dependent variable, employment status, and of the three control variables: race, age, and education. The definition and measurement of the three structural independent variables—class, economic sector, and business cycle—are considered in the chapters that follow. The third section sets out the logic of the log-linear techniques used in the analysis, describes the procedure for testing relationships and choosing a final model, and discusses the meaning of log-linear parameters.

DATA, SAMPLE, AND WEIGHTING PROCEDURES

The data used in the analysis is taken from the March Current Population Surveys for the 10-year span, 1969 to 1978. The Current Population Survey (CPS) is a monthly, national random sample of households conducted by the Bureau of the Census. The CPS was chosen because it is the only national survey that provides information on types of unemployment along with personal characteristics, occupation, and industry of individual workers, and that also contains a large enough sample of cases of unemployment for a

highly disaggregated analysis.[1] Further, since the CPS reproduces the same information over time it is possible to measure the effect of periods in the business cycle. The subsample chosen for this research is composed of white and black males ages 16–64, who are members of the experienced civilian labor force.[2]

---

[1]Two data sets other than the CPS were considered for the research: the National Longitudinal Survey (NLS) of adult workers and the Panel Study of Income Dynamics (PSID). Although the work-history information contained in the NLS provides the basis for determining incidences of unemployment, there simply are not enough cases to study unemployment in a disaggregated manner. If controls for personal characteristics of race, education, and age are introduced along with numerous categories of sector, class, and business cycle, the required sample size is much larger than that provided by the NLS. Unemployment for experienced members of the labor force averaged under 5% during the period from 1969 to 1978. The NLS would therefore provide only about 20 cases for any cross-sectional analysis. If about 20% of the labor force becomes unemployed sometime during the year this would leave only about 80 instances of unemployment to examine. The PSID is a larger sample and, besides reporting information on source of unemployment, it provides work-history data that would enable one to determine rates and incidences of unemployment. Nevertheless, it remains questionable whether the sample size is sufficiently large in view of the level of dissaggregation required by the study. If a consistent sample of the same men is desired, then clearly there are not enough cases. For instance, Corcoran and Hill (1980) report that "1251 men aged 35–64 . . . were household heads and labor force participants every year of the ten-year period 1968–1977 [p. 40]." If, in contrast, one is willing to use all the cases of male household heads and not just the ones in the sample for 10 years, then the number of cases of unemployed increases substantially. As Corcoran and Hill (1979) report, during 1976 there were 543 male household heads (out of a sample of 3269) who experienced a spell of unemployment. A more serious problem militating against use of this data set is that it contains only detailed (two-digit) occupation and industry classifications whereas the class and sector designations of my study required the specification of three-digit industry and occupation codes.

[2]Hispanics were included with whites and not treated as a separate group, for two reasons. First, the only indication of being a Hispanic in the CPS from 1969–1978 is having a Spanish surname. Such an indicator does not univocally distinguish those individuals we now consider socially important. Second, even if it were possible to determine the Hispanic population, there are not enough cases to properly "fill" the cells in a log-linear analysis dealing with unemployment. The CPS race category of "other" is excluded since groups included under that rubric, such as Japanese, are generally favorably placed in the labor market and thus data on their unemployment experience should not be allowed to confound that of blacks. Again, this group is relatively small and, even if included among the whites, would not change the results substantially.

A number of considerations kept me from including women in the analysis despite my original predisposition to do so. First, little sociological work has been done on employment and unemployment; thus the present research was conceived more as a theoretical argument establishing certain characteristics of the American economy than an empirical work estimating these relationships for either males or females. Second, due to the dirth of sociological literature on unemployment, the chapter was written in dialogue with economic research. This research emphasizes the importance of modeling the relationship of men and women to the labor force in

(continued)

Excluded are those who never worked (including those seeking their first job) and those who have given up searching for work.[3] The March surveys for 1969–1978 contain 341,568 cases that meet the subsample criteria. A specific weighting procedure was designed to adjust the given CPS weights for each case so as to provide true subsample weights. First, each case in the subsample was assigned the CPS case weight which inflated the total survey sample to match the demographic composition of the national population. These assigned weights were summed over the subsample and averaged. A new subsample case weight was calculated for each subsample case by dividing the case's original CPS weight by the subsample average. Each of these subsample case weights was then deflated by 25% (cf. Hauser and Featherman, 1978) to adjust for the nonrandom sample design of the CPS. This reduces the probability that significant statistical differences would emerge in the analysis of data. The deflated sample size entered into the analysis was 252,839.74.

OPERATIONALIZATION OF EMPLOYMENT STATUS AND PERSONAL CHARACTERISTICS

This research examines the impact of three structural variables on distributing workers to types of unemployment: class, economic sector, and business cycle. The argument is that over and above the impact of personal characteristics on determining the unemployment likelihoods of members of the labor force, these three structural variables are important. Thus, it is necessary to control for human capital characteristics in order to determine whether each of the structural variables makes a significant independent contribution to distributing members of the labor force to unemployment and to derive an unbiased estimate of this impact. Therefore, the analysis includes the dependent variable of employment status, three structural independent variables, and three human capital control variables. Table 3.1

---

different ways (cf. Cain, 1966; Mincer, 1963; Niemi, 1975; Rees, 1973; Watts and Rees, 1977). Consequently, for the sake of parsimony in this exploratory research I tested the impact of capital sector and job segment on unemployment only for males. I believe that the independent effects of sector resources and bargaining capacity may be similar for women but to show this would entail consideration of a series of further factors such as marital status, number of children, income, and the employment status of other members of the household.

[3] Discouraged workers are omitted from the analysis only because, being considered out of the labor force according to the Department of Labor criteria, no information is provided in the CPS survey concerning the type of unemployment by which they became severed from their last jobs.

lists these seven variables and the categories into which each is divided. The measurement of employment status and the human capital variables is discussed here, while the measurement of class, economic sector, and business cycle is discussed, respectively, in Chapters 4, 5, and 6.

TABLE 3.1
Variables and Their Categories Used in the Analysis

Variable	Categories
(1) Dependent variable employment status	a. Temporary layoff
	b. Indefinite layoff
	c. Firing
	d. Quit
	e. Employed
(2) Independent variables class segment	a. Self-employed
	b. Semi-autonomous employees: higher skill
	c. Semi-autonomous employees: lower skill
	d. Higher-skill managers
	e. Lower-skill managers
	f. Union-bargaining working class
	g. Skill-bargaining working class
	h. Partial wage-competition working class
	i. Full wage-competition working class
(3) Economic sector	a. Competitive
	b. Oligopoly
	c. State
	d. Construction
	e. Farm
	f. Utility
	g. Private nonprofit
(4) Business cycle	a. Peak
	b. Decline
	c. Trough
	d. Recovery
(5) Race	a. Black
	b. White
(6) Age	a. 16–19
	b. 20–24
	c. 25–54
	d. 55–64
(7) Education	a. Less than 4 full years of high school
	b. Four years of high school completed
	c. Less than 4 years of college
	d. Four or more years of college

Employment Status

The dependent variable, employment status, is composed of four categories of unemployment and the comparative category of employment. Unemployment is differentiated into temporary layoffs, indefinite layoffs, firings, and quits. This multicategory nominal variable is constructed to reflect real differences in firm vulnerability and class bargaining power. The four forms of job loss reflect different types and degrees of bargaining power and vulnerability of class positions, economic sectors, and individuals.

A basic distinction among types of unemployment is between voluntary and involuntary job loss, and within involuntary unemployment, between layoffs and firings. Layoffs differ from firings in that the former are job separations in which the unemployed have a contractural or informal expectation to be recalled to the position from which they were separated. Quits are a voluntary form of job separation in that workers presumably have chosen to leave a job. Not all forms of quits result in unemployment, only those in which a worker chooses to leave a job without already having obtained a new one.

Ideally, one would like to operationalize each form of job separation discussed in Chapter 2. No large national survey has ever attempted to measure all those forms, however. The only extensive representative sample conducted at regular intervals that makes a systematic attempt to distinguish types of unemployment is the Current Population Survey.

Temporary and indefinite layoffs are operationalized from the CPS monthly item inquiring why a worker was absent from work the previous week. Two of the eight possible responses to the question are "temporary layoff (under 30 days)" and "indefinite layoff (30 days or more or no definite recall date)." A later survey question, "Why did the person start looking for work?" is addressed to all the unemployed except those who had already indicated their unemployment status as a temporary or indefinite layoff. The category of "quit" in the dependent variable is measured simply by the response of "quit job" to this second question. The category of "firings" cannot be so directly ascertained from the CPS data. It is operationalized here as the unemployed who indicated they had "lost job" and who were not explicitly among those who were unemployed because they were laid off, had quit, had left school, wanted temporary work, or for some other such reason.

There are a number of problems with deriving measures of these variables from the CPS categories. The first is that the theory developed in later chapters is directly relevant to all forms of job separation including promotions, demotions, and quits that do not entail unemployment. It is

especially important to distinguish this last form quits by workers who move directly to new jobs, from quits that result in unemployment. Regrettably, the CPS survey does not provide any information on quits that did not result in unemployment. Consequently, the analysis of quits in the subsequent chapters refers to quits resulting in a spell of unemployment. Whenever quits not resulting in unemployment are treated, the two types of quits are explicitly distinguished.

A second problem is whether temporary and indefinite layoffs actually measure some capacity of bargaining power that makes them different from firings. The assumption is that unemployment with a formal or informal right to recall reflects different sector and class relations in the labor market than does involuntary job loss without such an expectation of recall. That many workers on layoff do in fact return to their original positions is substantiated by a number of researchers. Feldstein (1975, 1976) estimates that between 75 and 85% return. Figures reported by Medoff (1979) and Lillien (1977) suggest that between 66 and 88% on layoff return to their original jobs. Clark and Summers (1979:46–51), however, are not so optimistic. They calculate that the recall rate is closer to 50%. However, they admit that their estimate refers to the total number of persons on layoff at any particular time and that a larger proportion of the actual number of layoffs may result in recall. In any event, a good number of workers do not return to their former position. Presumably this is most likely the case for workers on indefinite layoff[4] although the formal process of granting indefinite layoffs does abound in the automobile and steel industries where contractual agreements directly guarantee the right of recall even to those on indefinite layoffs. In many cases an indefinite layoff may be closer to a permanent job separation or firing than the formal category may lead one to believe. Such ambiguities, however, do not render meaningless these distinctions among temporary layoffs, indefinite layoffs, and firings.

Issuing a temporary layoff, and even an indefinite layoff, rather than a firing reflects at least a minimal difference in the desire of a firm to keep workers attached during periods of unemployment. Regardless of whether the firm actually intends to recall the workers, or eventually does, the fact is that workers have a different expectation about returning to their original jobs than they would if they were fired. This is most true, of course, where the

---

[4]Clark and Summers (1979:49) claim that it is "reasonable to expect a smaller proportion of those with long spells of unemployment to return to the same job. This supposition is supported by the finding that 51 percent of those on temporary layoff in May [1976] who were employed in June returned to the same industry and occupation, while only 29 percent of persons who first became reemployed in August did so."

workers have a contractual right of recall. But, even where a formal agreement does not exist, a firm could not repeatedly layoff workers with no serious intent of recalling them, because to do so would eventually hurt the firm's ability to attract new workers since experienced workers would inform new entrants about the actual expectations for recall. Further evidence that, at least in the expectation of recall, firings differ from layoffs is provided by the CPS. The CPS explicitly recognizes that workers on layoff are different from those who are fired by counting them as unemployed but with a job. The only other group that is exempt from the Labor Department requirement that to be considered unemployed a worker must be without a job and actively looking for one are workers who are waiting to begin a new job in less than 30 days.

But, separate from this question of whether the expectation of recall differs for fired and laid-off workers is the issue of whether layoffs and firings measure different labor-market relations of classes and firms. That they do is argued in more detail in the next chapters. A prominent example of the difference is that layoffs dictated by a contractual agreement reflect bargaining power attached to employment positions. But even when not formally negotiated, a pattern of layoffs rather than firings may reflect the bargaining power of a position in an indirect way. If employment positions require firm investment in specific training of workers, then layoffs manifest an interest by the firm in retaining this investment during spells of unemployment. Thus, although layoffs, especially for an indefinite period, sometimes result in permanent job loss, the CPS distinctions do capture underlying sector and class variation in labor market vulnerability and power.

A third problem with using the CPS categories is that, as was mentioned earlier, firings are measured by the residual category of job loss. Directly asking whether a worker was fired, however, would risk as much if not more measurement error than is incurred through operationalizing firings by the less threatening category of job loss. More questionable is the fact that a job loss or firing is a composite category including a range of subcategories of firing—for example, disciplinary firings, firings that result from plant or division closings, firings that result from declines in demand or changes in technology. Despite this variation, the majority of firings are probably due to causes such as changes in technology and declines in demand. Given that these causes may also result in layoffs under different conditions of vulnerability and power, the distinction between firings and layoffs can be seen to reflect variation in these conditions.

A final data problem concerns the relation between the theoretical

argument and the empirical analysis. A more extensive discussion of the resolution of this problem is contained in Appendix A. What follows is a brief review.

The primary aim of the research is to examine the structural determinants of the distribution of workers to the pool of unemployed. I argue that the size of this pool and the pattern of unemployment types that it comprises reflect the adjustments of establishments to decreased requirements for labor. When demand for goods and services declines for a particular establishment or for the economy as a whole (as during a recession), involuntary job separation is created and the pattern of voluntary job separation changes. Although there are cases where particular workers simply replaced by other workers, many job separations represent strategies by establishments to save on their wage bills. These savings are captured by the proportion of workers unemployed at any point in time. To analyze the pool of unemployed—the dependent variable commonly studied in research on unemployment—requires data only on the number of unemployed in each type of unemployment and the size of the labor force. Such data, as provided by the CPS, is the direct object of investigation here.

Embedded in this argument, however, is a second argument, which is not as adequately measured by the proportion of persons in unemployment types. This is the argument that the proportion of unemployed at a point in time reflects the incidence or flows of job separation and reemployment which vary in a theoretically understandable way by class, sector, and business cycle. To analyze these flows requires data on the true rate or incidence of unemployment per unit of time. This second task is important because the theory specified in subsequent chapters argues, in part, that rates of types of job separation vary by classes and sectors, and over the business cycle. Regrettably, there is no direct measure of such incidences in the CPS. An approximation can be made by weighing the number of unemployed measured in the CPS cross section by the duration of the spells of unemployment. Although this appears to be a reasonable solution, it is marred by the fact that the CPS provides the duration only of unterminated spells of unemployment. Hence incidences or rates of unemployment calculated in this way reflect the truncation in the data on duration. Nevertheless, the present research is able to shed light on this problem of the rates of job separation since, as is in Appendix A, the average duration of a given type of unemployment does not vary substantially across sectors or across classes. Accordingly, the data on the number of unemployed by type by sector and class also validly approximate data on actual incidences of job separation. Consequently, the research simultaneously presents and tests a

theory that explains the pool of unemployed and, to a lesser extent, a theory that explains the generation of that pool.

Race, Age, and Education

The operationalization of race, age, and education is straightforward. Race is a dichotomous variable distinguishing whites from blacks. The CPS distinguishes a third category of "other" mainly composed of Orientals and native Americans. Cases falling into this category were not included in the analysis. Hispanics and Latin Americans are included among the whites.

Age is a nominal variable in which workers are grouped into the following four categories: (a) teens, 16–19; (b) youth, 20–24; (c) prime-age members of the labor force, 25–54; and (d) older members of the labor force, 55–64.

Education is also a four-category nominal variable composed of the following groups: (a) those with less than a high school degree; (b) those who have completed high school; (c) those with 1 to 3 years of college; and (d) those with 4 or more years of college.

TECHNIQUES OF ANALYSIS

The research findings reported in the next three chapters are derived from the techniques of log-linear analysis (cf. Bishop, Fienberg, and Holland, 1975; Fienberg, 1977; Goodman, 1972). Although this mode of analysis is frequently employed in sociological research, it remains a somewhat cumbersome and obscure tool. Nevertheless, it is possible to summarize in a fairly straightfoward manner the aspects of log-linear analysis that are most germane to the research. A more technical discussion of model determination and the interpretation of log-linear parameters is reserved for Appendix A.

Log-linear techniques are especially suited for the present analysis because both the dependent and independent variables are multicategory nominal variables. It is possible, of course, to employ regression techniques of multiclassification analysis where independent variables are nominal and the dependent variable is continuous. But since the dependent variable, employment status, is a five-category nominal variable, such a regression approach was not feasible. Fortunately, log-linear analysis serves the two major research purposes of (a) helping to establish a statistically significant model specifying the relationship between the dependent and independent

variables and (b) generating parameters that estimate the relationships contained in the chosen model.

Determination of the Model

The purpose of a model is to specify the variables and relationships between them in a way that reflects one's theory and allows for empirical testing. In log-linear analysis, this entails an effort to designate a theoretically derived model of relationships that is capable of approximating the actual or observed distribution of cases in the data. For instance, in the present analysis, each case is located in one cell of a large seven-dimensional table. The seven dimensions correspond to the seven variables in the analysis. Each of the dimensions has as many levels as there are categories in its corresponding variable. It so happens that it is possible to reproduce the empirical distribution exactly if one completely "saturates" a log-linear model, that is, allows every variable to interact fully with every other one, including all possible interactions with the dependent variable. This is analogous to obtaining a perfect fit of a regression line by including as many independent variables as there are cases. Constructing a model of this sort, however, proves useless for theoretical research where the object is to explain an empirical distribution by a limited set of the most relevant variables.

Searching out a parsimonious model of the determinants of employment status is important for two reasons. First, it provides the basis for arguing that certain key variables such as class and economic sector do indeed contribute significantly to explaining employment status outcomes. Second, it is the designated model that generates the log-linear tau-parameters that estimate the relationships between categories of the independent and dependent variables.

Selecting the model requires three sets of decisions. First, it is necessary to determine an appropriate starting or base-line model. The base-line model is not expected to approximate closely the empirical distribution. Rather, it serves as the point of departure for determining a model that does. My base-line model is model 1 in Table 3.2. In conventional Goodman notation it is summarized as (234567) (1), where the numbers 2–7 represent, respectively, class, sector, business cycle, race, age, and education, and where the number 1 represents the dependent variable, employment status. In this and all subsequent models, the notation (234567) indicates that the independent variables are saturated, that is, allowed to interact fully with each other as the research interest is the relationship of the independent variables to the

TABLE 3.2
Models for the Analysis of Employment Status and Independent Variables

Model	Fitted marginals	df	Likelihood Ratio χ^2	p
1	(234567) (1)[a]	17,296	18,668	>.5
2	(234567) (17)	17,284	16,698	>.5
3	(234567) (17) (16)	17,272	14,872	>.5
4	(234567) (17) (16) (15)	17,268	14,478	>.5
5	(234567) (17) (16) (15) (14)	17,256	13,041	>.5
6	(234567) (17) (16) (15) (14) (13)	17,232	9,767	>.5
7	(234567) (17) (16) (15) (14) (13) (12)	17,200	7,605	>.5
8	(234567) (17) (16) (15) (14) (13) (12) (156)	17,188	7,517	>.5
9	(234567) (16) (16) (15) (14) (13) (12) (156) (167)	17,156[b]	7,352	>.5
10	(234567) (17) (16) (15) (14) (13) (12) (156) (167) (157)	17,145[b]	7,278	>.5
11	(234567) (17) (16) (15) (14) (13) (12) (156) (167) (157) (136)	17,080[b]	6,871	>.5
12	(234567) (17) (16) (15) (14) (13) (12) (156) (167) (157) (136) (134)	17,008	6,764	>.5
13	(234567) (17) (16) (15) (14) (13) (12) (156) (167) (157) (136) (154)	17,068	6,855	>.5
14	(234567) (17) (16) (15) (14) (13) (12) (156) (167) (157) (136) (124)	16,984	6,758	>.5
15	(234567) (17) (16) (15) (14) (13) (12)(156) (167) (157) (136) (123)	16,888	6,487	>.5
16	(234567) (17) (16) (15) (14) (13) (12) (156) (167) (157) (136) (137)	17,008	6,759	>.5
17	(234567) (17) (16) (15) (14) (13) (12) (156) (167) (157) (136) (127)	16,984	6,713	>.5

(continued)

Table 3.2 continued

Models compared	Ratio of change in χ^2 to change in degrees of freedom	Change in degrees of freedom	Change in ratio χ^2	p
1 versus 2	164.9	12	1,979	<.001
2 versus 3	151.4	12	1,817	<0.001
3 versus 4	98.5	4	394	<.001
4 versus 5	119.8	12	1,437	<.001
5 versus 6	136.4	24	3,274	<.001
6 versus 7	67.6	32	2,162	<.001
7 versus 8	7.3	12	88	<.001
8 versus 9	5.2	32	165	<.001
9 versus 10	6.7	11	74	<.001
10 versus 11	6.3	65	407	<.001
11 versus 12	1.5	72	107	<.001
11 versus 13	1.3	12	16	>.10, <.25
11 versus 14	1.2	96	113	c..10
11 versus 15	2.0	192	384	<.001
11 versus 16	1.6	72	112	<.005
11 versus 17	1.6	96	158	<.001

[a] 1 Employment status (dependent variable)
  2 Class segment
  3 Economic sector
  4 Business cycle
  5 Race
  6 Age
  7 Education
[b]The degrees of freedom are adjusted to take into account the number of cases constrained to be zero. See the text on p. 74 for a discussion of this adjustment.

dependent variable and not the relationships among the independent variables. The notation (1) indicates, however, that in this model none of the independent variables is allowed to effect the dependent variable. In the process of model building, the base-line model functions as an initial null hypothesis. If the approximation of the empirical distribution of cases determined by the base-line model cannot be improved upon significantly by subsequent models, then the theory arguing for a relationship between the independent and dependent variables cannot be sustained.

As it turns out, the base-line model as well as a number of other relatively simple models may be rejected in favor of a model that supports the theory that the structural determinants of class, sector, and business cycle do make a significant impact on employment status. But, before reviewing the se-

quential process by which the final model was decided upon, it is necessary to discuss the second decision entailed in the choice of a model: that of selecting a criterion according to which various relationships may be included or excluded from the model. The conventional norm is to use a table of χ^2 values, degrees of freedom, and significance levels. This proved inadequate for the present research, however, since the number of cases in the study is so large that many relationships that are not theoretically meaningful or interpretable end up statistically significant. Ordinarily, this problem is alleviated in part by adding a second criterion. That is, once the theoretically central relationships are included, no further relationships need be added as long as the fit of the modeled or expected table to the observed table is greater than $p = .50$. This rule of thumb does not apply either, however. Even the base-line model (model 1) in Table 3.2 produces an expected table that meets this norm. Even without including interactions involving the dependent variable, the independent variables account for a great portion of the fit between the expected and observed tables. This would not occur if fewer independent variables had been included.

It is necessary, then, to choose another criterion for accepting and rejecting relationships for inclusion in the model. The criterion I chose is that for a relationship to be included the reduction of χ^2 that results from adding a relationship must be at least four times the associated reduction in degrees of freedom. This is more stringent than the conventional rule that the reduction of χ^2 be approximately two times the reduction in degrees of freedom. Nevertheless, this criterion is reasonable in view of the large number of cases.

The third decision in determining the final model involves testing whether particular relationships contribute significantly to explaining the distribution of workers to employment status. Table 3.2 presents a series of models and their corresponding χ^2, degrees of freedom, and level of significance. It also presents comparisons between models that test whether a particular additional interaction should be included. The degrees of freedom are adjusted to take into account the use of zeros as starting values in cells of the full table corresponding to the cells in the two- and three-way interactions that contained no cases. Since this constrains the parameters in these cells to be zero, the degrees of freedom for these interactions are reduced.[5]

Returning to Table 3.2, the baseline model is presented, followed first by a succession of models including the two-way interaction of employment status

---

[5]See Stevens (1977, Appendix C) for a discussion of how to estimate degrees of freedom for relationships in which some parameters are constrained to be zero.

with personal characteristics (models 2–4). After this, the two-way interactions of employment status with class, sector, and business cycle are
introduced (models 5–7). Next, the four three-way interactions that met the
significance criterion are presented (models 8–11). This is followed by a
number of models containing further three-way interactions selected from
among the remaining possible three-way interactions (models 12–17); all
proved to be statistically insignificant. The second panel of Table 3.2
presents the comparisons testing the significance of the various models
against an appropriate preceding model. The logic dictating the ordering of
the models and their comparisons is that a stronger case can be made for the
distribution of the structural variables of class, sector, and business cycle if
the interactions including these variables enter the model strongly significant
even after the human capital variables are allowed to explain as much as
possible.

As I indicated, models 2–4 introduce a sequence of relationships between
employment status and the personal characteristics, first of education, then
of age and race. The results summarized in the first three comparisons are
that the inclusion of each of these variables, singly and as a group, produces a
better approximation of the empirical distribution of cases than the base-line
model. This means that the age, education, and race of members of the labor
force affect their employment status. This expected finding confirms the
importance of demographic factors in explaining employment status outcomes. But the question remains of whether the structural determinants of
class, sector, and business cycle make additional contributions to the
determination of employment status. The comparisons indicate that the
successive inclusion of business cycle (model 5), sector (model 6), and class
(model 7) enhance the fit of the model to the observed data, thereby
confirming the fundamental thesis of the research.

But, as can be seen, the picture is more complicated. It is necessary to
consider various three-way interactions composed of the dependent variable
and two independent variables. The criterion for inclusion of additional
relationships to explain employment status allows only the interactions
introduced in models 8–11 to be incorporated in the final model. Model 8
confirms that race and age interact in producing employment status
outcomes. Model 9 does the same for the interaction of age and education.
Model 10 demonstrates the importance of the race and education interaction.
The only additional three-way interaction that meets the criterion for
inclusion in the model, and the only one involving a structural variable, is
that of sector, age, and employment status. This interaction is analyzed in
Chapter 5 in terms of its contribution to the theory of internal labor markets.
I argue there that, in sectors with substantial product market power, the fact

that older members of the labor force enjoy less vulnerability to negative employment-status outcomes provides indirect evidence of the existence of internal labor markets.

Interpreting Log-Linear Parameters

The difficulty in interpreting the tau-parameters generated from a log-linear model is a major reason why researchers often shy away from using log-linear analysis. The parameters, nevertheless, are meaningful in their own right and can be made more intelligible (a) by geometrically transforming them into various odds-ratio comparisons; and (b) by transforming the information they provide into cross-tabular form. All three modes of presentation of the parameters are used throughout the next three chapters. A technical discussion of the transformation of log-linear parameters into four types of odds ratios is provided in Appendix A. The issues of how the parameters themselves may be interpreted and how the information they contain may be summarized more intuitively in cross-tabular form are taken up in Chapters 4 and 5. In the meantime, a brief review of the fundamental meaning of each mode of interpretation is sufficient to indicate how the tau-parameters contribute to the analysis.

The tau-parameters that are calculated from the log-linear model of the relationships between employment status and the six independent variables are simply a way of estimating the relative effect of each category of an independent variable on each category of employment status. In the case of a two-way interaction between, say, class sector with 7 categories and employment status with 5 categories, the parameters will be arrayed in a 7 by 5 table with 35 cells. This table summarizes the relationship between the two variables, essentially controlling for all the other modeled effects. In the form presented in the subsequent analysis, the parameters in the table vary from 0 to infinity. A parameter of 1 in a cell indicates that the distribution of cases to that cell by the model is exactly proportional to the number that would be expected to occur on the basis of the size of the marginal distributions of the columns and rows of that cell. A parameter of less than 1 means that the number of cases in the cell is underrepresented relative to the expectation; a parameter greater than 1 means that the number of cases distributed to the cell is overrepresented. It should be cautioned, however, that the parameters do not reflect the absolute size of the cells. As will be seen, the most frequent form of unemployment for both the oligopoly and competitive sectors is firings and the least frequent form is temporary layoffs. What a parameter greater than 1 indicates in the cell for temporary layoffs in the oligopoly sector is that, given the relative size of the two sectors and the relative

frequency of firings and temporary layoffs, temporary layoffs are over-represented in the oligopoly sector.

Although all the information required to derive an interpretation of the results is contained in the tau-parameters, it remains difficult to estimate the *extent* to which firings are overrepresented in the competitive sector and temporary layoffs are overrepresented in the oligopoly sector. The absolute size of the tau-parameters may not be used in their raw form to make such interpretations. One way to derive meaningful numerical comparisons between cells is by transforming the tau-parameters into odds-ratio comparisons (cf. Daymont and Kaufman, 1979; Page, 1977). There are four types of odds-ratio comparisons, depending upon which sets of cells are being considered: within-category, cross-category, comparative, and generalized. Each of these is discussed in Appendix A along with the method for calculating them. But what remains important to note here is that such odds-ratio comparisons, although they facilitate the interpretation of results, may not always lift the shadow of obscurity from the exposition.

Where possible, therefore, and where doing so does not exaggerate the problem of interpretation even further, I have translated the information contained in the log-linear parameters into a cross-tabular form.[6] Details of this calculation are discussed in the next chapter. But essentially the methodology is to adjust the original, observed data by the parameters derived from the final model so that a cross-tabulation of employment status by class (Chapter 4) and by sector (Chapter 5) summarizes the same information more cryptically contained in the parameters.

---

[6] I am indebted to Robert Kaufman for suggesting how the tau-parameters could be translated into the cross-tabular mode of presentation.

4

Class Segments
and the Structure of Unemployment

$\mathbf{T}$his and the next two chapters analyze the structural determination of job-separation unemployment. The present chapter examines the relation of class segments to types of unemployment whereas the next two chapters study, respectively, the relation of economic sector and business cycle to unemployment. The analysis in this chapter is based on model 11 of Table 3.2 and, in order to capture the independent effect of class on unemployment, all the other relationships noted in model 11 are controlled. The composition of the dependent variable, employment status, and how it is operationalized are as described in Chapter 3.[1]

The first section of this chapter sets out the theoretical foundations for distinguishing the nine class segments or fractions used in the analysis: the self-employment segment (composed of petty-producer and small-employer positions); higher- and lower-skill managerial segments (composed of

---

[1] It is important to recall that the category "quit" only includes those who quit a job but did not yet obtain a new one. Also, the category "firing" includes those who were fired for disciplinary reasons as well as those who were fired due to labor force cutbacks. It is impossible to discern which type of firing actually occurred. But as we will argue in the following, it is reasonable to interpret firings from managerial positions as due more to employer dissatisfaction with an employee's performance and firings from working-class positions as due more to the need for cutbacks in the labor force.

managerial and foreman positions); higher- and lower-skill semi-autonomous segments (composed mainly of professional and technical positions), and four working-class fractions. These are the union- and skill-bargaining vacancy-competition segments, and the partial and full wage-competition segments. The second section formulates a set of hypotheses specifying the relationship between these class segments and unemployment. It also evaluates these theoretical propositions by reviewing the results from a log-linear analysis of unemployment data described in Chapter 3. The final section discusses implications for understanding the nature of unemployment, class structure, and class struggle.[1]

CLASS AND SEGMENT SOURCES
OF VULNERABILITY AND POWER

Sources of vulnerability and power vary, first, according to the type of control attached to a class position. Wright (1978) argues that this variation in control depends on whether a class exercises decision making over investments, the physical means of production, or labor. Capitalist class locations exercise all three forms of control whereas working-class positions sell their labor power and generally exercise no decision-making power. The petty-commodity class is similar to the capitalist class with the exception of not exercising control over the employment or work process of other workers. Small employers occupy a contradictory location between the capitalist class and the petty-producer class since the small employer, although hiring wage labor, combines a direct role in the labor activity with exertion of control in the spheres of economic ownership and possession (see Poulantzas, 1975). Managerial–supervisory positions are contradictory locations within the class structure between the capitalist and working classes.[2] Semi-autonomous class positions are located in the contradictory position between the working-class and petty-commodity producers.[3]

---

[2]These positions exert control directly, or at the behest of the capitalist class, over the labor process and the hiring and firing of workers. But they are constrained in their control over investment policies. Upper-level managerial positions are located closer to the capitalist class because of their fuller role in the sphere of possession. Lower-level managerial positions, including foremen and supervisors, are located more closely to the working-class positions since their control over decisions affecting work process and employment is more circumscribed.

[3]On the one hand, these positions enjoy the independence and self-direction of the petty-commodity producers in the labor process. On the other, these positions provide wage labor and remain subject to capitalist and managerial evaluation for pay, promotion, and job retension.

The second source of bargaining power derives from the resources of control that vary for positions within classes. These resources include (*a*) institutionalized arrangements such as collective bargaining agreements and due process procedures associated with unions and employment covered under civil service regulations; (*b*) technical requirements in the relations of production such as on-the-job training, the degree of technical skill level, and the degree of routinization, variability, and measurability of a task; (*c*) the degree to which positions shield workers from direct evaluation of their productivity by providing for internal monitoring of performance as is the case for professionals; and (*d*) the degree to which a position is free from supervision by being located at a higher level in the hierarchy of authority.

Such forms of bargaining power define class segments by determining the degree to which incumbents of positions are subject to or shielded from competitive labor market mechanisms such as evaluation of productivity, replacement by workers willing to work for lower wages, and the lowering of real wages during a recession or downturn of demand. Positions that grant workers such resources for deflecting or resisting these market relations correspond to what Sørensen and Kalleberg (1981) term *vacancy-competition positions*. Extending Thurow's (1975) notion of job-competition relations, Sørenson and Kalleberg define vacancy competition positions as those in which the employer must allow the employee some degree of control over job activity and over outcomes of the employment relationship. Characteristics of jobs is one aspect of resources; a second is the organization of workers. Resources are high when employment positions entail (*a*) the need for on-the-job training (especially employer-financed specific human capital) of new workers; (*b*) the need to induce worker acceptance of new technology; (*c*) promotion ladders that are established to elicit increased productivity, creativity, or initiative; (*d*) interdependence among jobs; (*e*) lack of measurability of output from a job; (*f*) collective organization among employees, such as unions; and (*g*) custom and legal relations that protect employees.

Positions that allow for a higher degree of vulnerability to employer decisions within a firm correspond to what Thurow (1975) calls *wage-competition market relations*. The labor market relations of wage competition positions are described by neoclassical price theory. A competitive labor market is cleared in the short run by wage rates; workers are hired and fired according to their physical productivity and the level of demand for labor. Consequently, wage-competition positions grant workers few, if any, resources for resisting market forces above and beyond what may result from a decrease in the supply of labor, relative to demand.

Operationalization of Class Fractions

Class fractions are operationalized according to detailed census occupation categories.[4] The categories comprising each fraction are listed in Appendix B. In order to distribute employment positions to class categories according to the criteria summarized in the preceding, it would be necessary to obtain direct measures of the type and degree of decision-making control, objective conditions of subordination or superordination, and relations to the means of production. Since no such data set is available, much less one that also contains the required unemployment information, class is operationalized by technical relations of production of work-task criteria. Although it is obvious that many ambiguities creep into the classification scheme, it is reasonable to argue that the main lines of class boundaries are captured by this approach. For instance, special care is taken to separate all self-employed persons from whatever occupational category into a distinct class. Also, foremen and supervisors classified by the CPS in nonmanagerial categories are joined to the managerial class.

The self-employed segment is composed of both small employers and independent small commodity producers. Included are all who are designated self-employed by the Current Population Survey employment status recode.

The semi-autonomous class is composed of the census occupation categories designated as professional and technical. The upper- or higher-skill segment includes those positions requiring over 2 years of specific vocational preparation (SVP),[5] whereas the lower-skill segment includes those positions requiring 2 years or less of SVP.

The managerial class includes all occupations designated as managerial,

---

[4]Three 1960 census occupation categories from the 1960 and 1970 CPS have been disaggregated further than is done by the census categories. The one category of retail and wholesale managers is separated by industry into retail and nonretail categories. Managers not elsewhere classified are separated by industry into two groups: (a) those dealing with individuals (retail, entertainment, recreation, and personal services) and (b) all others. Sales workers are divided into three categories: (a) those involved in sales to firms (manufacturing, wholesale, and advertising); (b) those involved in sales to individuals (retail, entertainment, recreation, and auto repair); and (c) a mixed category.

[5]According to the Department of Labor's *Dictionary of Occupational Titles* (1965), specific vocational preparation is "the amount of time required to learn the techniques, acquire information and develop the facility needed for average performance in a specific job worker situation [p. 652]."

supervisory, administrative, or foremen (including farm managers).[6] Theoretically the hope is to separate upper-level managers from lower-level ones. Such a dichotomy proved impossible to construct with the present data, however. Instead I use specific vocational preparation as a way to obtain a crude approximation of what hierarchical divisions might look like. But because no direct measure is made of rank in the hierarchy, the findings are, at best, only suggestive of differences between upper-level and lower-level managerial positions; consequently, we will refer to these segments as higher-skill and lower-skill. Included among higher-skill managerial positions are those with SVP greater than 2 years whereas lower-skill ones are those with SVP of 2 or fewer years.

In the working class, four segments or fractions are designated. The two vacancy-competition positions are divided into union-bargaining and skill-bargaining segments. The former is composed of positions in occupations that are more than 40% unionized.[7] The latter are composed of (a) positions with between 30 and 39% unionization that require more than 6 months of SVP and (b) positions of any level of unionization less than 30% that require more than 2 years of SVP.

Positions with few resources of bargaining power are divided into partial and full wage-competition segments. The partial wage-competition segment is composed of positions that belong to occupational categories with unionization between 30 and 39% but SVP requirements of 2 years or less. The full wage-competition segment is composed of positions that belong to

---

[6]Operationalizing the managerial class in this manner—according to their technical relations of production or formal job title is, of course, far from ideal. However, the Current Population Survey that provides information on types of unemployment does not provide a direct measure of supervisory capacity that would enable us more accurately to define employment positions according to their role in the relations of authority.

[7]The measure of unionization for occupation categories included in the working class is derived from the weighted average of unionization levels for occupations calculated from individual data in the March 1971, May 1973, and May 1976 Current Population Surveys (see Freeman and Medoff, 1979, for a comparable set of calculations). Since, with the exception of the March 1971 CPS, none of the other nine March surveys from 1969–1978 included information on unionization, occupations were assigned an average unionization score. This approach serves the purpose of the research since the goal is to develop a measure of unionization as a characteristic of the incumbent. The cutoff point of 40% as the level of unionization sufficient to include an occupation in the union-bargaining fraction is based on the assumption that when unionization covers 40% of the jobs in an occupation, union power extends not only to the directly unionized jobs, but through spillover and threat effects, to all positions in the occupation.

occupational categories with less than 30% unionization and SVP requirements of 2 years or less.[8]

Class and Occupation

The operationalization of class segments by occupational categories raises
an important question concerning the analytic distinction between class and
occupation. This question asks something more fundamental than whether it
is valid to map occupations into class categories. Although there are
substantial problems with such an approach, there often is no alternative for
researchers requiring large government samples. Instead, the issue I wish to
address concerns the theoretical justification for an allegiance to class rather
than occupation as the way to conceptualize the most significant aspects of
employment positions that are consequential for labor market outcomes.

This, of course, is not a new debate. Wright (1980), for instance,
summarizes many of the elements embedded in the controversy. Although
sociologists generally define classes "as largely *determined* by occupations
(italics in original)," Marxist theory, Wright points out, adopts "a totally
different stance":

> Occupations are understood as positions defined within the *technical* relations of
> production; classes, on the other hand, are defined by the *social* relations of
> production. Occupations are thus defined by an array of technical functions or
> activities. . . . Classes, on the other hand, can only be defined in terms of their social
> relationship to other classes, or in more precise terms, by their location within the
> social relations of production [p. 177; italics in original].

From this vantage point, it is a matter of great consequence whether a person
technically trained as a plumber runs a major plumbing firm, is self-
employed, supervises a construction site, or is employed as a heating-
systems installer by a contractor. In the case of this plumber, it is not difficult
to appreciate how differences in class position produce substantial within-

---

[8]It should be pointed out that both the skill-bargaining and partial wage-competition segments
are conceptually intermediate between the union-bargaining and full wage-competition segments. Also, they contain relatively few cases (see Table 4.4). As such, they are both
theoretically and empirically less important in the analysis. However, they are treated as
separate categories rather than merged with the two larger segments in order to (a) test the
validity of my conception of bargaining power by showing that segments with intermediate forms
of bargaining power evidence unemployment patterns between the two larger segments; and (b)
preserve the conceptual integrity of the two larger segments.

occupation differences in economic outcomes. But it remains more problematic to separate the domains of class and occupation for a manager because the specific skill and training requirements associated with the task of management converge with the class-based tasks of exercising control at the point of production.

On one level the issue may be resolved theoretically by arguing for the analytical priority of class over occupation. According to Kalleberg and Griffin (1980), this is in fact what is done by Braverman (1974) in arguing that the technical division of labor is itself the object of class-based decisions. But even where this can be demonstrated historically (cf. Wallace and Kalleberg, 1982), the empirical and theoretical problem of the distinct explanatory power of class and occupation remains unresolved. In explaining the distribution of labor market outcomes, is there a within-class variation in economic outcomes that is due to occupation-based differences in skill and training that cannot be captured by class variables? Put differently, what are the aspects of labor market dynamics and labor market outcomes that continue to reside in occupations and that make significant and independent contributions to explaining labor market outcomes, even where these processes can be explained by a broader class theory?

These questions are especially relevant to the analysis in this chapter. Research on the relation between occupation and unemployment (e.g., Corcoran and Hill, 1979) cannot be written off simply as the misspecification of class relations by occupational categories. Even after taking into account characteristics of employment position associated with class relations (such as control over labor process and employment decisions), other aspects of bargaining power related to occupational skill and training remain consequential for the determination of employment outcomes. To take a telling example: The thesis of the reserve army is one way class theory incorporates the economic forces of supply and demand into an explanation of unemployment, job rewards, and working conditions. Nevertheless, this thesis will remain incapable of explaining more intricate patterns of inequality in job outcomes and rewards within and across classes unless it also takes into account variations in the labor market demand for occupational skills and training. Instructive in this regard is Kalleberg and Griffin's (1980) investigation of the distinct class and occupation effects in the determination of income and job fulfillment. Incorporating measures of class and occupation, the authors conclude that "both class and occupation represent distinct and important sources of inequality and that *both* are necessary to understand the positional sources of job rewards [p. 763; italics in original]." Class categories are required to explain within-occupation differences in job rewards whereas occupational distinctions are needed to explain within-class differences.

Thus, by focusing on class as a variable I am not advancing the dogmatic position that other dimensions of employment relationships are inconsequential. In fact, by operationalizing class in terms of occupational categories, the impact of some occupationally based forces are included nonetheless. Moreover, both class and occupation themselves capture some nonstructural aspects of labor market dynamics. Controlling for various personal characteristics filters out much of the impact of human-capital effects in a multivariate analysis. But the social selection processes whereby certain individuals become mapped into employment positions make it impossible to completely isolate the structural contribution of class and occupation from all human-capital effects. Hence, the focus on class, as opposed to occupation, as a structural determinant of unemployment remains a positive one. I deny neither the importance of within-class variations due to factors captured in occupational skill and training nor the penetration of class by human-capital effects. Rather, the choice of class categories reflects my endeavor to emphasize the job-based aspects of vulnerability and power that are derived from the relations of production.

ANALYSIS

The analysis proceeds in three steps. First, I establish the independent explanatory power of class in determining the distribution of workers to unemployment. I then analyze the relation of classes and class segments to unemployment in general. Finally, I analyze the relation of class segments to types of unemployment.

The Independent Contribution of Class

The statistical significance of an effect is established through a process of testing a series of models with and without the effect included. If including the effect or variable in the model significantly reduces the unexplained χ^2 for a given number of degrees of freedom (df), the effect may be considered as contributing to the explanation of the dependent variable.

Table 4.1 presents a series of models and comparisons of models relevant to establishing the independent effect of class. The findings here demonstrate the validity of the general theoretical proposition that the degree and type of bargaining power associated with a class location helps determine the proportion and type of unemployed. Even controlling for economic sector, personal characteristics, and business cycle, class location retains a strong independent effect on the distribution of job losers. This independent

TABLE 4.1
Models for the Analysis of Employment Status and Class Segment

Model	Fitted marginals[a]	df	Likelihood ratio χ^2	p
1	(234567) (1)	17,296	18,668	>.5
2	(234567) (12)	17,264	13,975	>.5
3	(234567) (13) (14) (15) (16) (17)	17,232	9,797	>.5
4	(234567) (13) (14) (15) (16) (17) (12)	17,200	7,605	>.5
1 versus 2				
3 versus 4				
5[b]	(234567) (12) (13) (14)	32	4,693	<.001
	(15) (16) (17) (136)	32	2,192	<.001
	(156) (157) (167)	17,080[c]	6,871	>.5

[a] 1 Employment status (dependent variable)
   2 Class segment
   3 Economic sector
   4 Business cycle
   5 Race
   6 Age
   7 Education
[b] Model 5 is the basis for the analysis reported in the text. All interactions are included that met the criterion that to be included an interaction must reduce the likelihood ratio χ^2 by a factor of at least four times the reduction in the degrees of freedom. This more stringent criterion was chosen because of the large number of cases in the study.

[c] The degrees of freedom are adjusted to take into account the number of cases constrained to be zero.

contribution is demonstrated by the substantial reduction in χ^2 that occurs when class is introduced into the model both before and after all the other direct effects have been introduced. When entered first, class segment reduces χ^2 by 4693 corresponding to a reduction of 32 df. This is significant at $p < .001$. A more stringent test of the independent contribution of class segment is to enter class segment last. This allows the other variables to account for their own direct impact and any joint contribution they may make with class segment. In this case class segment reduces χ^2 by 2192 corresponding to a reduction of 32 df. This too is significant at $p < .001$.

Class Variation in the Proportion of Unemployed

The results from the log-linear analysis specifies the qualitative difference in unemployment and type of unemployment associated with each of the

class segments. In this and in the following section, I study this specific impact of class segment on employment by analyzing the log-linear parameters in Table 4.2 derived from fitting the observed data to model 5 of Table 4.1. The tau-parameter in each cell of this table represents the number of cases relative to all other cells under the specified final model. These parameters do not represent absolute numbers of cases. Each tau-parameter is to be read as the relative likelihood that a case will be in a particular category of employment status within a particular class segment.[9]

CLASS AND UNEMPLOYMENT

From the overview of class and segment sources of vulnerability and power, I predict that the self-employment class will have the lowest proportion of unemployed because members of this class enjoy the greatest degree of control over their work decisions.[10] It also is predicted that the semi-autonomous and the managerial class will have a greater proportion of unemployed than the self-employment class but a lower proportion than the working class. On the one hand, this is because working class positions afford less control over the relations of production than do semi-autonomous positions. On the other hand, this is because working-class positions have less control in the relations of authority than do managerial positions and

---

[9]For instance, comparing the cells for temporary layoffs in the union-bargaining and full wage-competition segments, the parameters reveal that relative to other categories of employment status and relative to all other segments, temporary layoffs are more likely in the union-bargaining than in the full wage-competition segment. The relative likelihood of unemployment for any segment (as opposed to the relative likelihood of a particular type of unemployment) is given by the inverse of the tau-parameters for these cells. These tau-parameters may be transformed into odds ratios (cf. Daymont and Kaufman, 1979; Page, 1977). It should be recalled that these parameters are taken to represent the relative likelihood of members of a class position to *be* unemployed as well as the relative likelihood to *become* unemployed. In the first instance the parameters represent relative labor force adjustments by class segment. Such adjustments, measured by the relative number of members of the labor force in the status of unemployed, reflect both the incidence and duration of unemployment spells. In the second instance, the parameters represent the relative incidence of unemployment since duration of unemployment types do not vary substantially by class segment (see Appendix A, pp. 197–205).

[10]It must be cautioned, however, that these relationships are complex and for the most part neglected in existing literature. Also, many aspects of the relationship between class segments and unemployment are theoretically indeterminate and can be interpreted only as the analysis progresses. Finally, data restrictions make it impossible to operationalize class segments or unemployment types in a manner completely congruent with the conceptual and theoretical definitions. Accordingly, the emphasis will be to establish the broad qualitative relationships between class segments and unemployment types rather than to obtain a precise estimation of these relationships.

TABLE 4.2
Tau-Parameters for the Net Relationship of Employment Status and Class Segment[a]

Employment status	Self-employed	Semi-autonomous[b]		Managerial[c]		Working Class[d]			
		h	l	h	l	ub	sb	pwc	fwc
Temporary layoff	.7411	.7932	1.1450	.9488	.7039	1.5273	1.3455	1.1348	.9539
Indefinite layoff	.4367	.9604	1.1753	.8160	.9754	1.5349	1.1838	1.5675	.8947
Firing	.5246	1.3719	1.0260	.8869	1.3069	.9706	.9951	1.0370	1.1667
Quit	1.5414	.7308	.8835	1.0038	1.2070	.7624	.9343	.9026	1.2890
Employed	3.8210	1.3093	.8198	1.4507	.9227	.5765	.6753	.6006	.7791

(Header: Class segment)

[a]Controlling for the other modeled relationships of economic sector, business cycle, race, age, and education
[b]Semi-autonomous: h = higher-skill; l = lower skill.
[c]Managerial: h = higher-skill; l = lower skill.
[d]Working class: ub = union-bargaining; sb = skill-bargaining; pwc = partial wage-competition; fwc = full wage competition.

because firms are reluctant to dismantle the social relations of authority during downturns in demand. The log-linear parameters in Table 4.2 show that the self-employed are the least likely to be unemployed and that incumbents of the working-class segments are the most likely to be unemployed. Cross-segment odds ratios[11] calculated from these parameters and presented in Table 4.3 estimate that the self-employed are between 3.8 and 6.8 times less likely to be among the unemployed than employees holding semi-autonomous positions, and between 3.4 and 5.9 times less likely to be unemployed than employees employed in managerial positions. Also the self-employed are from 7.3 to 10.6 times less likely to be unemployed than those employed in the working class.

CLASS SEGMENTS AND UNEMPLOYMENT

Findings concerning the relative number of unemployed within classes show that next to the self-employment class, employees of higher-skill managerial positions are the least likely among all the segments to be unemployed. But the difference is great between the two segments of the managerial class. Members of the higher segment are 1.8 times less likely to be unemployed than those of the lower-skill segment.

Within the working class, I expect that positions with greater vacancy-competition bargaining power (especially the union-bargaining segment) will have a large proportion of unemployed due to the inability of employers to lower real wages and adjust prices when demand turns down (see Schervish, 1981).[12] In contrast, I expect that positions with the least bargaining power (especially the full wage-competition segment) will be associated with the least unemployment. Such positions afford workers few resources for resisting declines in real wages since the competitive labor market keeps their wages in competition even during downturns of demand. This enables their employers to adjust by lowering labor factor costs and thus the prices of output. This in turn mitigates unemployment. A key finding is that, as predicted but contrary to what ordinarily may be expected, positions with the least bargaining power have relatively fewer unemployed whereas positions

---

[11]See Appendix A (p. 206) for a discussion of the method for calculating cross-segment odds ratios.

[12]In this research I found that incumbents of primary positions were less likely than incumbents of secondary positions to be unemployed. However, this difference was due to the fact that primary positions included both vacancy-competition working-class positions as well as managerial and professional–technical positions. It is important that the findings suggested that primary positions were more likely to be associated with layoffs and quits whereas secondary positions were more likely to be associated with indefinite layoffs and firings.

TABLE 4.3

Cross-Segment Odds Ratios Comparing Employment and Unemployment Likelihoods for Class Segments[a]

	Self-employed	Semi-autonomous[a]		Managerial		Working class			
		h	l	h	l	ub	sb	pwc	fwc
Self-employed	—	3.81	6.85	3.36	5.91	10.63	8.73	10.10	7.30
Semi-autonomous									
Higher-skill	.26	—	1.80	.88	1.55	2.79	2.29	2.65	1.91
Lower-skill	.15	.56	—	.49	.86	1.55	1.27	1.48	1.07
Managerial									
Higher-skill	.30	1.14	2.04	—	1.76	3.17	2.60	3.01	2.18
Lower-skill	.17	.65	1.16	.57	—	1.80	1.48	1.71	1.24
Working class									
Union-bargaining	.09	.36	.64	.32	.56	—	.82	.95	.69
Skill-bargaining	.11	.44	.78	.38	.68	1.22	—	1.16	.84
Partial									
wage-competition	.10	.38	.68	.33	.58	1.05	.86	—	.72
Wage-competition	.14	.52	.94	.46	.81	1.46	1.20	1.38	—

Note: To obtain the relative likelihood of a worker's being employed rather than unemployed in segment A in contrast to segment B, find segment A's row and read across to the column of segment B. To obtain the relative likelihood of a worker's being unemployed rather than employed in segment A in contrast to segment B, find segment A's column and read down to the row of segment B. See Appendix A (p. 206) for the method of calculating these odds ratios.

[a] See Table 4.2 for key to abbreviations

with strong union-bargaining power have the greatest proportion of unemployed relative to the size of the segment. Cross-segment odds ratios demonstrate that although the union-bargaining and partial wage-competition segments have almost identical unemployment propensities, the union-bargaining segment is 1.5 times more likely than the full wage-competition segment to have workers in unemployment.

A number of conclusions can be drawn from this analysis. First, there is a strong relation between unemployment likelihoods and class and, within classes, between unemployment likelihoods and class segments. Classes with greatest control over the social relations of authority and production have relatively fewer unemployed; and within the semi-autonomous and managerial class locations the segments with greater bargaining power have relatively fewer unemployed. The self-employment class has the lowest unemployment proportion followed by managerial and professional–technical classes. In contrast, the working class has the greatest relative frequency of unemployment. Positions in this class afford workers the least control over relations of authority and production and hence over the ability to retain their jobs during downturns in demand. Nevertheless, within the working class, different working class segments vary in unemployment according to theoretical expectations about the degree and type of bargaining power associated with these positions.

The Relation of Class Segment and Unemployment Type

These findings concerning class differences in overall unemployment rates are only half the story. Class variations in type of unemployment reveal further dimensions of the class structure, bargaining power, and the value of decomposing unemployment into its constituent components.

SELF-EMPLOYMENT CLASS

Members of the labor force who hold self-employment positions have the greatest control over decisions within their enterprises. Thus I predict that the unemployment proportion for members of this class will be low. When cutbacks in the labor force occur, members of the self-employment class who make decisions about unemployment will of course remove others from the payroll before themselves. For these same reasons the form of unemployment expected to be associated with self-employment positions is quits. Here, as is the case throughout, I am interested in examining the variation by

class segment around the average distribution across classes of layoffs, firings, and quits.

Although all the information needed for this task is contained in the log-linear tau-parameters, the findings are made intuitively more understandable when translated into cross-tabular form in Table 4.4. Table 4.4 is derived by fitting the observed distribution through a process of iterative proportional adjustment to the log-linear parameters of Table 4.2. This produces a cross-tabulation of cases of employment and unemployment by class and class segment controlling for the modeled effects (see Table 4.1) of economic sector, business cycle, race, age, and education. For instance, column 3 of Table 4.4 shows that, on average, temporary layoffs are 6% of unemployment across classes whereas temporary layoffs are 24%, firings 55%, and quits resulting in unemployment 15%.

The findings confirm that within the self-employment class firings followed by quits are the most common reason for being unemployed. As we shall see, the predominance of firings and quits in absolute numbers occurs throughout the class structure. What is more consequential for our purposes is the degree to which various classes and segments diverge from the average predominance of these two types of unemployment. In the self-employment class, I find from columns 3 and 4 of Table 4.4 that the proportion of unemployed who quit (38%) is 153% greater than occurs on average across classes. This overrepresentation of quits relative to overall employment is greater by far than for any other segment. All the other forms of unemployment, in contrast, are underrepresented in relation to the average pattern. Such quits represent the termination of a firm, office, or establishment without the proprietor or owner moving directly to a new job or starting a new business. It is difficult to explain, however, the existence of some layoffs and firings in this class. It may be that such involuntary job separation represents the special employment relation in which self-employed real-estate agents, salespersons, and other freelance workers who contract with an entrepreneur or establishment have this relation terminated. Still, these involuntary job losses are few in absolute number and—with the exception of temporary layoffs—their relative propensity is lower among the self-employed than in any other segment.

MANAGERIAL CLASS

We have already noted that the managerial class has a low proportion of unemployed because the kinds of control and decision-making activity carried out by incumbents of these positions continue even when decreased demand curtails employment in other class segments. Given this overall low

TABLE 4.4
Net Distribution of Employment, Unemployment, and Labor Force by Class Segment

Class segment	Number (1)	Percentage (2)	Percentage of unemployed (3)	Percentage deviation of (3) from average distribution (4)	Percentage of total (5)	Percentage of total unemployment–Percentage of total labor force (by category) (6)
Total						
Employed	241838	95.65			100.00	1.00
Unemployed[a]	10993	4.35	100.00		100.00	1.00
Temporary layoff	654	.26	5.95	—	100.00	1.00
Indefinite layoff	2626	1.04	23.89	—	100.00	1.00
Firing	6052	2.39	55.05	—	100.00	1.00
Quit	1661	.66	15.11	—	100.00	1.00
Labor force	252830	100.00			100.00	1.00
Unemployment ratio[b]		4.55				
Self-employed						
Employed	24680	99.39			10.21	
Unemployed	152	.61	100.00		1.38	−7.12
Temporary layoff	9	.04	5.92	−1	1.38	−7.12
Indefinite layoff	20	.08	13.16	−82	.76	−12.92
Firing	65	.26	42.76	−29	1.07	−9.18
Quit	58	.23	38.16	+153	3.49	−2.81
Labor Force	24831	100.00			9.82	
Unemployment ratio		.62				
Semi-autonomous (total)						
Employed	31089	96.64			12.86	−1.29
Unemployed	1082	3.36	100.00		9.84	

(continued)

TABLE 4.4 (continued)

Class segment	Number (1)	Percentage (2)	Percentage of unemployed (3)	Percentage deviation of (3) from average distribution (4)	Percentage of total (5)	Percentage of total unemployment– Percentage of total labor force (by category) (6)
Temporary layoff	51	.16	4.71	−26	7.80	−1.63
Indefinite layoff	218	.68	20.15	−19	8.30	−1.53
Firing	676	2.10	62.48	+13	11.17	−1.14
Quit	137	.43	12.66	−19	8.25	−1.54
Labor force	32170	100.00			12.72	
Unemployment ratio		3.48				
Semi-autonomous (higher-skill)						
Employed	19281	97.11			7.98	
Unemployed	574	2.89	100.00		5.22	
Temporary layoff	21	.11	3.66	−63	3.21	−1.50
Indefinite layoff	100	.50	17.42	−37	3.81	−2.45
Firing	390	1.96	67.94	+23	6.44	−2.06
Quit	63	.31	10.98	−38	3.79	−1.22
Labor force	19854	100.00			7.85	−2.07
Unemployment ratio		2.98				
Semi-autonomous (lower-skill)						
Employed	11808	95.88			4.88	−1.05
Unemployed	508	4.12	100.00		4.62	−1.06
Temporary layoff	50	.24	5.91	−1	4.59	

	N	%	%	Change		
Indefinite layoff	118	.96	23.23	−3	4.49	−1.08
Firing	286	2.32	56.30	+2	4.73	−1.03
Quit	74	.60	14.57	−4	4.46	−1.09
Labor force	12316	100.00				
Unemployment ratio		4.30			4.87	
Managerial (total)						
Employed	36341	97.16			15.03	
Unemployed	1063	2.84	100.00		9.67	−1.53
Temporary layoff	45	.12	4.23	−41	6.88	−2.15
Indefinite layoff	189	.50	17.78	−34	7.20	−2.05
Firing	635	1.70	59.74	+9	10.49	−1.41
Quit	194	.52	18.25	+21	11.68	−1.27
Labor force	37404	100.00				
Unemployment ratio		2.93			14.79	
Managerial (higher-skill)						
Employed	23129	97.95			9.56	
Unemployed	484	2.05	100.00		4.40	−2.12
Temporary layoff	27	.11	5.58	−7	4.13	−2.26
Indefinite layoff	91	.39	18.80	−27	3.47	−2.69
Firing	273	1.16	56.40	+2	4.51	−2.07
Quit	93	.39	19.21	+27	5.60	−1.67
Labor force	23614	100.00				
Unemployment ratio		2.09			9.34	
Managerial (lower-skill)						
employed	13212	95.81			5.46	
Unemployed	579	4.20	100.00		5.27	−1.03
Temporary layoff	18	.13	3.11	−91	2.75	−1.98
Indefinite layoff	98	.71	16.93	−41	3.73	−1.46
Firing	362	2.63	62.52	+14	5.98	+1.10
Quit	101	.73	17.44	+15	6.08	+1.12

(continued)

TABLE 4.4 *(continued)*

Class segment	Number (1)	Percentage (2)	Percentage of unemployed (3)	Percentage deviation of (3) from average distribution (4)	Percentage of total (5)	Percentage of total unemployment– Percentage of total labor force (by category) (6)
Labor force	13790	100.00			5.45	
Unemployment ratio		4.38				
Working class (total)						
Employed	149728	94.51			61.91	
Unemployed	8696	5.49	100.00		79.10	
Temporary layoff	549	.35	6.31	+6	83.94	+1.26
Indefinite layoff	2199	1.39	25.29	+6	83.74	+1.34
Firing	4676	2.95	53.77	−2	77.26	+1.34
Quit	1272	.80	14.63	−3	76.58	+1.23
Labor force	158425	100.00			62.66	+1.22
Unemployment ratio		5.81				
Working class (union-bargaining)						
Employed	75923	94.02			31.39	
Unemployed	4829	5.98	100.00		43.93	
Temporary layoff	360	.45	7.45	+25	55.05	+1.38
Indefinite layoff	1415	1.75	29.30	+23	53.88	+1.72
Firing	2470	3.06	51.15	−8	40.81	+1.69
Quit	584	.72	12.09	−25	35.16	+1.28
Labor force	80753	100.00			31.94	+1.10
Unemployment ratio		6.36				
Working class (skill-bargaining)						
Employed	5206	95.03			2.15	

Unemployed	273	4.98	100.00	+17	2.48	+1.14
Temporary layoff	19	.35	6.96	-2	2.91	+1.34
definite layoff	64	1.17	23.44	-2	2.44	+1.12
Firing	148	2.70	54.21	+2	2.45	+1.13
Quit	42	.77	15.38		2.53	+1.17
Labor force	5478	100.00				
Unemployment ratio		5.24			2.17	
Working class (partial wage-competition)						
Employed	16549	94.01			6.84	+1.38
Unemployed	1055	5.99	100.00	-12	9.60	+1.23
Temporary layoff	56	.32	5.31	+20	8.56	+1.65
Indefinite layoff	302	1.71	28.63	-5	11.50	+1.31
Firing	552	3.14	52.32	-10	9.12	+1.25
Quit	145	.82	13.74		8.73	
Labor force	17604	100.00				
Unemployment ratio		6.38			6.96	
Working class (full wage-competition)						
Employed	52050	95.35			21.52	+1.07
Unemployed[a]	2539	4.65	100.00	-13	23.10	-1.24
Temporary Layoff	114	.21	4.49	-45	17.43	-1.36
Indefinite Layoff	418	.77	16.46	+8	15.92	+1.15
Firing	1506	2.76	59.31	+31	24.88	+1.40
Quit	501	.92	19.73		30.16	
Labor force	54590	100.00				
Unemployment ratio		4.88			21.59	

[a] The unemployment rate is the total number of workers unemployed through temporary layoffs, indefinite layoffs, firings, and quits divided by the total in the labor force.

[b] The unemployment ratio is the total number of unemployed in the four categories divided by the number of employed.

[c] Totals may not be exact since the table is calculated by rounding weighted cases whose values are not integers.

proportion of unemployment the question is what is the relative composition of unemployment types.

Column 6 of Table 4.4 indicates that, for the managerial class as a whole, the proportion of the total and each type of unemployed is lower than the proportion of the labor force. Keeping this in mind, I ask what types of unemployment predominate in this class and its segments. I expect that the measured proportion of quits and firings will be disproportionately high whereas the number of layoffs will be disproportionately low. This is because, on the one hand, layoffs are an unattractive option for employers when dealing with incumbents of managerial positions and, on the other, because of the meaning of firings and quits in this class.

First, layoffs are an unattractive option because layoffs effectively dismantle the hierarchy of command at least temporarily and because managers, with much firm-specific training, embody a costly investment by the firm that would be lost should a manager on layoff obtain employment elsewhere (see Oi, 1962). Second, relative to the trend across classes, we expect firings to be more frequent in the managerial class since managers are subject to evaluation based on the performance of their units or subordinates over which they are in charge. Consequently managers can be expected to be fired for poor performance; recalling that they will not be likely to be laid off, the result is an above average proportion of fired managers and a below average proportion of laid-off managers. Finally, quits without a new job are expected to be relatively more frequent than average partly as a function of the lower proportion of layoffs, partly because career ladders for managers often entail movement from one firm to another, and partly because managers are often accorded the opportunity to register their involuntary dismissal as a quit.[13]

---

[13]In the abstract, quits represent the voluntary side of job separation. In reality, however, quits may be induced not only by workers' discovering more rewarding, immediately available jobs but also by their negative evaluation of the short- and long-range worth of their present jobs. Also, it is important to distinguish two types of quits: those undertaken with a new job in hand and those undertaken with a new job still to be found. Technically, the former type is not a form of unemployment; the latter type entails either unemployment or leaving the labor force. What is common to all quits is that workers, rightly or wrongly, discern that their present job has become less valuable—either because expectations have changed, new job opportunities have opened up, more leisure is desired, wage rates relative to inflation or in absolute terms have decreased, the employer is about to fire the worker, or work assignments or pace have become more rigorous. What differs among quits is the degree to which workers enjoy a position of strength in their present job. Workers in high resource positions can generally accomplish more of their search for a new job while still employed. Furthermore, they can more easily time their quit to coincide with favorable labor market conditions. On the other hand, workers in low resource positions will be more vulnerable to a range of market forces that induce quits. Consequently, they will be more likely to quit without a new job, thereby entering the ranks of the unemployed.

These predictions are generally borne out by the findings. Column 4 indicates that, for the class as a whole and for the two segments, the composition of the unemployed is more than average for firings and quits and less than average for layoffs. In the *higher-skill segment* the most striking aspect of the distribution of the unemployed is that persons in indefinite layoffs are 27% fewer than occurs on average and unemployed persons due to quits are 27% more frequent than is the case across classes.

In the *lower-skill managerial segment* there is a similar pattern of fewer than average layoffs and more than average firings and quits. Two differences from the higher-skill segment are important. First, the level of unemployment of each type is greater than in the higher-skill segment. Second, given this higher level the distribution of unemployed is even more toward firings and away from layoffs. Temporary and indefinite layoffs are, respectively, 91 and 41% lower than average. Also, unlike in the higher-skill segment, the proportion of unemployed by firings and quits is even greater than the proportion of the labor force employed in this segment. For instance, whereas the ratio of temporary and indefinite layoffs to firings is .43 in the higher-skill segment, the ratio is .32 in the lower-skill segment. This means that although the number of unemployed is few in absolute numbers, the distribution of unemployed leans heavily toward firings and, to a lesser extent, toward quits than in other segments. Compared to other segments only the higher-skill semi-autonomous employees have a lower ratio of layoffs to firings than the lower-skill managerial employees. Also, only the weakest bargaining segment of the working class has a proportion of quits greater than the managerial segments. And even here it is important to note that these figures do not include the number who quit with a new job in hand. As I said, since managerial positions often form career ladders across firms, the incumbents of such positions are frequently able to quit without suffering a spell of unemployment. For instance, one study reported in the *Wall Street Journal*, claims that 29% of corporate managers are circulating résumés, while still at their present jobs.

Taken together, the results from the analysis of unemployment in the managerial segments appear similar to what occurs in the full wage-competition segment of the working class. This pattern of the composition of the unemployed reflects two aspects of vulnerability especially in the lower-skill managerial segment. First, compared to the higher-skill segment, lower-skill positions such as foremen are less crucial in the hierarchy of authority, more akin to working-class positions in task, and less likely to be salaried. Second, the relatively higher ratio of unemployed who were fired as opposed to those who quit indicates that incumbents of the lower-skill managerial positions are less able than their counterparts in higher-skilled positions either to translate firings into quits or to risk a self-induced period of unemployment and job search by quitting.

Still it should be pointed out that the social meaning of quits and firings in the managerial class differ from the meaning in the weakest segment of the working class where the pattern is similar. First, the absolute number and, hence, vulnerability to unemployment is much lower for managerial positions. And second, although there is no evidence in the present research to confirm this, it is reasonable to argue that quits in the managerial segment are more connected to building careers than is the case in the working-class wage-competition segments where quits are more a function of negative job characteristics (see Osterman, 1980). Finally, firings in the managerial segments—as few as there are—are probably connected more to a criteria of evaluation of the incumbents than in the wage-competition segments of the working class where firings more commonly represent labor force *adjustments* in numbers of workers rather than *replacements* of workers with better workers.

Semi-Autonomous Professional–Technical Class

I have already noted that the below average unemployment proportion for this class confirms the proposition that semi-autonomous positions are less susceptible to unemployment than the working class. Semi-autonomous positions[14] gain their bargaining power from skill certification and licensing, high measures of job-specific skills, and the inability of employers to evaluate productivity directly. Thus I expect that among types of unemployment, these vacancy-competition positions will be associated with an above average propensity of layoffs since, even when the labor force is cut back, employers will desire to keep workers attached to the firm. Also, workers in these positions are expected to be associated with a lower than average proportion of quits that lead to unemployment. This is due to the strong bargaining resources that enable incumbents of these positions to search for a job when employed and to quit only when a new job has been found.

---

[14]The semi-autonomous class is composed of numerous census occupation categories designated as professional and technical. As with the managerial class, there are problems in operationalizing these positions by occupational categories describing the technical relations in production or tasks carried out by incumbents. Theoretically, semi-autonomous class positions are distinguished by their partial independence in the sphere of possession or work process. Yet as Wright (1978) points out, professional and technical positions are with some exceptions generally included in the semi-autonomous class locations. Moreover, the problems of operationalization are partially alleviated by the designation of two segments for this class: higher-skilled (generally professional) positions that may be considered closer to the self-employed petty producers in their class relations and lower-skilled (generally technical) positions that may be considered closer to the working class.

These predictions generally are confirmed for the lower-skill semi-autonomous positions but prove less adequate to explain the findings for higher-skill positions in this class.

In analyzing the unemployment pattern for the semi-autonomous class as a whole and for the class segments within it, I again focus on the variation from the overall pattern. Column 6 of Table 4.4 shows that for every form of unemployment the semi-autonomous class and its segments are under-represented relative to their size in the labor force. Given this low unemployment propensity, column 4 then indicates the relative distribution among these types of unemployment. We can see that the unemployed from this class are more likely to be fired (+13%) and less likely to be temporarily laid off (−26%) than the average across classes. Also the unemployed in this class are 19% less likely than the average to be so by quits or by indefinite layoffs. This class pattern, however, obscures important differences in the unemployment pattern of the two segments that comprise this class.

The findings indicate that virtually all of the divergence from the average pattern results from the distribution of unemployment in the higher-skill segment. The findings also indicate that the expectation that layoffs be relatively common was incorrect, especially for the higher-skill segment.

In accord with my expectations, in the *higher-skill segment* the relative proportion of the unemployed who are unemployed from quits is lower than in any other segment (11%). In contrast to what I predicted, a greater proportion than I expected of the unemployed members of this segment are in this status due to firings (23% more than average) and a lower proportion than expected are unemployed due to layoffs (63% less than average). Although obtaining a general shelter from unemployment, employees in higher-skill semi-autonomous positions suffer disproportionately from firings when unemployment does occur. The proportion of fired among the unemployed (68%) is greater than for any other segment, including the weakest segment of the working class. The findings that workers in this segment are from 22 to 45% underrepresented among the unemployed suggest that only when a firm is faced with extreme curtailment of production or when workers prove undesirable for continued employment will an employee in this segment be counted among the unemployed. Apparently, layoffs are not a favored form of unemployment in this segment. This seems to be true despite the fact that layoffs enable employers to decrease payroll costs while retaining some hold on workers even during periods of unemployment.

In the instance of incumbents of higher-skill semi-autonomous positions employers do not seem to be willing to take such a risk. As I will argue more fully in the discussion, on-the-job training and other sunk costs in these employees serve to protect employees from firings but not necessarily from

the "intermediate" form of involuntary unemployment—layoffs. In the case of semi-autonomous employees, the secular expansion of these positions over the past decade adds the factor that temporary declines in demand may be met not by such layoffs but by decreasing the rate of new hiring. Thus when involuntary unemployment occurs, it takes the form of firings, but only when either of two situations come about. The first is when a firm's economic prospects become so dire that it considers it necessary to separate these employees permanently. Such seems to have occurred during the early 1970s when both the Northwest and New England experienced substantial economic declines in defense-related aeronautics and telecommunications industries. The second situation in which firings take place is when a firm critically assesses an individual's suitability for continued employment as happens, for instance, when universities deny tenure to assistant professors.

The findings for the *lower-skill semi-autonomous segment* are more congruent with the predictions. First, employees in these positions are more vulnerable to unemployment than any of the non-working-class segments with the exception of the lower-skill managerial positions. Employees in these positions are more likely to be counted among the unemployed in each type of unemployment than their higher-skill counterparts. For instance, column 6 of Table 4.4 indicates that the unemployment likelihood ranges from only 3 to 9% below the number that would be expected on the basis of their size in the labor force. Nevertheless, depending on the type, the propensity of these semi-autonomous employees to be unemployed remains substantially lower than for the working class. Given this, however, the fact remains that these employees are distributed to unemployment types in a pattern most similar to the skill-bargaining segment of the working class. Although not strongly supporting the expectation, the unemployed in this segment are slightly underrepresented in the category of quits and—far more than is the case for higher-skill semi-autonomous employees—virtually at the average in their proportion of temporary and indefinite layoffs. Finally, they are only 2% more likely than average to be fired. Overall, then, this segment evidences a pattern and a propensity of unemployment similar to that for the two vacancy-competition working-class segments: namely, a tendency away from firings toward layoffs and a tendency not to quit without a new job in hand. Such a pattern, again, reflects a general shelter from unemployment associated with job-specific skills, a lower inducement to quit without a better job, and some protection (through layoffs) when unemployment does occur.

WORKING CLASS

Working-class positions exercise little or no decision-making power in either economic ownership or possession; their incumbents are attached to these positions by entering a contract to exchange labor power for wages. Being employed in a working-class position in and of itself subjects a worker to forms of unemployment associated with the competitive labor market: involuntary job loss through firings and voluntary job loss through quits. Without added resources of bargaining power provided by unions or high-skill requisites, workers may be removed from employment at the discretion of employers and are vulnerable to wage rates and working conditions that may induce quits without a new job.

Compare the figures in column 6 of Table 4.4 for the entire range of class segments: Only in the working class does the proportion of unemployed outstrip the proportion of the labor force. The working class as a whole is 26% more likely to be unemployed than average. Among types of unemployment, it is 34% more likely to have laid-off workers, 23% more likely to have fired workers, and 22% more likely to have workers who quit without moving immediately to a new job. More dramatic than the contrast to average unemployment levels is the contrast to the other segments. For instance, the proportion of unemployed in the working class is 63% greater than in the semi-autonomous class and 93% higher than in the managerial class.

As many writers (e.g., Aronowitz, 1973; Edwards, 1979; Hodson, Schervish, Stryker, and Yago, 1980; O'Connor 1973; Rosenberg, 1975) have pointed out, however, the working class is not a unidimensional reality. Instead it is segmented into fractions, each with qualitatively different labor market resources, rewards, and processes. Here I have defined four fractions of the working class in order to examine such divergence in relation to unemployment. Two fractions are imbued with vacancy-competition forms of bargaining power and two others are subject to wage competition in the labor market.

VACANCY-COMPETITION POSITIONS
OF THE WORKING CLASS

On-the-job training or specific human capital financed by the employer, unionization, the lack of measurability of tasks, and other sources or bargaining power enable workers to resist being fired and replaced by others

from the labor pool. When firms face decreased demand for their output, workers are able to deflect the more costly consequences from their work history. Workers with high resources, then, are more likely to be laid off or to quit with another job in hand (see Schervish, 1981).

Quitting with a job in hand or when job prospects are favorable is a reasonable outcome or index for being employed in positions of high bargaining power. Why layoffs reflect high bargaining power may be more difficult to appreciate, since they entail involuntary job separation for the worker. The notion of layoff used here emphasizes the "beneficial" aspects of this form of unemployment relative to firings or to quits due to job dissatisfaction. The aspect of layoffs that proves relatively beneficial to workers is that being laid off rather than fired involves, for the most part, an ability to retain a hold on one's position even while unemployed. When positions are reopened the laid-off worker retains either a formal–legal or an informal–customary priority in being reinstated. The significant connection to high resource positions is that the pattern of being laid off and reinstated reflects an underlying bargaining relationship between workers and employers in which workers have struggled to reduce their vulnerability in the labor market. Thus, in its most institutionalized form, this bargaining process is formalized in union contracts guaranteeing procedures for layoffs. As Feldstein (1976) says, "Most of those who are laid off know that they will soon return to their employer, protected by seniority arrangements and by their job-specific human capital [p. 938]." He supports this assertion by showing that in manufacturing, 75–85% of workers are rehired after being laid off (1975, 1976).

In the managerial and semi-autonomous classes, bargaining power becomes translated into a lower proportion of unemployed. In the case of vacancy-competition working-class positions, bargaining power does not have this effect. Instead it affects the type of unemployment and, if anything, may actually increase the frequency of unemployment. How this comes about reveals aspects of the structure of class relations not discernible from studies of income alone. As working-class positions, vacancy-competition jobs are generally vulnerable to absorbing the impact of firm policies to adjust to economic declines.

But given this general vulnerability, vacancy-competition bargaining power—especially when based on unionization—both raises wages and insulates them, at least in part, from real declines due to inflation. This stability in wage rates, in turn, constrains employers to adjust to downturns more by curtailing output and employment than by lowering wage costs and prices. Ironically, the bargaining resources that provide wage security can be expected to contribute as well to more unstable employment. But the impact

of these bargaining resources does not stop here, the form of this augmented unemployment is also affected by this bargaining power. The resources of vacancy-competiton relations grant workers the capacity to break from market forms of labor turnover. Institutionalized bargaining power through unionization or high levels of on-the-job training provides property rights over jobs. Thus I expect that even though firings will continue to be the major source of the unemployed, the proportion of layoffs relative to firings will be *higher* than in wage-competition segments. Moreover, these same resources tend to attach workers permanently to positions of employment. Specific training, seniority systems, and pension rights constrain workers in these positions from quitting, especially when such quitting is not for a better job already obtained. Consequently, workers in union vacancy-competition positions will be expected to have a higher than average proportion of layoff and a lower than average proportion of firings and quits that result in unemployment.

Even in the absence of a high frequency of unionism for occupations, high-skill requisites and long periods of on-the-job training still provide vacancy-competition resources of bargaining power. The higher the specific skill level and the greater the on-the-job training, the fewer are the number of workers in the labor pool able to replace a specific worker. Also, the employer will be more dependent on workers to train each other and thereby will be forced to provide workers with job conditions and protections that make workers amenable to accepting new technology without fear of job loss (cf. Thurow, 1975). Thus, positions with such requisites provide resources of bargaining power that result in a tendency for many to be laid off rather than fired since employers seek to retain their investment in specific human capital for when production increases. These positions also will have lower than average rates of quits that result in unemployment since the same job-specific skills that induce layoffs rather than firings also attach workers to positions until a better job is obtained.

In sum I suggest that the working-class positions with the greatest bargaining power will evidence the greatest job security but not necessarily the lowest unemployment rate among working-class segments. The findings confirm this expectation. Table 4.4 indicates that among the unemployed from the vacancy-competition positions with *union-bargaining* power the proportion of layoffs is greater than in any other segment; the proportion of quits is lower (with the exception of the high-skill semi-autonomous segment) than in any other segment; and the proportion of fired is lower (with the exception of the self-employed) than in any other segment. In the union-bargaining segment, according to column 4 of Table 4.4, layoffs (temporary or indefinite) are over 23% greater than average; firings are 8% less than

average; and quits are 25% less than average. Moreover, this pattern of distribution of the unemployed coincides with the fact that, in relation to the size of the segment, all forms of unemployment are overrepresented for this segment: most for layoffs and least for quits. Column 6 shows that layoffs are 72% overrepresented, indefinite layoffs 69% overrepresented, firings 28% overrepresented, and quits 10% overrepresented.

The unemployment pattern in the *skill bargaining segment* reflects the theoretical expectations less fully. First, although the unemployed are overrepresented in this segment, the overrepresentation is not nearly as high as the theory of restricted wage adjustment and firm investment in specific human capital would lead one to expect. Note that in contrast to the 38% overrepresentation of unemployed in the union-bargaining segment, the skill-bargaining segment is only 14% overrepresented. This 14% is composed of an overrepresentation of 34% in temporary layoffs, 12% in indefinite layoffs, 13% in firings, and 17% in quits. Second, the pattern of unemployment types among this number of unemployed follows the predictions closely only in the case of temporary layoffs where workers are unemployed at a level 17% greater than the average. In contrast to the union-bargaining segment, indefinite layoffs are actually 2% less than average. Apparently, where the direct union impact is less and workers depend more on skill-requisites of positions for protection in unemployment, temporary layoffs continue to reconcile the needs of firms to adjust the size of the labor force and the demands of workers for employment security. But when longer-term adjustments are anticipated by the firms, it appears that in the absence of strong union power, the tendency is to bypass indefinite layoffs and to fire workers. At the same time the unemployed who quit are 2% greater than average indicating a tendency for workers in this segment to bank on their training, risk voluntary separations, and invest in the search for a comparable or better job. It is important to point out that the interpretation of these quits as essentially positive because they entail efforts at building a career differs from the mainly negative interpretation of unemployment quits found to be so prominent among the full wage-competition segment where quits reflect the *lack* of job-specific skills and career ladders across firms.

Being so vulnerable to unemployment is the general plight of members of the working class, yet these findings indicate that the high unemployment rate in these segments actually reflects their high bargaining power in two ways. First, because positions in the segments grant workers power to resist lower wages, employers adjust to decreased demand by lowering output and increasing unemployment. Such is the plight even of workers holding positions of strong bargaining power: Wage security won in one arena of struggle results, ironically, in greater vulnerability in the arena of un-

employment. but this is not the end of the story. Once the decision is made to reduce the labor force, a second source of bargaining power comes into play. Due to both worker organization and other vacancy-competition resources, more of the unemployed are in layoffs, especially temporary layoffs, than in other segments.

WAGE-COMPETITION POSITIONS
OF THE WORKING CLASS

In wage-competition positions with low resources of bargaining power, workers retain little or no control over the processes of unemployment and reemployment. When firms close down and positions are permanently ended, workers are left without jobs. A more important type of firing, both statistically and theoretically, occurs when positions are ended temporarily or not ended at all but workers are separated permanently from their jobs with no priority for reinstatement. Workers with low resources are subject to those market forces within the firm described by neoclassical theories of marginal productivity. Workers are hired and fired according to their productivity, rather than in accord with institutional constraints imposed on employers. The relative value of a worker to an employer is a function of the amount of productivity provided by the worker relative to the costs of to the employer. When firms face increased competition, decreased demand, or incentives to lower costs, they will release workers that are more costly and hire those that are less costly. This does not mean that such replacement happens simultaneously, only that in the absence of worker power, adjustments in the labor force are accomplished through labor turnover.[15] Workers are separated from positions permanently and, when demand turns up, different workers are employed.

In line with this logic, it is hypothesized that compared to vacancy-competition segments of the working class, these segments will have lower proportions of unemployed because of the ability of employers to adjust by lowering real wages when demand for labor decreases. Among types of unemployment, I expect that these segments will be more associated than vacancy-competition segments with forms of labor turnover resulting from the competitive workings of the labor market such as quits that result in unemployment and firings.

---

[15]Neoclassical research on worker-financed specific human capital (cf. Parsons, 1972) treats this phenomenon in a narrower framework but implicitly lends support to this thesis that workers with little or no control over employer decisions will face lowered relative wages and will be fired rather than laid off with the right of recall.

The findings presented in Table 4.4 confirm the expectations for the full wage-competition segment but not for the partial wage-competition segment with its middle level of bargaining power. (Recall that the findings for the two vacancy-competition segments revealed that the theoretical expectations were more solidly supported for the larger union-bargaining segment than for the smaller, skill-bargaining segment.)

As with all working-class segments, employees of the *partial wage-competition segment* are overrepresented among the unemployed, both in general and for each type of unemployment. This overrepresentation is equal to that of the union-bargaining segment, however, and thus challenges the proposition that weaker bargaining power allows for more wage-negotiation and hence lower unemployment. Likewise, the relative distribution of the unemployed by types does not fully confirm the expectations. For instance, relative to the average pattern, temporary layoffs are 12% less, indefinite layoffs 20% more, firings 5% less, and quits 10% less. Thus although the likelihood of temporary layoffs is low and in the predicted direction, the high likelihood of indefinite layoffs and the relative underrepresentation of firings and quits appear contrary to predictions.

One possible way to reconcile these findings with the expectations is suggested by the concurrence of a relatively low proportion of temporary layoffs and a relatively high proportion of indefinite layoffs. This pattern, in contrast to that of the union-bargaining segment (where both temporary and indefinite layoffs are more than 23% greater than average) suggests that in the absence of strong union- or skill-bargaining power, indefinite layoffs in this partial wage-competition segment may be proxies for firings. Whereas in the union-bargaining segment the high propensity of temporary layoffs suggests that layoffs do indeed represent separations from jobs with expectation of recall, in the partial wage-competition segment the relatively low propensity of temporary layoffs may indicate that indefinite layoffs are structurally less like extended layoffs and more akin to firings: that is, with only a circumscribed guarantee, if any, of actual recall despite the label of "layoff."

This interpretation is congruent with the fact that unemployment is so strongly overrepresented in this segment. Taken together, then, the findings suggest the following picture. The moderate level of bargaining power attached to these positions (*a*) makes wages less flexible than in the full wage-competition segment thereby inducing a higher level of unemployment; and (*b*) encourages a moderate, but not overriding, concern among employers to keep workers attached to the firm through unemployment spells thereby producing an above average propensity of indefinite layoffs (that often approximate firings) and the slightly lower than average measured

proportion of fired workers among the unemployed. Finally, this interpretation is consistent with the less than average propensity for the unemployed to have quit without a job. The moderate level of bargaining power makes employment in these positions relatively beneficial for the workers but without encouraging quits for career building.

In contrast, the findings for the *full wage-competition segment* of the working class strongly support the theoretical expectations. Contrary to popular and even social science imagery, the proportion of unemployed is lower than for any segment of the working class. I also find that the unemployed are more predominantly those who were fired and quit than in the other working-class segments. Column 6 of Table 4.4 shows that the unemployed are only 7% overrepresented in the segment in contrast to the 26% overrepresentation in the working class as a whole and the 38% overrepresentation in the union-bargaining segment. Moreover, this aggregate 7% overrepresentation conceals larger contradictory trends among the forms of unemployment suffered by the workers of this segment. Unemployed from temporary and indefinite layoffs are strongly (24% and 36%) underrepresented relative to the size of the labor force whereas firings and quits are significantly overrepresented (15% and 40%). This trend in the relative number of the unemployed is complemented by the distribution of types of unemployment relative to the average and, more important, relative to the union-bargaining segment.

Column 4 shows that temporary and indefinite layoffs are, respectively, 13% and 45% fewer than the average across classes whereas firings are 8% greater than average and quits are 31% greater than average. Compared to all other working-class segments, the unemployed are quite unambiguously in that status as a result of turnover forms of unemployment—namely, firings and quits. Workers employed in positions with traditional forms of market, wage-competition relations are more prone to become separated permanently from their jobs rather than remain tied to them through layoffs during spells of unemployment. The proportion of unemployed who quit or were fired is greater than in any other working-class segment. In fact the proportion of unemployed who quit is exceeded only in the self-employment class; the proportion who were fired is exceeded only in the higher-skill semiautonomous and the lower-skill managerial segments where the level of unemployment is far lower.

Contrasting the distribution of the unemployed in the two numerically and theoretically more important segments—the union-bargaining and the full wage-competition segments—highlights the significance of differentiating types of unemployment and fractions in analyzing unemployment in the working class. Not only do I find that the proportion of unemployed is 29%

greater in the strongest bargaining segment, but the distribution of the unemployed among the types also differs significantly. For instance, the proportion of unemployed by temporary layoffs is 66% greater among workers in the union-bargaining segment than in the full wage-competition segment and the proportion of unemployed by indefinite layoffs is 78% greater. In contrast, the proportion of unemployed by firings is 16% greater in the full wage-competition segment whereas the proportion of unemployed by quits is 63% greater. Moreover, as previously discussed, the weaker the bargaining power of the segment, the more likely quits reflect the negative or dead-end characteristics of positions rather than positive ones such as skill training and other forms of experience that support a career-oriented decision to quit without a job.

DISCUSSION

The analysis of the relationship between class segments and employment status reveals a systematic class difference in unemployment rate and types of unemployment. Class position contributes to the relative type and degree of bargaining power of a worker. The location of a position in the employment structure provides its incumbent with various types and degrees of resources for affecting labor market outcomes or rewards. Wright (1979) has established and interpreted the independent contribution of class position in determining the level and process of income attainment of the labor force. This present research makes a similar argument concerning the proportion and type of unemployment.

We have found that the position of employment defined in terms of the relations of production and the relations of authority (as opposed to occupation defined as a task in the technical relations of production or as an indicator of socioeconomic status) makes a statistically and theoretically significant impact on determining the unemployment level and type for incumbents of various classes. This relationship, moreover, holds even controlling for personal characteristics, business cycle, and economic sector. Drawing on a growing body of research stressing the theoretical and political importance of class fractions and types of unemployment, I have distinguished rates and types of unemployment for the self-employment class, for two fractions each within the semi-autonomous and managerial classes, and four fractions within the working class. The findings from the analysis suggest a series of implications concerning (a) the nature of unemployment, (b) the structure of class relations, and (c) the theory of class struggle in advanced capitalism.

Concerning *unemployment*, the research supports the proposition that unemployment is not a unidimensional phenomenon. Columns 3 and 4 of Table 4.4 show that hidden beneath the variation in the proportion of unemployed across classes and fractions is a complex relationship between types of job separation that comprise this aggregate proportion. A prime example is the variation in unemployment types within the working class. The popular belief that secondary positions entail higher unemployment is not necessarily correct. Instead, the greatest unemployment propensity occurs in the strongest (union-bargaining) working-class segment. Some of this difference may be due to an underestimation of unemployment in the weakest working-class segment. This results from the greater tendency of workers in this fraction to leave the labor force after job separation and thus not to be counted among the unemployed. Nevertheless, the point is that even if the workers in the full wage-competition segment are proportionately less likely to be among the unemployed, the sensitivity that "secondary" workers are less well off than other members of the working class is not undercut. Rather it forces us to turn to a more basic understanding of unemployment as deprivation than is given by examining comparative levels of overall unemployment.

What makes full wage-competiton positions "secondary" is their predominant type of unemployment (firings and quits) and the underlying vulnerability to competitive labor markets reflected in these types of unemployment. Similarly, the "anomalous" finding that the union-bargaining segment may have the highest unemployment rate reflects the presence rather than the absence of bargaining power. Union-bargaining power deters wage adjustments by firms, hence increasing unemployment, but this same bargaining power transforms involuntary job separation into layoffs.

These conclusions entail *implications for theory and research* in two areas of labor market studies. First, it suggests one possible path through the debate regarding the extent of wage flexibility (factor price elasticity of demand) in determining the demand for labor. Nadiri and Rosen (1973) and Hamermesh (1976) argue that wage flexibility is a negligible component in estimating the demand for labor and that the demand for labor reflects, instead, the level of output and the cost of physical capital. In contrast, Clark and Freeman (1980) argue that the price of labor itself and not just its price relative to the price of capital determines the demand for labor. The findings presented in the preceding pages suggest that the two arguments may offer complementary rather than competing interpretations. The findings provide some evidence for the proposition that the relation of wage flexibility to labor demand differs in different segments of the labor market. The higher unemployment in the union-bargaining segment, I have argued, reflects the

inflexibility of wages and the existence of quantity adjusting in this labor market. In contrast, the lower unemployment proportion in the full wage-competition segment reflects a labor market with flexible wages and hence a more immediate impact of the price of labor in the determination of labor demand.

A second contribution of the research to current analysis of unemployment is its modification of the application of Oi's (1962) theory of labor as a quasi-fixed factor to explaining relative differences among positions in their unemployment propensities. According to Oi, labor varies in the extent to which it entails more than a variable cost. The cost of labor is valued at the wage or salary plus the value of the sunk costs entailed in the hiring and training of a worker. In order to avoid the risk of losing such investment, employers, even in downturns, will be more likely to retain rather than fire those workers in whom they have invested substantially. The implication, then, is that unemployment should be lower among segments of the labor market where labor embodies these fixed costs since the employer will avoid the risk of losing these costs by dismissing a worker. This theory helps to explain the relatively low unemployment rate among the employees in the managerial and semi-autonomous positions and, to a lesser extent, the moderate unemployment proportion among workers in the skill-bargaining segment.

My findings indicate that, without some revision, however, Oi's formulation falters when applied to the working class. Specifically, these results question Oi's expectation that fixed costs reduce involuntary unemployment. There is a higher relative proportion of unemployed from the union-bargaining segment where fixed costs are high than from the full wage-competition segment where, presumably, fixed costs are low. In fact, this measure of the difference in overall unemployment between the two segments actually underestimates the differences in involuntary unemployment because the proportion of quits in the union-bargaining segment is lower than in the full wage-competition segment. What needs to be added to Oi's theory to reconcile his expectations with the pattern of unemployment in the working class is an understanding of the theoretical and empirical importance of layoffs, especially temporary layoffs. Since layoffs are a form of involuntary unemployment that tend to attach a worker to a firm even during spells of unemployment, it seems appropriate to recast the application of the theory of labor as a quasi-fixed factor to take this fact into account. In view of the findings, this would mean that in the working class, at least, the fixed costs of labor do indeed reduce the indicidence of firings as predicted, but, contrary to expectations, do not reduce the proportion of total involuntary unemployment. This is because employers are able to turn to layoffs—a form of

unemployment that enables them to reduce labor costs while protecting, to a great extent, their investment in hiring and traning costs. Minimally the implication for the application of the theory of fixed labor-factor costs to unemployment is that fixed labor costs do not necessarily reduce (and may even increase) the likelihood of unemployment in those segments of the labor market where layoffs allow for labor force reductions but with a lower risk to employers of losing their investments in such fixed costs.

The second major implication of this study is that it brings to the fore a class segment's *relative vulnerability to market relations* as a fundamental characteristic of class relations and thus as an important category or lens for understanding the class structure. Such vulnerability derives from four sources: personal characteristics, the business cycle, economic sector of a firm, and class position. The research reported here highlights how class segments can be defined by their capacities to employ or circumvent competitive market mechanisms in pursuing their interests.

Third, the analysis suggests that the historical development of capital is simultaneously a development of the capacities for *class struggle* and of the objective interests over which inter- and intra-class struggle takes place. Edwards (1979), Braverman (1974), and Burawoy (1979) document how the transformation of capital entails a parallel transformation of the class structure and the systems of control embedded in the labor process. As the "middle layers" of managers and semi-autonomous employees expanded, new forms of control emerged, and the working class was fractionated. Although the research reported here is cross-sectional, it confirms the theoretical and empirical relevance of this historical analysis. It shows that the most recent epoch of capitalist evolution provides an instance of the dialectical proposition that the transformation of the class structure is simultaneously the development of capacities for struggle. As Burawoy (1978) also insists, economic and social outcomes reflect more than the one-sided application of capitalist will. The findings also imply that differences in unemployment proportions and types reflect class and fraction differences in what Wright (1978) calls the structural (embedded in the workplace) and organizational (purposefully constructed unions, associations, and parties) capacities to transform further or resist labor market forces in fulfilling their interests. I have called such capacities bargaining power. I have shown how in the case of unemployment a position's location in the class structure and its ties to organizational resources reflect the segmented structure of contemporary capitalism and result in differing patterns of unemployment.

Thus the present research goes beyond documenting the important, but short-run, need for targeting worker, state, or union employment strategies in accord with the uneven distribution of rates and types of unemployment

across class segments. More fundamentally it shows that class differences in unemployment are not random but systematically reflect and reinforce divisions between and within classes, especially within the working class. This is because such variation in unemployment is due to underlying differences in vulnerability to market forces, differences in capacities for class struggle, and differences in immediate interests surrounding employment, job security, and the distribution of the social wage. I find both in wages and in unemployment that contemporary class relations subordinate the working class while undercutting a unified working-class response by imposing objectively different patterns of unemployment on different fractions of the working class.

5

Economic Sectors and the Distribution of the Unemployed

Chapter 4 examined the effect of class on the distribution of members of the labor force to types of unemployment. This chapter analyzes the independent effect of the second dimension of employment structure— economic sector—on determining the employment status of labor force members. It also studies the interaction effect of economic sector and age by analyzing how age variation in unemployment varies by sector. Again, these analyses control for all the modeled effects of personal characteristics, business cycle, and class indicated in model 11 of Table 3.2. Although the discussion of class segment investigated the impact of job characteristics common to positions across sectors, the treatment of economic sector (defined by industry) examines the impact of firm characteristics common to positions across class segments. In particular, I examine the relationship between the extent of market power of firms in the product market and the extent and type of job separation and unemployment in the labor market.[1]

Previous research has examined this firm aspect of segmentation as a

---

[1] Only persons who are employed or who have lost jobs through layoffs, quits, or firings are included in the study. Not included are those among the officially unemployed job searchers who were reentering the labor force or entering the labor force for the first time.

function of each detailed census category of industry (Stolzenberg, 1975), as a function of capital sectors (Beck, 1980; Beck *et al.*, 1978; Edwards, 1979; Hodson, 1978), or by more general product categories such as durable and nondurable manufacturing, service, retail, construction (e.g., Bluestone, Jordan, and Sullivan 1981; Bluestone and Stevenson, 1980; Weiss, 1963, 1966b). Consistent throughout the various strains of this literature is the argument that oligopoly, competitive, and state sectors differ in their market power in determining the quantity and price of outputs, the stability of revenue, and the stability of their demand for labor. Though valuable as the starting point for the present study, the previous research evidences two shortcomings. First, the research usually (but not exclusively) focuses on income, wages, or profits as the outcome differentiated among sectors (see Scherer, 1980), rather than unemployment. Second, the research that does examine unemployment (e.g., Best, 1981; Bolle, 1981; Buchele, 1976; Cornfield, 1981; Doeringer and Piore, 1975; Feinberg, 1979; Mueller, 1972; Norris, 1978; Schervish, 1981) fails to distinguish types of unemployment or fails to control for personal characteristics, business cycle, or occupational class composition.

The thesis of this chapter is that the rate of unemployment associated with a firm is a function of (*a*) the type of vulnerability to market downturns of the firm and (*b*) the range of options available to a firm to adapt to this vulnerability. Differences in the vulnerability of a firm to market mechanisms of supply and demand in the product market result in differences in the proportion of types of job-separation employment associated with the firm.

This chapter proceeds in four steps. First I set out three aspects of vulnerability that provide the theoretical basis for distinguishing unemployment proportions by type among economic sectors. I focus especially on the competitive, oligopoly, and state sectors. Four further sectors, however, are distinguished that either are difficult to classify among the three major sectors or are theoretically distinct: the construction, farm, utility, and private nonprofit sectors. Second, propositions are formulated and tested concerning the relative number of unemployed in general and by type in these seven sectors. The propositions are tested by a log-linear analysis of unemployment data for the sample designated in Chapter 3. Third, in a brief discussion, I explore some issues of internal labor markets from the vantage point of how the sectoral impact on employment status varies for different age groups. The final section discusses implications for understanding the nature of unemployment and the nature of sectoral segmentation in the American economy.

FIRM VULNERABILITY

Three aspects of vulnerability[2] of a firm to market relations determine the proportion and type of unemployment associated with that firm. First is the extent to which a firm is vulnerable to downturns in income. This is largely a function of whether the product or service of the firm is vulnerable to fluctuations in demand controlling for changes in national income represented by the business cycle. This price elasticity of demand determines whether a firm will be forced to make systematic rather than occasional or individual cutbacks in its demand for labor.[3]

Second, when a firm faced with decreased product demand must make some adjustment in its factor and product markets, it may react in either of two ways, depending on how it strives to maintain its revenue. That is, the degree to which a firm is a price taker or price administrator in the product market indicates the extent to which it will be a price adjuster or output adjuster in the face of decreased demand (cf. Feinberg, 1979; Means, 1935; Weiss, 1977). This influences whether the firm or industry will carry out a systematic curtailment in the demand for labor or will, instead, minimize the reduction in demand for labor by reducing wages. Although it is difficult to establish any hard and fast rule, the economic research cited previously as well as other studies (cf. Scherer, 1980:350–362) have shown the theoretical

---

[2]The distinction between vulnerable and nonvulnerable firms is more than a tautalogical argument that firms in industries with low unemployment are nonvulnerable. Rather the argument is that industries that are growing or that have stable sources of income because demand for their product or service is inelastic are theoretically and empirically distinct from those that do not. Any number of specific industrial markets are not vulnerable to significant decreased demand. This is the case, for instance, with the dairy, petroleum, and tobacco industries. Since the more theoretically important distinction being analyzed here is that between the competitive, oligopoly, and state sectors, however, and since these and other industries with similarly inelastic product markets do not comprise a large proportion of employment, these particular nonvulnerable industries are included among the competitive and oligopoly sectors. This is not the case for two other substantially large industrial sectors: the utilities, and the so-called nonprofit, voluntary sector. These sectors are not only relatively large employers but also are distinctive in their relatively stable sources of income and insulation from downturns of demand (see footnote 5, p. 121).

[3]Overall vulnerability of a firm is a function of the price and income elasticity of demand. This, in turn, reflects such factors as the secular change in demand for a product, entry or growth of competing firms, and the relative availability of substitute goods. Although examining each of these factors and determining their relative importance for particular industries is beyond the scope of this research, Haveman and Golladay (1976) do investigate these aspects in detail.

and empirical correspondence between vulnerability to market prices and (*a*) the degree to which a firm will be price adjusting in the product market and (*b*) the degree to which it will be able to maintain production and hence its demand for labor. It is generally argued that competitive firms will be price adjusters in the product market, will tend to maintain output, and will retain its labor force. On the other hand, oligopolistic firms will tend to be price administrators. In the face of decreased product demand these firms will maintain prices, lower output, and decrease demand for labor.

Although the first and second aspects of vulnerability concern the level of unemployment generated by a sector, a third aspect concerns the type of unemployment. The extent to which a firm is required or able to provide wages to induce a stable work force, even in the face of decreased demand, will influence the type of unemployment faced by workers. First, techno-logical and organizational aspects of a firm create employment requirements that affect the type of unemployment. Firms that employ more advanced technology and mechanization of production and that are larger in absolute size will tend to contain positions that are hierarchically structured, interdependent, and job-specific in training or skills. Firms with less elaborate technology will tend to be more labor intensive and to contain positions that require job skills that are general, easily learnable, or similar to those embodied in the labor force of competitors. Firms of the first kind, generally oligopoly firms, are thus more vulnerable to the loss of specific workers. Workers who have obtained either an integrated role in a managerial hierarchy or a job-specific skill from on-the-job training represent an investment by the firm (see Oi, 1962). I expect that firms will seek to maintain a stable labor force and will attempt to keep workers tied to the firm even when decreased output requires adjustment in the size of the labor force. As we shall see, this enables us to understand how oligopoly firms, while more vulnerable to higher rates of unemployment will, at the same time, create a type of unemployment that ties workers to the firm. In this way, instability of employment sometimes coincides with a stable labor force. More particularly—short of major recessions—firms with more elaborate technology, larger hierarchies of authority, and greater on-the-job training will be expected to lay off workers with an expectation of recall rather than to fire workers outright. In contrast, firms that are less dependent on workers with specific human capital are able to benefit from hiring workers with the greatest general human capital endowments at the lowest market wage will tend to fire workers during downturns rather than pay the wage premiums necessary to retain its labor force intact during periods of unemployment.

Just as technological and organizational characteristics of firms create the desirability of retaining a stable labor force, certain characteristics of a firm's income-generating process make such retension of the labor force a

possibility. Firms vary in the extent to which they are able to pay wage premiums or unemployment insurance. Although research on the so-called monopoly wage premium continues to debate the source of such premiums, it does concur that imperfectly competitive firms do in fact obtain excess income from their oligopoly product market structure (cf. Scherer, 1980:358–362). Thus when and where income is stabilized over time (for instance in the oligopoly and state sectors), the labor force receives wages that induce the attachment of these workers to their firms even during periods of unemployment. Moreover, even when unemployment occurs, the firm's pricing structure enables it to sustain higher unemployment insurance taxes that otherwise would exert a greater disincentive to curtail employment.

This research designates seven sectors. Each of these sectors differs in its relative vulnerability to declines in income; and given such declines, the sectors differ too in their methods of adjustment to such declines and in the types of unemployment used in this adjustment. The logic of the argument requires that I distinguish each sector by its relationship to the three aspects of vulnerability. The first step is to determine whether a sector is relatively vulnerable or nonvulnerable to downturns in income. Second, among the vulnerable sectors, we need to distinguish between those that adjust by price and wages, thereby decreasing output and employment. Finally—given different levels of unemployment due to the first two dimensions—what factors contribute to the types of unemployment that will occur in the various sectors? Table 5.1 diagrams the applicability of the three aspects of vulnerability to the seven sectors designated in the analysis.

OPERATIONALIZATION OF ECONOMIC SECTORS

The dependent variable in the analysis again is a person's employment status. It is the five-category qualitative variable operationalized in the manner described in Chapter 3.[4] Economic sectors are operationalized by three-digit census categories of industry and the CPS employment status recode. Although the theoretical argument about the relation of economic sector to unemployment is ultimately a theory about firm behavior, firm-specific data is unavailable either on the scale or range necessary to conduct this research on unemployment. This is due, in part, to the fact that job-separation unemployment during the period 1969–1978 averaged under 5%. Unless a survey is exceptionally large, it is impossible to obtain enough cases to carry out quantitative analysis without eliminating controls for personal

---

[4]See footnote 1 of Chapter 4 (p. 79) for some cautions concerning the meaning and operationalization of employment status.

TABLE 5.1
Aspects of Vulnerability across Economic Sectors

	Capital sector						
	Competitive	Oligopoly	State	Farm	Construction	Utility	Private nonprofit
I Vulnerability to declines in revenue	+	+	−	∓	+	−	∓
II Vulnerability to market prices and price-adjustment[a]	±	∓	n.a.	+	−	n.a.	mixed[b]
III Vulnerability to need for attaching employees to positions	±	±	±	−	±	±	mixed

Note: + indicates the applicability of the criterion to a sector; − indicates the nonapplicability of the criterion to a sector; ± indicates partial applicability of the criterion to a sector; ∓ indicates the minimal applicability of the criterion to a sector.

[a]The inverse of this relationship is that a sector is output adjusting.

[b]Because the private nonprofit sector is composed of units with such diversity, no predictions are indicated. The table shows, for instance that the competitive, oligopoly, and state sectors vary in their process of obtaining income and in their vulnerability to decreases in revenue. Thus they vary in their means of adjusting their labor supply through unemployment. Competitive and oligopoly firms obtain income through the sales of goods and services. Firms in these two sectors face the possibility of decreased income (+ in row I) and must then pursue strategies to curtail factor costs of labor. The competitive firm does this largely but not exclusively by decreasing prices and wages (± in row II), thereby maintaining production after some initial, short-term, reduction. The oligopoly sector confronts decreased demand mainly through output adjustment and price stability and only minimally by price-adjustment (∓ in row II). In contrast, the state sector obtains its income from taxation and, through deficit spending, can legally allocate funds for employment even when revenues are depleted (− in row II and n.a. in row II). Finally, the figure indicates that the oligopoly and state sectors share the need to retain their investments in specific training of employees (± in row III), whereas in the competitive sector this is less true (∓ in row III).

characteristics, class segment of an employment position, and business cycle. The alternative is to employ CPS data that covers a sufficient number of cases for each type of unemployment but does so only with industry-level data. Consequently, even though I recognize the potential for misclassifying particular firms, I operationalize sectors by detailed census industry codes. The oligopoly and competitive sectors are determined according to Hodson (1978) who distinguishes these sectors on a number of criteria, especially the Shepherd concentration ratios. The major exception is that here I include in the state sector all employees from whatever industry who are designated as employed by the state in the CPS employment status recode. For comparative purposes and in order to avoid confounding the results by including industries that are difficult to categorize as either competitive or oligopolistic, the construction, farm, utility, and private nonprofit sectors are treated as separated categories of the capital sector.[5] Appendix C lists the census categories and the number of weighted cases comprising each sector.

UNEMPLOYMENT AND ECONOMIC SECTOR

Competitive Sector

Traditional economic theory contends that competitive firms face perfect elasticity of demand in the product market. When demand for the firm's

---

[5]The utility sector is a prototypical example of a monopoly industry. Barriers to entry are great; local product markets are divided by, at most, two firms; and there is little or no challenge from substitution of alternative products. Utilities are analyzed here separately from oligopoly sector firms. This is done in order to avoid obscuring the differences between oligopoly and competitive sectors by including in the former a large industry that does not face the general market forces confronting the oligopoly sector despite the oligopoly sector's ability to stabilize income through pricing. A second sector, the private nonprofit voluntary sector, is distinguished from the oligopoly sector for many of the same reasons. The nonprofit sector is relatively large and its vulnerability to downturns is low. Unlike the utility sector, the nonprofit sector is not easily classified as either oligopoly or competitive. Appendix C shows the industrial composition of this sector. Many of the industries in this sector also are included in the state sector since various welfare, educational, and health institutions are also in the public sector. As to its place in the oligopoly or competitive sector, the private nonprofit sector is ambiguous. On the one hand, hospitals are oligopolistic and are often price makers; they enjoy the benefits of stable income from third-party payers and often serve a particular geographic area alone or with only a few other hospitals. On the other hand, private social and welfare organizations, voluntary organizations, and private educational institutions are subject to competition for funding and clients. Despite this internal ambiguity, this sector is separated from the state, oligopoly, and competitive sectors once again in order to increase the homogeneity of these latter three sectors and to reduce the distortions in the analysis and difficulties of interpretation that would ensue if such a separate category were not introduced.

product falls, competitive firms may initially lower production and reduce the work force. In the medium and long runs, the competitive firm will respond to decreases in demand (due to changes in tastes and in real prices) by lowering prices in an effort to maintain income through increased volume. Unless prices are lowered these price-taking firms would be driven out of the market. Consequently, dismissal of workers should be curtailed by this competitive constraint and by their ability to lower prices of products and the costs of labor inputs. Thus, although I expect a moderate amount of layoffs and firings to coincide with reductions in output, the second aspect of firm vulnerability (price adjusting) results in competitive firms being associated with unemployment due to quits. In their attempt to lower production costs, real wages are decreased and workers find their jobs less valuable.

The third aspect of vulnerability, the extent to which firms seek to retain their labor force even during spells of unemployment, results in competitive firms tending to fire rather than lay off workers. It also results in these firms tending not to pay wage premiums to curtail quits. Competitive firms are more constrained than oligopoly firms in their application of technology and mechanization and in their obtaining and paying out in wages the revenues generated by monopoly pricing. Consequently, compared to the oligopoly sector, and controlling for class composition, the competitive sector is less likely to attract, train, or need to retain workers with higher skills. Moreover, the structure of the competitive sector, with many firms producing essentially the same goods, provides for each firm a pool of prospective workers from the ranks of the employed workers among its competitors. Accordingly, I expect that the proportion of layoffs will be less than average whereas the proportion of firings and quits that result in unemployment will be greater than average.

Oligopoly Sector

A second sector that is vulnerable to decreased demand is the imperfectly competitive or oligopolistic sector. Given this first aspect of vulnerability, the second aspect asks whether this sector will adjust to decreases by curtailing output and employment.

Economic research again supports the proposition that firms with greater market concentration will respond to decreased demand by lowering output and decreasing the demand for labor. This will mainifest itself in a higher rate of involuntary job separations. For instance, Means (1935) documents the connection between degree of concentration and degree to which a firm is output rather than price adjusting. Feinberg (1979) takes the next step, arguing that concentrated industries have less flexible downward pricing and

more unstable employment than do less concentrated, nonoligopolistic industries.[6]

Robinson (1969:70–71) details four sources of change in demand affecting imperfectly competitive firms: (*a*) the number of buyers of the firm's product decreases; (*b*) the wealth of the existing group of buyers for the product decreases; (*c*) the number of rival sellers increases; or (*d*) the cost of some rival commodity decreases. Since imperfectly competitive firms face downward sloping demand and marginal revenue curves, the demand for labor by these firms is a function of both real wages and the elasticity of demand. If any of these four changes occur, the demand for the firm's goods is decreased while the elasticity of demand increases. Decreased demand, then, coupled with increased elasticity of demand compounds the need to decrease output. This outcome is compounded once again by the fact than many factors that make these firms imperfectly competitive in the first place, also impose institutional constraints on their ability to decrease real wages when demand slows. These firms generally have high requirements for on-the-job training, for winning worker compliance to technological and organizational innovations, and for inducing established workers to pass on training to new workers (cf. Thurow, 1975). All these aspects lead me to predict, therefore, that imperfectly competitive firms will tend to be associated with layoffs and firings.

Still it is possible to be more precise in predicting the proportions of these two forms of involuntary unemployment. Turning to the third aspect of vulnerability—the capacity of a firm to keep its labor force attached even

---

[6]That oligopolies diverge in pricing behavior from the neoclassical model is argued in many different forms by a wide spectrum of theorists. The empirical foundations of the argument is that market power of oligopoly firms grants them the capacity to "set their margins above normal production costs, so that they can generate sufficient cash flow to finance from internal sources much of the investment expenditure they wish to undertake [Keynon, 1979:38–39].[33] The assumption is that oligopoly enterprises do not maximize short-run profits but set prices in order to ensure lone-run stability, growth, and profit. A number of reasons for this price rigidity are cited by Feinberg (1979): (a) oligopoly firms may set prices lower than the short-run profit-maximizing level in order to limit entry by other firms; (b) oligopolies keep price constant in order to avoid price wars, especially when declines in demand are expected to be temporary; (c) oligopolists "collect" cost and demand changes over a period of time in order to make price coordination easier; (d) oligopolists face a kinked demand curve and so maintain prices even when demand is curtailed; and (e) oligopoly firms pursue the managerial goal of profit and revenue stability that is enhanced by stabilizing prices and varying output when necessary. Other researchers have posited similar institutional arguments for oligopoly price stability. Okun (1973, 1975) and Eichner (1973) postulate that cost-based or cost-plus pricing has superseded market pricing but with the caveat from Okum that this does not apply just to oligopoly firms. Kenyon (1979) suggests that oligopoly price stability is based on a combination of mark-up pricing directed at ensuring resources for planned investments and normal-cost pricing directed at maintaining a standard or expected rate of capacity utilization over the long term.

during periods of unemployment—I argue that oligopoly firms, in contrast to competitive firms, reduce quits and tend to transform firings into layoffs. Two interrelated aspects of oligopolistic firms—monopoly pricing and technological complexity—result in a coincidence of worker and firm interests in ensuring the long-term attachment of workers to jobs. On the one hand, the greater managerial and technological complexity, interdependence of jobs, and on-the-job training of employees result in greater firm investment in worker-specific human capital. As a consequence, there will be an attempt to retain the attachment of workers to the firm even during unemployment. Hence, the tendency is for output adjustment in the product market to become translated into layoffs rather than firings when there are cutbacks in employment. On the other hand, the ability of oligopoly firms to extract monopoly rents (a factor often disputed [cf. Stafford, 1968; Weiss, 1966a, 1968]) results in the ability of these firms to provide higher wage rates and greater opportunities for promotion and other various benefits. This will result in the reduction of quits leading to unemployment even though quits with new jobs already in hand may not have been curtailed.

State Sector

Until the recent spate of property-tax limitation initiatives and federal cutbacks in civilian spending, the state sector experienced a stable or growing demand demand for its services. This was especially true for the 1969–1978 period. Also, until recently, state expenditure patterns were not significantly constrained by fluctuations in revenue. Therefore, due to its ability to stabilize its economic relations during the 10-year period being investigated, the state sector sector is expected to enjoy a lower proportion of unemployed than the competitive or oligopoly sectors. Moreover, since the state sector underwent little fluctuations in demand for its services, there will be a low proportion of involuntarily unemployed.

Given this, I expect that involuntary unemployment will tend to be firings rather than layoffs. This is because the removal of incumbents from positions is due not so much to the ending of positions as to the decision by the state employer that a particular individual is not competently completing an assigned task. But even here, it must be remembered that despite coverage of many workers by civil service protections and regulations for job tenure, many workers are hired as limited term employees and thus face firing when the task for which they were employed is terminated. Thus, although relatively infrequent, the proportion of fired employees firings is expected to be a greater than average whereas the proportion of laid-off employees is expected to be lower than average.

Finally, it is reasonable to expect that workers will quit state positions. The proportion of quits is difficult to predict, however. On the one hand, the existence of promotion and pension systems incorporated in the bureaucratic structure of state employment induces workers to remain attached to their positions. On the other hand, many workers take state jobs only as a second choice to employment in the private sector; and the skills learned at or used in state jobs are often transferable to employment in the private sector. Moreover, to the extent that skills are transferable to the private sector, there is some reason to expect that quits resulting in unemployment will be only a small proportion of the total number of quits.

Farm and Construction Sectors

For purposes of clarity in the analysis, four other economic sectors are distinguished over and above the competitive, oligopoly, and state sectors: the farm, construction, utility, and private nonprofit sectors. The farm and construction sectors are treated separately for two reasons: (a) it is difficult to categorize them univocably as either oligopoly or competitive and (b) the workings of the product market for each of these large industries is relatively unique. The farm sector is generally competitive in food production; however, in the growing of some basic fruits and vegetables, it is increasingly concentrated (cf. Morgan, 1979; Zwerdling, 1979). At the same time, the farm sector is special in that agricultural production is regulated not simply by the free market but also by government price supports, large government-to-government food sales, and by production quotas of various sorts.

Similarly, the construction industry is ambiguously located between the competitive and oligopoly sectors. On the one hand, because of the difficulty in transporting the products of this industry, the relevant market for determining market concentration is local rather than national. In many local markets, therefore, the construction industry does exist as an effective oligopoly, or, as it is sometimes called, a local or regional monopoly (as often is the case with hospitals or taxi companies). Second, the product market of the construction industry, unlike that of the farm industry, is highly mercurial. The demand for construction goods is not just cyclically volatile (here controlled for). It is also seasonally variant as well as strongly dependent on fluctuations in the supply of money regulated through the administration of interest rates. Because of these two reasons and because of the relatively large volume of employment (and unemployment, in the construction industry) the farm and construction sectors are treated as categories distinct from the competitive and oligopoly sectors.

Unemployment in the construction sector is expected to be high with the proportion of layoffs, being greater than average and the proportion of firings and quits being below average. This is due to the high wages in this sector as well as to other factors characteristic of oligopoly firms. Indefinite layoffs will be especially overrepresented due to the seasonal nature of the industry. The farm sector is expected to evidence unemployment patterns similar to those of the competitive sector. The skill requirements of employment are generally lower for most workers in this sector, and wage rates reflect the availability of a large labor pool able to compete for these jobs. Consequently, workers will tend to quit or be fired rather than be laid off.

Utility and Private Nonprofit Sectors

The utility and nonprofit sectors also are included in the analysis as distinct sectors. The utility sector is composed of the nonstate, private employment positions located in the water, natural gas, and electricity industries (see Appendix B). Firms in this sector may be considered classical instances of monopoly. With a few exceptions, utilities are the sole providers of necessary commodities to a geographical area. They differ from firms included in the oligopoly sector, however, according to the criterion of general vulnerability to downturns in revenue and product demand. This is because the utility sector faces a relatively inelastic demand for its products. Also, state-controlled rate schedules ensure a regularized rate of return on investment, stable profits, and funds for expansion or improvement of productive capacities. Consequently, this sector is expected to be associated with a low proportion of unemployed. Since this is a function of clearly discernible product characteristics, the utility sector is analyzed as a separate category from the oligopoly sector. Due to the stable demand for utility services and the firm-specific skills of employment positions, I expect that relative to other sectors the proportion of involuntarily unemployed to be low and, among types of unemployment, for the proportion of laid-off employees to be greater than average, and the proportion of fired employees to be lower than average.

The private nonprofit sector is composed of employment positions located in nonstate educational, health, and welfare institutions as well as various nonprofit professional organizations, social associations, and foundations (see Appendix B). Although a growing body of research is attempting to establish the theoretical and empirical characteristics that unify this sector (cf. Weisbrod, 1977), it remains a composite of many diverse enterprises. Included, for instance are the Red Cross, Catholic relief agencies, private

hospitals, private prep schools, and fraternal organizations. Even though these institutions are similar only in that each is formally a nonprofit organization outside the state sector, it is important to separate these organizations from the other sectors because of their peculiar insulation from market pressures entailed in generating revenue.

It would be reckless to formulate strong predictions concerning the proportion or types of unemployment associated with this heterogeneous sector. But it is reasonable to expect that due to moderately stable revenue the level of unemployment will be relatively lower than for the more vulnerable competitive, ologopoly, and construction sectors. Due to the relatively large number of positions in this sector that entail low or general job-training and that are subject to low wage rates and less intrinsically rewarding tasks, it would not be surprising to find a substantial propensity for workers to be unemployed as a result of quitting without a new job in hand.

ANALYSIS

The data and sample are described in Chapter 3. The analysis proceeds in three steps: (a) I establish the independent explanatory power of economic sector in determining the distribution of workers to unemployment; (b) I analyze the relation of this averaged effect of sector to unemployment in general; and (c) I estimate sectoral differences in their relative frequency of types of unemployment.

The Independent Contribution of Sector

The most general empirical finding is that the sector in which a person is employed makes a significant independent contribution to explaining the employment status of the person. This obtains controlling for all the modeled effects of class segment, period in the business cycle race, age, and education.

Table 5.2 shows that sector significantly reduces the amount of unexplained χ^2 when it is introduced both first and last in the hierarchical models describing the relation between the series of independent variables and employment status. When introduced as the first two-way interaction to the model containing all the one-way main effects of the dependent variable on employment status, the reduction in χ^2 is 4134 whereas the reduction is df 24. This is significant at the level of $p < .001$.

TABLE 5.2
Models for the Analysis of Employment Status and Economic Sector

Model	Fitted marginals[a]	df	Likelihood ratio $\approx^2$	p
1	(234567) (1)	17,296	18,668	>.5
2	(234567) (13)	17,272	14,534	>.5
3	(234567) (12) (14) (15) (16) (17)	17,224	10,505	>.5
4	(234567) (12) (14) (15) (16) (17) (13)	17.200	7,605	>.5
1 versus 2		24	4,134	<.001
3 versus 4		24	3,100	<.001
5[b]	(234567) (12) (13) (15) (16) (17) (136) (156) (157) (167)	17,080[c]	6,871	>.5

[a] 1 Employment status (dependent variable)
2 Class segment
3 Economic sector
4 Business cycle
5 Race
6 Age
7 Education
[b] Model 5 is the basis for the analysis reported in the text. All interactions are included that met the criterion that to be included an interaction must reduce the likelihood ratio χ^2 by a factor of at least four times the reduction in the degrees of freedom. This more stringent criterion was chosen because of the large number of cases in the study.
[c] The degrees of freedom are adjusted to take into account the number of cases constrained to be zero.

The more stringent test of significance also confirms the argument that the second dimension of the employment structure, economic sector, makes an independent contribution to distributing workers to employment status. Introducing the two-way effect of economic sector on employment status after all the other significant two-way effects have been added to the model still results in the reduction of 3100 χ^2 for a reduction of the 24 df.

The Relation of Economic Sector and Unemployment

Table 5.3 presents the tau-parameters generated by the log-linear analysis of the relation of employment status and capital sector controlling for personal characteristics, business cycle, and class position. The lower the tau-parameter for the category of employment status designated "employed" the higher the relative propensity of workers in the sector to be unemployed.

TABLE 5.3
Tau-Parameters for the Net Relationship of Employment Status and Economic Sector[a]

Employment status	Competitive	Oligopoly	State	Capital sector Construction	Farm	Utility	Nonprofit
Temporary layoff	.9318	1.0644	.6108	1.2248	1.1114	1.2282	1.0115
Indefinite layoff	.8884	1.3479	.5527	2.0639	1.4886	.8689	.5154
Firing	1.0675	.8961	1.0915	1.3699	.9483	.6963	.9302
Quit	1.2383	.8952	1.2444	.6786	.8160	.7215	1.4879
Employed	.9133	.8756	1.9219	.4338	.7889	1.8045	1.3847

[a]Controlling for the other modeled relationships of economic sector, class segment, business cycle, race, age, and education.

Table 5.4 presents the cross-sector odds ratios[7] that calculate the relative frequency of workers to be employed rather than unemployed in each sector compared to every other. These odds ratios show that the construction sector has by far the largest unemployment propensity whereas the state sector followed by the utility and nonprofit sectors, have the lowest. The unemployment propensity for the competitive and oligopoly sectors is similar and slightly lower than that for the farm sector. The likelihood of unemployment in the construction sector is 5.7 times more likely than in the state sector.

These findings corroborate the predictions concerning sector unemployment. I argued that the state sector would experience low unemployment due to its ability to generate revenue and due to its stable and even increased demand for services when other sectors face declining demand. People apply for more income transfers, return to school, attend to medical needs, and turn to the state for employment when faced with declining economic prospects.

The expectation from empirical research by Feinberg (1979) and from theory was that the oligopoly sector would have higher unemployment propensities than the competitive sector. The findings indicate that the competitive sector is only slightly less prone to unemployment. This finding, however, does not by itself call into question the oligopoly–employment instability hypotheses. The findings reported in Chapter 6 show that when the effect of business cycle unemployment is analyzed, the types of unemployment characteristics of the oligopoly sector are dramatically increased in a downturn whereas the forms of unemployment that characterize the competitive sector do not increase as much. Moreover, the findings presented in the next section show that the relative propensity of types of unemployment differs sharply between the competitive and oligopoly sectors.

Table 5.4 also confirms that the utility and nonprofit sectors are less vulnerable to conditions that produce unemployment than any sector with the exception of the state. Both of these sectors share a low vulnerability to decreased demand. But the ability of the utility sector to escape wage and price adjustments reduces the need for involuntary job separations; and the extensive firm-specific training in this sector curtails voluntary separations. Accordingly, the cross-sector odds ratios comparing the utility and nonprofit sectors indicates that the former is 1.4 times less likely to induce unemployment than the former. Again the findings point to the importance of

---

[7]See Appendix A (p. 206) for a discussion of the method for calculating cross-sector odds ratios.

TABLE 5.4
Cross-Sector Odds Ratios for Comparing the Employment and Unemployment Likelihoods for the Economic Sectors

	Competitive	Oligopoly	State	Construction	Farm	Utility	Nonprofit
Competitive	—	1.05	.42	2.38	1.19	.45	.62
Oligopoly	.95	—	.40	2.27	1.13	.43	.59
State	2.38	2.50	—	5.68	2.83	1.08	1.47
Construction	.42	.44	.18	—	.50	.19	.26
Farm	.84	.98	.35	2.01	—	.38	.52
Utility	2.21	2.32	.93	5.28	2.63	—	1.36
Nonprofit	1.63	1.71	.68	3.87	1.93	.73	—

Note: To obtain the relative likelihood of being employed rather than unemployed in sector A in contrast to sector B find sector A's row and read across to the column of sector B. To obtain the relative likelihood of being unemployed rather than employed in sector A in contrast to sector B find sector A's column and read down to the row of sector B.

See Appendix A for the method of calculating these cross-sector odds ratios.

distinguishing types of unemployment in order to explain sectoral differences in the general levels of job separation.

The Relationship of Economic Sector and Unemployment Type

I have already implied that variation in the relative frequency of unemployment by sectors conceals a more complex pattern of variation in the sectoral composition of forms of job separation. Examining how sectors with different vulnerability to market forces vary in type of unemployment is the topic of this section.

The tau-parameters in Table 5.3 are the basis for these analyses. The findings may be presented in a more intuitively understandable fashion by translating the findings summarized in Table 5.5. This table is computed by fitting the observed distribution through a process of iterative proportional adjustment to the log-linear parameters of Table 5.3. Table 5.5 then indicates the distribution of cases of employment and unemployment by economic sector controlling for the other modeled effects designated in Table 5.2. For example, column 3 of Table 5.5 indicates that, on average, employees on temporary layoffs are 6% of the unemployed across sectors whereas employees on indefinite layoffs are 24% of the unemployed, those fired are 55%, and those having quit are 15%.

COMPETITIVE AND OLIGOPOLY SECTORS

It was predicted that in contrast to the unemployed in the oligopoly sector, the unemployed in the competitive sector would be more likely to have been fired or to have quit than to have been laid off. The findings summarized in Tables 5.3 and 5.5 confirm these predictions. I have already noted (Table 5.3) that overall proportions of unemployment are virtually identical in the competitive and oligopoly sectors. Column 6 of Table 5.5 shows this too. Relative to the size of the labor force, the number of unemployed is 5% underrepresented in the competitive sector and 6% underrepresented in the oligopoly sector.

In the competitive sector, however, this underrepresentation results from a combination of an underrepresentation of temporary (11%) and indefinite (43%) layoffs, from an overrepresentation of quits (21%), and from a proportional representation of firings. In relation to the average distribution of unemployment types, column 4 shows that the unemployed in the competitive sector are 6% less likely to have become unemployed by

TABLE 5.5
Net Distribution of Employment, Unemployment, and Labor Force by Economic Sector

Economic Sector	Number (1)	Percentage (2)	Percentage of unemployed (3)	Percentage deviation of (3) from average distribution (4)	Percentage of Total (5)	Percentage of Total Unemployment/ Percentage of Total Labor Force (by category) (6)
Total						
Employed	241842	95.65				
Unemployed[a]	11002	4.35	100.00		100.00	1.00
Temporary layoff	653	.26	5.94	—	100.00	1.00
Indefinite layoff	2626	1.04	23.87	—	100.00	1.00
Firing	6063	2.40	55.11	—	100.00	1.00
Quit	1660	.66	15.09	—	100.00	1.00
Labor force	252844[c]	100.00			100.00	1.00
Unemployment ratio[b]		4.55				
Competitive						
Employed	85471	95.85			35.34	
Unemployed	3697	4.15	100.00		33.60	-1.05
Temporary layoff	207	.23	5.60	-.06	31.70	-1.11
Indefinite layoff	650	.73	17.58	-.36	24.75	-1.43
Firing	2133	2.40	57.70	+.05	35.18	1.00
Quit	707	.80	19.12	+.27	42.59	+1.21
Labor force	89168	100.00			35.27	
Unemployment ratio		4.33				
Oligopoly						
Employed	79933	95.88			33.05	
Unemployed	3438	4.12	100.00		31.25	-1.06

(continued)

133

TABLE 5.5 (continued)

Economic Sector	Number (1)	Percentage (2)	Percentage of unemployed (3)	Percentage deviation of (3) from average distribution (4)	Percentage of Total (5)	Percentage of Total Unemployment/ Percentage of Total Labor Force (by category) (6)
Total						
Temporary layoff	231	.28	6.72	+.13	35.38	+1.07
Indefinite layoff	962	1.15	27.98	+.17	36.63	+1.11
Firing	1746	2.09	50.79	−.09	28.80	−1.14
Quit	498	.60	14.49	−.04	30.00	−1.10
Labor force	83371	100.00				
Unemployment ratio		4.30			32.97	
State						
Employed	35377	98.13			14.63	
Unemployed	675	1.87	100.00		6.14	−2.32
Temporary layoff	27	.07	4.00	−.49	4.13	−3.45
Indefinite layoff	80	.22	11.85	−1.01	3.05	−4.68
Firing	429	1.19	63.56	+.15	7.08	−2.01
Quit	140	.39	20.74	+.37	8.43	−1.69
Labor force	36052	100.00			14.26	
Unemployment ratio		1.91				
Construction						
Employed	20135	89.22			8.33	
Unemployed	2433	10.78	100.00		22.11	+2.48
Temporary layoff	135	.60	5.55	−.07	20.67	+2.31
Indefinite layoff	749	3.32	30.79	+.30	28.52	+3.19
Firing	1357	6.01	55.77	+.01	22.38	+2.51
Quit	192	.85	7.89	−.91	11.57	+1.30

	Number	%	% of unemployed		Unemployment ratio	Unemployment ratio
Farm						
Employed	10333	95.23			.43	
Unemployed[a]	518	4.77	100.00		4.71	+1.10
Temporary layoff	35	.32	6.76	+.14	5.36	+1.25
Indefinite layoff	152	1.40	29.34	+.23	5.79	+1.35
Firing	265	2.44	51.16	−.08	4.37	+1.02
Quit	65	.60	12.55	−.20	3.92	−1.09
Labor force	10851	100.00			4.29	
Unemployment ratio[b]		5.01				
Utility						
Employed	2984	98.42			1.23	
Unemployed	48	1.58	100.00		.44	−2.73
Temporary layoff	5	.16	10.42	+.75	.77	−1.56
Indefinite layoff	11	.36	22.92	−.04	.42	−2.86
Firing	25	.82	52.08	−.06	.41	−2.93
Quit	7	.23	14.58	−.03	.42	−2.86
Labor force	3032	100.00			1.20	
Unemployment ratio		1.61				Unemployment ratio
Private nonprofit						
Employed	7608	97.51			3.15	
Unemployed	194	2.49	100.00		1.76	−1.76
Temporary layoff	13	.17	6.70	+.13	1.99	−1.55
Indefinite layoff	22	.28	11.34	−1.10	.84	−3.68
Firing	109	1.40	56.19	+0.2	1.80	−1.72
Quit	50	.64	25.77	+.71	3.01	−1.03
Labor force	7802	100.00			3.09	
Unemployment ratio		2.55				

[a] The unemployment rate is total number of workers unemployed through temporary layoffs, indefinite layoffs, firings, and quits divided by the total in the labor force.

[b] The unemployment ratio is the total number of unemployed in the four categories divided by the number of employed.

[c] Totals may not be exact since the table is calculated by rounding weighted cases whose values are not integers.

135

temporary layoffs; 36% less likely to have become unemployed by indefinite layoffs; 5% more likely to have become unemployed by firings; and 27% more likely to have become unemployed by quits.

In contrast, the pattern of unemployment in the oligopoly sector is heavily skewed toward layoffs. First, the 6% underrepresentation of total unemployment hides the contrasting overrepresentation of layoffs (7% and 11%) and the underrepresentation of firings and quits (14% and 10%). Given this pattern of unemployment propensities, column 4 indicates how this pattern compares to the average across sectors. The unemployed from the oligopoly sector are 13% more likely than average to be in temporary layoffs; 17% more likely to be in indefinite layofs; 9% less likely to be in the status of fired; and 4% less likely to be unemployed by a quit.

Comparing these patterns reveals one of the major findings of the research. Despite the similarity in aggregate unemployment rates, the types of unemployment that undergird these aggregate rates diverge sharply. Although firings and quits predominate in the competitive sector, temporary and indefinite layoffs predominate, as predicted, in the oligopoly sector.

I conclude that the competitive sector tends to have forms of unemployment such as firings and quits that are connected to traditional notions of labor turnover. In these two forms of unemployment, workers—by their own choice or through the decision of their employer—become permanently separated from their position. In the oligopoly sector, where traditional competitive mechanisms have become constrained in the factor and product markets, the prevalent forms of unemployment reflect constraints on the market mechanisms that separate workers from jobs. The oligopoly sector is more characterized by a form of unemployment in which workers remain attached to jobs even when the latter are temporarily ended.

The difference between the two sectors is accentuated by comparing the relative propensity of particular unemployment types directly against each other instead of each against the average. For instance, comparing the percentages in column 3 of Table 5.5 we find that the unemployed in temporary layoffs are 20% greater and the unemployed in indefinite layoffs are 59% greater in the ologopoly than in the competitive sector. In contrast, the proportion unemployed in firings is 14% greater and the proportion unemployed in quits is 32% greater in the competitive than in the oligopoly sector.

STATE SECTOR

I have already discussed the low unemployment propensity of the state sector. Table 5.5 indicates too that the unemployed in the state sector are 132% underrepresented relative to the size of the labor force in the sector.

Only the utility sector has a lower unemployment propensity. Moreover, the underrepresentation of the unemployed in the state sector extends across all types. Gien this low proportion, the question remains concerning the relative propensity of different types of unemployment. Column 4 indicates that the unemployed in the state sector are the least prone to be in either form of layoff and, accordingly, are above average in the proportion in firings or quits.

Compared to the competitive and oligopoly sectors, the state sector evidences a pattern of firings and quits similar to the former but a pattern of layoffs much lower than either. These findings confirm the general proposition that the proportion of unemployed will differ by type in a theoretically meaningful way. More specifically they confirm the expectation that over and above the lower overall propensity of unemployed, the state sector will evidence a marked stability of positions (as shown by the low proportion of layoffs). Also, even though firings are a large proportion of the unemployed in this sector, they are relatively few in number during the period 1969–1978 before the current wave of state and local fiscal crises, tax abatement initiatives, and direct policy decisions increased involuntary state unemployment. Finally, the high proportion of unemployed who quit without a job from the state sector (21%), which is surpassed only in the somewhat comparable private nonprofit sector (26%), reflects the sector's function as a training ground for employment in the private sector. It also reflects the general administrative and professional nature of positions in the sector that make job-specific skills used or obtained in the state sector readily transferable to employment in other sectors.

CONSTRUCTION SECTOR

The construction sector produces the highest total unemployment proportion, 11%, which is 148% higher than average. In terms of numbers of unemployed, all forms of unemployment are strongly overrepresented. Column 4 of Table 5.5 shows that the distribution of this large number of unemployed tends toward indefinite layoffs and away from quits. No other sector approaches the 30% greater than average proportion of indefinite layoffs and 91% less than average proportion of quits. Temporary layoffs are slightly less than average, reflecting the seasonal pattern of employment and unemployment: Namely, the March CPS data for 1969–1978 captures the construction industry at the end of its winter lull and just before its spring rehiring so that most recorded layoffs would be indefinite rather than temporary. The high overrepresentation of all types of unemployment clearly reflects both the yearwide and seasonal fluctuation in the demand for construction employees. Given this, however, the proportion of unemployed

by type shows (a) a strong instability of employment positions due to seasonal and business demand variations; (b) a strong tendency for this involuntary unemployment to take the form of layoffs in order to ensure the retention of employees with high job skills; (c) a pronounced tendency, nevertheless, for the unemployed to have been fired, reflecting the large variation in demand suffered by the construction industry; and (d) a low proportion of quits resulting in unemployment, reflecting the generous wage and benefit structure of the construction industry.

FARM SECTOR

The level of unemployment in the farm sector—4.8%—is second only to the level in the construction sector; still, this is only 10% above the average. This 10% overrepresentation is composed of a strong overrepresentation of layoffs, an average representation of firings and a slight (9%) under-representation of quits. This shows that involuntary unemployment is more prominent than in any other sector except the construction sector. In comparison to the average distribution, the most pronounced status for the unemployed is in temporary and indefinite layoffs (14% and 23%). In contrast the fired and those who quit are 8% and 20% below the average distribution. Like the construction sector, the farm sector is vulnerable to changes in demand for products due to competition and secular trends. But also important is the vulnerability of these two sectors to seasonal fluctuations in the demand for labor. The CPS data from March reflect this seasonal fluctuation especially in the high propensity for indefinite layoffs. Seasonal factors also affect the measured proportion of quits. During the period of the CPS surveys (early spring) it would be expected that little excess labor would remain employed. Once curtailment of the labor force due to the temporary and even permanent ending of positions occurs, there are fewer workers remaining for whom voluntary separation is an issue. Thus for the farm, as for the construction sector, a high level of unemployment is not simply a function of unstable workers choosing to quit or undesirable workers who are fired. Rather, unemployment derives in large part from the instability of employment positions themselves.

UTILITY SECTOR

The calculations in Table 5.5 indicate that the utility sector produces the lowest proportion of unemployed; it is underrepresented by 173%. As I have argued, this reflects the low vulnerability of this sector to changes in demand and to the need to adjust to the product market by decreased output or lowered prices and wages. In view of the relative infrequency of unem-

ployment in general, the most pronounced types compared to other sectors are temporary and then indefinite layoffs. The number of cases of unemployed employees, however, is so sparse that it is impossible to claim that the distribution in Table 5.5 necessarily reflects a genuine pattern of unemployment types. Nevertheless the data, such as they are, do support the contention that although the monopolized utility sector differs from the oligopoly sector in its low proportion of unemployed, the prevalence of layoffs rather than market forms of unemployment (such as quits and firings) is similar. With little vulnerability to seasonal fluctuations in demand, with little possibility of accumulating excess inventory, and with stable revenues and profit margins guaranteed by regulation, there is virtually no need for involuntary unemployment. But among the involuntarily unemployed, the proportion due to firings and quits without a job is quite low whereas the proportion due to layoffs is high. This prominence of layoffs is due to the high degree of quasi-fixed labor costs and of job-specific training in this advanced-technology industry that employers do not wish to forfeit through layoffs. In turn, the low number and proportion of quits is due to the fact that positions in this sector entail wage and training benefits that reduce voluntary separations without new employment in hand. We find that a monopoly industry, as opposed to an oligopolistic one, is characterized by very low unemployment when the services provided by that industry are essential, growing secularly, and have a guaranteed rate of return. When unemployment does occur, however, it tends to be characterized by labor conditions that induce the temporary rather than permanent separation of workers from jobs and a pattern of instability of positions rather than of workers.

NONPROFIT SECTOR

The nonprofit sector is composed of a diverse amalgamation of organization, institutions, and foundations. Besides the nonprofit legal status of these enterprises (an aspect that often distinguishes them little from either state or private organizations), the major similarity is their low degree of vulnerability to fluctuations in demand for their goods or services. This explains the 76% underrepresentation of unemployed shown in Table 5.5. Explaining the pattern of types of job separation, however, requires speculation since the sector is composed of such diverse enterprises. Column 4 shows that employees on temporary layoffs are 3% greater than occurs on average across sectors, employees on indefinite layoffs are 110% less than on average, and those who are unemployed by a quit are 71% greater than on average.

Although it is important not to make too much of these differences, I

suggest that the low proportion of indefinite layoffs mirrors the insulation of this sector from declines in demand due to seasonal variation or inventory surplus. The high proportion of voluntary job-leaving without a new job may reflect, as in the state sector, a combination of sources of job dissatisfaction with the possibility of job mobility. The nonprofit sector is composed largely of educational and health-related institutions such as hospitals. Many positions in these service industries are not covered by civil service regulations or other forms of job or wage protections. Also, many positions are relatively low paying (such as those in parochial schools) relative to comparable positions in the state sector, have job skills that are transferable to the state of private profit-making sectors, entail few opportunities for promotion, and have few benefits attached to employment longevity. Although this explanation cannot be directly supported, the fact remains that the nonprofit sector is characterized more than any other sector by the prevalence of voluntary job separation.

INTERNAL LABOR MARKETS: AGE, ECONOMIC SECTOR, AND EMPLOYMENT STATUS

The effect of economic sector on employment status just analyzed portrays the impact of sector on employment status averaged over the variation in this impact across categories of the other independent variables. In determining the model for analysis (Chapter 3), I found that with one exception this averaged sector effect adequately captured sectoral variation across categories of the other independent variables. The one exception was in the case of age. Table 3.2 indicates that the three-way interaction of age, economic sector, and employment status meets the criterion for inclusion in the model: Namely, this interaction reduces the level of χ^2 by at least four times the associated reduction in degrees of freedom. This three-way interaction means that the impact of age on employment status varies across sectors. I argue here that sectoral variation in the age effect on employment status reveals a further dimension of vulnerability and power in determining unemployment outcomes. The empirical question is in what sectors and to what extent age differences affect employment status. The theoretical issue is how structural factors associated with particular sectors mediate the impact on age on unemployment and how this is related to the theory of internal labor markets.

Table 5.6 presents the generalized odds ratios for the relation of sector, age, and employment status. The generalized odds ratios are direct transformations of the tau-parameters for this interaction. (See Appendix A,

TABLE 5.6
Generalized Odds Ratios for the Analysis of Age, Economic Sector, and Employment Status

Panel A: Generalized odds ratios—Age and employment status[a]				
	Age			
Employment status	16–19	20–24	25–54	55–64
Temporary layoff	1.2086	.8912	.8732	1.0934
Indefinite layoff	.4423	1.2127	1.1986	1.3820
Firing	1.2343	1.0831	.9773	.7882
Quit	2.5730	1.4873	0.6015	.4895
Employed	.6177	.5741	1.5536	1.5947

Panel B: Generalized odds ratios—Age and employment status by economic sector[a]

Competitive sector				
Temporary layoff	.9684	.5799	1.2689	1.4997
Indefinite layoff	.4498	1.2564	1.0977	1.4374
Firing	1.1089	1.2158	.9415	.8119
Quit	2.2423	1.6801	.6814	.4329
Employed	.9366	0.6460	1.1265	1.3818

Oligopoly Sector				
Temporary layoff	.8062	.8317	1.5695	.9530
Indefinite layoff	.7058	1.4952	1.0617	.7961
Firing	1.1925	0.9764	.8118	1.1011
Quit	3.3116	1.6845	.4106	.4982
Employed	.4565	.4928	1.8095	2.2904

State sector				
Temporary layoff	2.4901	1.0458	.3646	.0[b]
Indefinite layoff	.2655	1.5451	1.9232	1.0878
Firing	2.2054	1.3148	.5449	.6471
Quit	2.1605	1.1212	.8979	.5199
Employed	.4134	.4452	2.1469	2.4716

Construction sector				
Temporary layoff	.8354	.9794	1.2046	1.0027
Indefinite layoff	.3082	1.2096	1.4419	1.6135
Firing	.9341	.7921	1.0332	1.3308
Quit	4.3500	1.3322	.4405	.4660
Employed	.9927	.8049	1.2464	.9659

Farm sector				
Temporary layoff	1.1015	.8574	1.0976	.9760
Indefinite layoff	.4188	1.3815	.8732	1.7821
Firing	1.1560	1.0938	1.1220	.7217

(continued)

TABLE 5.6 *(continued)*

Panel A: Generalized odds ratios—Age and employment status[a]

Employment status	16–19	20–24	25–54	55–64
			Age	
Quit	2.2932	1.6010	.7102	.4263
Employed	.8424	.4845	1.2871	1.7940
		Utility sector		
Temporary layoff	.0	.0	.0	.0
Indefinite layoff	1.3100	.0	.4105	1.4673
Firing	3.7338	1.4050	.8794	.2618
Quit	.0	1.1765	.7604	.0
Employed	.0857	.4995	3.1999	4.8661
		Nonprofit sector		
Temporary layoff	2.1585	1.2521	.3486	1.1035
Indefinite layoff	.4374	.6894	1.5651	1.8394
Firing	.7734	1.1147	1.7743	.6578
Quit	18340	1.6042	.6175	.6195
Employed	.8168	.6504	1.4360	1.2226

[a]See Appendix A for an explanation of the formulae for calculating generalized odds ratios.

[b].0 indicates a cell in which no cases occurred.

pp. 207–208, for a discussion of the method of calculating and interpreting generalized odds ratios for a three-way interaction.) The odds ratios in Table 5.6, panel A indicate the relative chances of being in a particular cell of age and employment status rather than in any other. The odds ratios in Table 5.6, panel B indicate the relative chances of being in a particular cell of age, employment status, and sector rather than any other. The odds ratios entered in each cell of the subtables of panel B vary around the corresponding cells in panel A. The deviation of a sector–age entry in panel B from the corresponding averaged-effect entry in panel A signifies how the relationship of age to employment status varies for the sector. For instance, panel A specifies that across sectors, 55 to 64 year-old men are 1.59 times less likely to be unemployed than the average for all ages (see the odds ratio, 1.5947 for "employed" and ages "55–64"). However, comparing this averaged odds ratio to the corresponding employment status–age entries for the competitive and oligopoly sectors, we find that the age advantage is greater than the average in the oligopoly sector (2.2904) but less than the average in the competitive sector (1.3818).

Three major trends can be discerned from Table 5.5. First there is a general tendency for unemployment propensities to decrease with age. Even

in the four sectors where youth are more likely to be unemployed than teens
(a finding that may reflect the sparseness of cases of teen unemployed), teens
are still more likely to be unemployed than either prime-age or older
workers.

Second, the parameters disclose that with the exception of the farm and
construction sectors (where productive capacity is related to age), the trend is
for firings and quits to be relatively more pronounced among teens and for
layoffs to be relatively more pronounced among prime-age and older
workers. Over and above the variation by sector in the distribution of workers
to rate and type of unemployment, we find that within sectors the younger the
workers the more vulnerable they are to turnover forms of unemployment
(quits and firings). In contrast, the older the workers, the more likely they are
to be separated from their jobs through layoffs.

Third, the findings show that in sectors subject to competitive production
markets, the added dimension of vulnerability represented by the age–sector
interaction is not as important as in the sectors shielded from competition in
the product market. In the competitive and farm sectors, the vulnerability of
young age makes less of an impact than in the oligopoly, state, construction,
and utility sectors. For instance, comparing the age effect averaged across
sectors (the last row in each subtable of panel B), we find that age differences
are mitigated in the competitive sector but exaggerated in the oligopoly and
state sectors. Within the competitive sector, teens and youth are more likely
to be unemployed than prime-age and older workers. Among types of
unemployment, the trend is for teens and youth to undergo relatively more
quits and firings than layoffs and for prime-age and older workers to be
relatively more likely to be laid off than to have been fired or to have quit. In
the oligopoly and state sectors, the trend for unemployment to *decrease* as
age *increases* is even more pronounced. This parallels the tendency for the
relative frequency of quits to decrease dramatically as workers get older.

These findings indicate that the age–employment-status relation differs
across sectors. The more vulnerable a sector to market relations in the
product market, the less variance there is in age–employment-status relation.
In the presence of institutional or organizational constraints in the product
market, the tendency is for age differences to be more consequential in the
labor market. Apparently these structural factors provide some increased
return to age in terms of unemployment just as they do in terms of income
(see Kalleberg, Wallace, and Althauser. 1981).

These results are elucidated by the theory of internal labor markets and, in
turn, suggest some new implications for the theory. An *internal labor market*
was defined in Chapter 1 as an allocation mechanism by which persons and
jobs within a particular establishment or occupation are matched. In
contrast, an *external labor market* functions to recruit new employees by

matching persons to jobs at ports of entry to an establishment. Doeringer and Piore (1971) emphasize the role of internal labor markets in augmenting the allocative efficiency of a firm and enhancing the bargaining power of workers. Burawoy (1979:106–108) argues that internal labor markets not only increase stability and predictability in worker relations but serve as well as "part of a system of bureaucratic control." By rewarding seniority in a bureaucratically regulated manner, internal labor markets foster in workers "a commitment to the enterprise," a consciousness of individual rather than class interests and antagonisms, and the identification of workers with the execution of management-directed tasks.

The findings suggest that the sectors that internal labor-market literature identifies as evidencing age-based job and benefit ladders (e.g., oligopoly, construction, state, and utility sectors) also appear to provide age-based insulation from unemployment in general and from turnover forms of unemployment in particular. In contrast, sectors that remain linked to external labor markets for recruitment to a full range of positions (e.g., farm and competitive sectors) do not offer an added source of seniority-based shelter from job separation.

I cautiously conclude that sectors capable of circumventing or overcoming vulnerability to competitive product markets maintain unemployment and not just employment practices that create careers for workers while obtaining the benefits of worker compliance, motivation, and efficiency. Not only are career ladders and internal labor markets constituted by patterns of job linkages and wage structures but by patterns of unemployment as well. Viewing internal labor markets from the vantage point of unemployment highlights, on the one hand, how such structures enhance the productive efficiency of certain sectors by enabling firms to retain workers with desired skills and experience even over periods of unemployment. On the other hand, this perspective on internal labor markets emphasizes how unemployment may afford mechanisms of control at the workplace. That is, the inverse relationship in certain sectors between age and unemployment, in general, and between age and firings and age quits without a job, in particular, enchance bureaucratic control (Edwards, 1979). Such control is the type needed to elicit the internalized initiative, discipline, and creativity required to counteract new capacities of bargaining power derived from the social organization of work in enterprises with complex production technologies and where more obstrusive levels and types of unemployment would otherwise threaten the balance of productive efficiency and labor compliance.

DISCUSSION

I have argued that the distribution of the unemployed to types of unemployment is partly a function of the sector in which they were employed. Within the limitations of the data discussed previously, I have tested a theory of the relation between sectoral vulnerability and employment status. The analysis confirms that the distribution of the unemployed results from three aspects of sector vulnerability: (a) the vulnerability of the establishment to declines in demand for their products; (b) the vulnerability to traditional market mechanisms for adjusting to such declines in income; and (c) the vulnerability to the need to stabilize, socially control, and retain workers with enterprise-specific skills. A number of conclusions about the structural determination of unemployment are derived from this analysis.

First, controlling for the modeled effects of other independent variables, the economic sector in which a worker is employed makes an independent contribution to the distribution of workers to employment status. The proportion of unemployed in the state, utility, and private nonprofit sectors is lower than in the competitive, oligopoly, construction, and farm sectors.

Since the analysis controlled for the business cycle, the remaining sources of decline in product demand that induce unemployment are seasonal fluctuations, the possibility of accumulating excess inventory, and the constancy of demand for goods and services. Accordingly, we found that the state and utility sectors enjoyed the lowest relative unemployment levels. Both of these sectors share a relatively inelastic demand for their products and generally are less confronted by choices between output and price adjustment to declines in product demand. In the state sector, low unemployment results from its ability to generate constant revenues and to execute deficit spending. This combines with a growing secular demand for services and a further increase in this demand when other sectors create unemployment. In the case of utilities, constant and often growing demand for services combine with monopoly pricing through regulatory profit guarantees to ensure low unemployment. Similar arguments—made cautiously—explain the low level of unemployment in the diverse nonprofit sector.

The highest unemployment level by far is in the construction sector. This is explained by the congruence (a) of its vulnerability to seasonal and to local, noncyclical fluctuations in demand for its durable products and (b) of its characteristics as a local oligopoly that dictate a pattern of output rather than price adjusting. As with the second highest unemployment sector, the farm

sector, the fact that the data for this research is taken from March CPS surveys accentuates the seasonal aspect of unemployment. Evidence for the prominence of this seasonal factor is the relatively large proportion of indefinite layoffs in these two sectors. Also, the oligopoly sector, producing many durable goods, has a high proportion of indefinite layoffs due to the ability to produce excess inventory.

Second, because the relative frequency of unemployment types also varies from sector to sector, the fuller story of the sectoral effect is revealed only by investigating the sectoral differences in types of job separation. It was predicted that the oligopoly sector would be confronted by greater instability of employment due to its output rather than price adjusting tendency. This was expected to be accentuated by this sector's production of durable goods. The findings indicated, however, that the representation of unemployed in the oligopoly is virtually equal to that of the competitive sector. Nevertheless, this finding is not interpreted to mean that the concentration–employment instability hypothesis is incorrect. This is because the competitive and oligopoly sectors differ in the forms of unemployment that constitute their similar overall levels.

Just as the oligopoly sector has developed various nonmarket mechanisms to resist or adjust to product market forces, the forms of unemployment associated with this sector, temporary and indefinite layoffs, likewise differ from the types of unemployment associated with neoclassical models of labor turnover. Oligopoly firms, with longer time horizons and greater capacities for ensuring long-range investment plans, appear to have developed various mechanisms for retaining their workers even through spells of unemployment. The precise nature of the mechanisms are impossible to determine from this research. I suggest, however, that the larger size, higher profit margins, and desire for stability in the work force enable oligopoly firms to pay the type of wages, create a structure of promotions, and provide a system of pensions that result in forms of unemplyment in which employees remain attached to their jobs even when the positions are temporarily ended.

In contrast, the pattern of unemployment in the competitive sector reflects the continued prevalence of market relations both in the sector's mechanisms for adjusting to declining demand and in its relations to the labor market. The higher frequency of quits and firings, as opposed to layoffs, reflects the sector's tendency to deal with declines in demand through price adjustments. This results in efforts to lower production costs, including the cost of labor. Some curtailment of employment through layoffs and firings follows. But more than for the oligopoly sector, the consequence of price adjustment is the lowering of real wages and inducing workers to quit. Even when there are no direct declines in demand, competitive forces confronting firms in this sector

create a constant downward pressure on wages for many positions within the firm. Also, the shorter time-horizon of the competitive firm and the lower investment in firm-specific human capital lead to a higher proclivity of firings. Employees need not be retained by the firm through wages and benefits that would induce employees not to search for jobs during unemployment as is the case with layoffs. Also the fact that these firms are competitive means that workers can be fired since a pool of similarly trained or easily trainable workers is more readily available than for oligopolistic firms.

These results then indicate one important method for reconciling the theoretical expectations concerning the greater employment instability of the oligopoly sector with the findings. By decomposing the types of unemployment that comprise aggregate unemployment proportions, we find that the oligopoly sector evidences a greater instability of positions. Although it is impossible to know whether firings in either sector represent the ending of positions or simply the replacement of one worker by another, it is clear that the oligopoly sector does have a greater instability of positions whereas the competitive sector has a greater instability of workers.

Third and finally, the results from the analysis of the interaction of age, sector, and employment status shed light on how sectoral resources mediate the impact of age on employment status. The findings disclosed that age differences in unemployment propensities are greater than average in the oligopoly, state, utility, and construction sectors although less than average in the competitive and farm sectors. It appears that in sectors with internal labor markets seniority structures augment protection from unemployment in general and turnover forms of unemployment, in particular. These age-based structural resources elicit compliance and creativity in the performance of tasks and establish a mutual interest between employees and employers in job tenure and seniority. This accounts, in part, for the lower relative frequency of quits and firings and a higher relative frequency of layoffs that keep employees attached to positions even during spells of unemployment.

6

Business Cycle, Economic Sector, and Unemployment

T he previous two chapters examined the static or cross-sectional association between types of unemployment and differing class positions and market structures. These analyses controlled for the business cycle.[1] Accordingly, the analyses represented the impact of class and firm market power in determining unemployment outcomes due to movement along a demand curve rather than to a shift of demand. This chapter examines the impact of changes in national income on the number and types of unemployment.

Many theories of the business cycle have been derived from the neoclassical, Keynesian, and Marxist traditions. It is not the purpose of this chapter to review the history of the theory of the business cycle with its complex debates between and within the various paradigms.[2] Instead, the focus will be on formulating and testing the fundamental proposition that cyclical change in demand produces a pattern of expansions and con-

---

[1] Besides controlling for business cycle, each analysis in Chapters 4 and 5 controlled for all the other modeled effects of the structural and demographic independent variables not considered in that specific analysis.

[2] For a review of the different theories and their historical evolution, see Alcaly, 1978; Dornbusch and Fischer, 1978; Shaikh, 1978; Sherman, 1979; Weisskopf, 1978; Wright, 1978.

tractions, the consequences of which are distributed unevenly across economic sectors. Although this general proposition is not novel, what is new is the attempt to tie together existing research on the business-cycle consequences for unemployment to the present research on the sectoral determinants of unemployment.

Two relationships comprise the focus of the analysis: (a) the relationship between the dependent variable of employment status and the business cycle averaged over class, sector, race, age, and education; and (b) the interaction effect of business cycle and economic sector on unemployment. These relationships provide insight into economic segmentation not stressed in the previous chapters. The averaged effect of business cycle on employment status shows that the relative frequency of unemployment types is not constant across periods of the cycle. The interaction effect of business cycle and sector estimates how the relation of sector and employment status varies over the business cycle. This second relationship is especially relevant since sectoral differences in labor-force adjustments over the cycle are directly related to an important body of theory and research on the nature of contemporary recessions.

The dependent variable studied in this chapter—employment status— again is the five-category nominal variable composed of four types of unemployment due to job loss (temporary layoffs, indefinite layoffs, firings, and quits) and the comparative category of employed. The operationalization of this variable is described in Chapter 3.

The independent variable, business cycle, is composed of four categories: (a) peak of the business cycle, (b) decline, (c) trough, and (d) recovery. Each month of March for the years 1969 to 1978 was placed into one of these four periods according to the official definitions of recession and business cycle determined by the American Statistical Association and the National Bureau of Economic Research (NBER) published monthly by the Department of Commerce in the Business Conditions Digest (BCD). These sources demarcate the boundaries of a business cycle by retrospectively analyzing the direction, duration, and magnitude of fluctuations in aggregate business conditions. No single economic indicator is used to date the peaks and troughs. Rather, according to Moore (1980), the NBER uses the following more comprehensive definition formulated by Burns and Mitchell (1946) who modified the definition published by NBER in 1927:

> Business cycles are a type of fluctuation found in the aggregate economic activity of nations that organize their work mainly in buiness enterprises: a cycle consists of expansions occurring at about the same time in many economic activities, followed by similarly general recessions, contractions, and revivals which merge into the expansion phase of the next cycle [Burns and Mitchell, 1946: 3].

Data from the 10 March surveys were distributed to the 4 business-cycle categories in the following way:

(1) Peak
    March 1969
    March 1973
(2) Decline
    March 1970
    March 1974
(3) Trough
    March 1975
(4) Recovery
    March 1971
    March 1972
    March 1976
    March 1977
    March 1978

The second independent variable is economic sector. This variable and its operationalization is described in Chapter 5. There is one difference, however, in the way the variable is categorized in the present chapter. In Chapter 5, seven industrial sectors were distinguished whereas in the analysis that follows only five are defined. The competitive, oligopoly, state, and construction sectors remain unchanged. The farm, utility, and nonprofit sectors are collapsed into one category, however. This is done in order to reduce the number of sampling zeros or empty cells in the three-way observed table passed to the programs that calculate the expected table and associated log-linear parameters. When sampling zeros are frequent in the observed table, the calculations of the log-linear parameters for three-way tables become distorted. Combining the three categories into a single category eliminates this problem. At the same time the parameters generated for the competitive, oligopoly, construction, and state sectors remain comparable to their counterparts generated in the analysis using all seven categories (compare Table 5.3 and Table 6.3).

The analysis proceeds in several steps. The first section reviews the issues at the heart of the theory of the relation of the business cycle to structural segmentation. Next the findings are presented that confirm the impact of the business cycle on distributing workers to types of unemployment and that estimate the changing prevalence of these types of job loss over the cycle. The third section turns to the complex theoretical and empirical controversies over how the effect of the business cycle is mediated by the segmented industrial structure. A set of specific propositions concerning this

effect are formulated and tested. The final section summarizes a series of implications of this research for the debate on the relation of segmented market power to inflation and unemployment over the business cycle.

BUSINESS CYCLE AND UNEMPLOYMENT

The fundamental proposition is that the business cycle—as one further structural source of segmentation—generates variation in the relative frequency of types of unemployment and that the composition of this variation is due, in part, to systematic differences in sectoral vulnerability to the business cycle.

The history of the analysis of the business cycle parallels that for the theory of firm behavior and labor markets. Over time, business-cycle research has moved from assuming that the economy is self-regulating to analyzing explicitly the internal structural forces that produce and exaggerate business fluctuations. Early theory and research assumed the classical Marshallian view. Competitive markets determine the price and quantity of inputs and outputs, and establish a self-equilibrating match of aggregate supply and demand. The conviction that a self-regulating economy will never suffer and endogenous or "natural" depression was shattered, however, by the events of 1929 and their aftermath. Such happenings spawned the theoretical revolution of Keynes (1936) and Samuelson (1939). These two economists developed a theory of the business cycle, unemployment, and inflation that stressed the need for fiscal intervention in the troughs in order to counteract the self-perpetuating tumble toward depression due to successive phases of business disinvestment, reduced wages, and lowered consumer demand. But as Sherman (1976:91) points out quoting Hicks (1950:1), Keynesian economics, in spite all that it has done for our understanding of business fluctuations, has beyond doubt left at least one major thing unexplained; and that thing is nothing less than the business cycle itself."

Various researchers set out to discover the inherent characteristics of market economies that make them inevitably vulnerable to cyclical fluctuations. Two general approaches were proffered by both conventional and Marxist researchers. The first is the underconsumptionist view argued by the liberal economist Hobson (1922, 1930) and Marxists such as Sweezy (1958). In this view, as profits rise in an expansion, the ability to produce outstrips consumer demand. As total national income grows in an expansion, the share of the increase going to labor diminishes while the share going to investors increases. Despite some countertendencies such as unionization

and the passing along of monopoly profits to workers in that sector in the form of higher wages (see Wright, 1978), the rate of increase in productivity and productive capacity in general remains greater than the rate of increase in wages and, hence, purchasing power of the work force as a whole. Thus the crisis of underconsumption: More can be produced than is demanded at the existing level of purchasing power. As the actual rate of consumption and accumulation falls relative to the rate of potential profit, investment is curtailed and a decline sets in. Moreover, according to the Keynesian logic, the decrease in consumer demand at the peak of the cycle is not sufficiently offset by increased investment demand because consumer demand comprises a larger proportion of total demand.

An alternative to the underconsumptionist explanation is the over-investment view. This version also has been advocated by traditional (e.g., Fellner, 1951; von Hayek, 1933) as well as Marxist theorists who offer either an "exhaustion of the reserve army" version (wage-push) (e.g., Boddy and Crotty, 1975; Glyn and Sutcliffe, 1972) or a "rise in organic composition of capital" version (e.g., Dobb, 1945; Shaikh, 1978; Yaffe, 1973). Although differing on the particular dynamics and causes of overinvestment, the common thread is that expansion-induced rises in the cost of production outpace increments in the rate of profit. Whether due to relative rising costs of labor, capital, or money; or due to the inability to maintain productivity in the face of excess capacity generated by competition; or due to the falling rate of profit induced by the rising organic composition of capital; the result is that lower profit margins lead to decreased rates of investment, lowered output and employment, and, finally, falling aggregate demand.

Although both the undercomsumptionist and overinvestment perspectives argue that business cycles are endogenous to market economies, the earliest formulations of these theories failed to include the segmented structure of advanced capitalism as a central factor in the dynamics of the business cycle. Recently, a number of researchers remedied this deficiency. For instance, Wright (1978) argues that, in the current stage of advanced monopoly capitalism, institutional rigidities in class relations and firm behavior exacerbate the business cycle, produce simultaneous inflation and unemployment ("stagflation"), and make traditional monetary and fiscal solutions inadequate. In this latest stage of capitalist development, the underlying source of crisis is underconsumption of the surplus produced by excess capacity. The New Deal solution of state expenditures to bolster demand directly and through redistribution of income, faltered, however. First, due to the organizational and electoral power of the working class, these state expenditures expanded faster than excess surplus. This produced a secular decline in the profit rate, restricted capital expansion, and increased the

volatility of the economy. Along with class-based constraints, the contemporary economy confronts a second structural complication. The concentration of product markets aggrevates the crisis and distorts or displaces fiscal and monetary policies designed to level the ebb and flow of the economy. The oligopoly sector becomes sheltered to a significant degree from price and wage adjustments dictated by the Keynesian logic. Moreover, such insulation mitigates the impact of macroeconomic policies on other sectors, including the competitive sector, again making the economy as a whole less responsive to initiatives designed to ameliorate cyclic swings.[3]

Although a full analysis of the impact of institutional structures on the nature and mechanics of the business cycle would require an examination of a host of factors, the present research is not so ambitious. I limit my exploration of contemporary business-cycle dynamics to what can be garnered from a scrutiny of (a) the changing composition of unemployment over the business cycle and (b) the cyclical variation by sector in the level and type of unemployment. The first task, to which I turn in the next section, is fairly straightforward and is largely descriptive. It sets the stage for the second, more analytic, task by decomposing the cyclical changes in unemployment into their constituent parts. The second task, however, exploring how sectors vary over the business cycle in their level and composition of unemployment, returns us to the theoretical considerations of business-cycle dynamics just outlined. Although not taking up the debate on which theory of the business cycle is more adequate, the empirical analysis of unemployment will demonstrate the relevance of business cycle theories that incorporate notions of structural segmentation.

EFFECT OF BUSINESS CYCLE ON UNEMPLOYMENT

In this section I discuss the findings on the direct effect of business cycle on employment status. First, the gross variation in unemployment types over

---

[3]Drawing on Weisskopf (1978), Sherman (1979) also synthesizes the various strands of crisis theory by arguing that the squeeze on profits is related to structural factors. In *early expansion*, the profit rate rises because hourly wages change little while productivity climbs, utilization of capacity increases, and the output–capital ratio rises. In *late expansion*, the profit rate falls because increasing investment in the early phase lowers the wage share, the propensity to consume and, hence, the utilization of capacity. Moreover, labor militancy increases as unemployment declines in an effort to advance or retain labor's income share. This raises prices, lowers productivity, and leads to disinvestment, excess capacity, a lower output–capital ratio, and a further squeeze on profits. As a result of the assault on profits from both the cost and demand side, profits turn down, investment becomes curtailed, and a recession ensues. Also see Sherman (1968, especially Chapter 11).

periods of the cycle is presented. Second, the effect of the business cycle net of the other modeled independent variables is established. The final part of this section estimates the impact of this net business cycle effect on unemployment types.

Variation of Unemployment over the Business Cycle

The CPS data from the March surveys (1969–1978) for men in the labor force ages 16–64 demonstrate that as the economy moves from the peak to the trough of the cycle total involuntary job separation increases while voluntary job separation decreases. The increment in involuntary unemployment reflects, however, the simultaneous decline in the proportion of firings and increase in the proportion of layoffs—especially indefinite layoffs. Thus, despite the aggregate increase in unemployment from the peak to the trough the percentage of quits and firings decreases and the percentage of layoffs increases. Specifically, Table 6.1 shows that the unemployment ratio[4] for the peak is 3.02% whereas for the trough it is 8.86%. For the years included in the decline it is 3.67% whereas for the years in the recovery it is 5.52%. At the peak, the total unemployment rate is composed of 23% layoffs, 55% firings, and 22% quits. In contrast, in the trough the three categories of job separation are, respectively, 40% layoffs, 50% firings, and 10% quits.

The Net Effect of Business Cycle

To establish the independent contribution of business cycle, I test whether the structural effect of business-cycle variations makes a significant contribution to the distribution of workers to employment status controlling for the direct effects of the other independent variables. With some differences,[5] the test of this independent contribution is similar to those conducted on the other relationships considered in Chapters 4 and 5.

---

[4]The unemployment rate is the number of unemployed through job loss divided by the number in the labor force. The unemployment ratio is the number of unemployed divided by the number of employed. Though the two statistics tell the same story, the latter is more directly comparable to the unemployment likelihood ratio (discussed in the following), which is a measure of the propensity for unemployment in relation to employment rather than in relation to the total labor force.

[5]The analysis presented here differs from that treated in Chapters 3–5 in that economic sector and class are defined as five-category variables. Also, the three-way interaction between

(continued)

Table 6.2 presents a series of models with different relationships included and excluded along with their respective likelihood ratio χ^2 and associated df. It also presents calculations of the relative differences between models and the significance levels of these differences. The table shows that the two-way interaction between employment status and business cycle is strongly significant both when added first and when added after all other two-way effects have been allowed to make their contribution. When added first, the business cycle effect reduces the χ^2 by 1297 with a reduction of 12 df. This is significant at the $p < .001$ level. When added last the reduction in χ^2 of 1433 is significant at the $p < .001$ level. These findings substantiate the independent contribution of this third structural variable, business cycle, on distributing members of the labor force to employment status. In the following analysis, this relationship should be interpreted as the effect of business cycle averaged over—but controlling for—the modeled effects of class, sector, and personal characteristics.

Estimation of the Net Effect of Business Cycle on Employment Status

The final aspect of these descriptive considerations is to estimate the net effect of business cycle periods on the changing relative propensities of unemployment. Although Clark and Summers (1979) examine the effect of the business cycle on unemployment and labor-force participation of various demographic groups, the focus here is on the effect of the business cycle on the component types of job loss that underlie the variation in the aggregate rate of unemployment.

Table 6.3 presents the log-linear tau-parameters for the averaged effect of

---

employment, status, class segment, and capital sector is included since in this collapsed version meets the criterion for including relationships employed in Chapters 4 and 5. That is, for an effect to be included it must contribute to a reduction in χ^2 at least four times the associated reduction in ds. This is shown in Table 6.8 by the comparison between model 4 and model 5, which includes the interaction of employment status, segment, and capital sector. Although this interaction becomes more strongly significant, this finding does not throw into doubt the analysis of Chapters 4 and 5 because we have collapsed the number of categories of sectors from seven to five and the number of categories of classes from nine to five. Thus the classes and sectors that evidence such an interaction of employment status, class, and sector are given relatively more weight. That is, the test of the significance of the interaction reflects the fact that the measured variation of employment status across class segments and economic sectors is now extended across only 125 cells (5 × 5 × 5) instead of 315 cells (5 × 7 × 9). For the same reason the interaction of employment status, sector, and business cycle also increases in significance when tested for this collapsed model.

TABLE 6.1
Gross Distribution of Employment, Unemployment, and Labor Force by Business-Cycle Period

Period	Number	Percentage	Percentage of unemployed	Percentage of total	Percentage of total unemployment–percentage of total labor force (by category)
Total					
Employed	217,165	95.24		100.00	
Unemployed[a]	10,847	4.76	100.00	100.00	1.00
Temporary layoff	645	.28	5.88	100.00	1.00
Indefinite layoff	2,602	1.14	23.95	100.00	1.00
Firing	5,988	2.63	55.25	100.00	1.00
Quit	1,611	.71	14.92	100.00	1.00
Labor force	228,012[c]	100.00		100.00	
Unemployment ratio[b]		4.99			
Peak					
Employed	42,415	97.07		19.53	-1.63
Unemployed	1,279	2.93	100.00	11.79	-1.57
Temporary layoff	79	.18	6.14	12.17	-2.27
Indefinite layoff	219	.50	17.06	8.43	-1.63
Firing	702	1.61	54.95	11.72	-1.10
Quit	279	.64	21.84	17.34	
Labor force	43,694	100.0		19.16	
Unemployment ratio		3.02			
Decline					
Employed	43,169	96.46		19.88	-1.34
Unemployed	1,584	3.54	100.00	14.60	1.00
Temporary layoff	126	.28	7.91	19.56	

	Number	% of labor force	% of unemployed		Ratio
Indefinite layoff	360	.80	22.60	13.82	−1.42
Firing	803	1.79	50.56	13.41	−1.46
Quit	295	.66	18.64	18.31	−1.07
Labor force	44,753	100.00		19.63	
Unemployment ratio		3.67			
Trough					
Employed	21,496	91.86		9.90	
Unemployed	1,904	8.14	100.00	17.55	+1.71
Temporary layoff	143	.61	7.49	22.25	+2.17
Indefinite layoff	610	2.61	32.06	23.45	+2.29
Firing	961	4.11	50.49	16.05	+1.56
Quit	189	.81	9.95	11.71	+1.14
Labor force	23,400	100.00		10.26	
Unemployment ratio		8.86			
Recovery					
Employed	110,085	94.77		50.69	
Unemployed	6,080	5.23	100.00	56.06	+1.10
Temporary layoff	297	.26	4.97	46.02	−1.11
Indefinite layoff	1,413	1.22	23.33	54.30	+1.07
Firing	3,523	3.03	57.93	58.82	+1.15
Quit	848	.73	13.96	52.64	+1.03
Labor force	116,165	100.00		50.95	
Unemployment ratio		5.52			

[a] The unemployment rate is total number of workers unemployed through temporary layoffs, indefinite layoffs, firings, and quits divided by the total in the labor force.

[b] The unemployment ratio is the total number of unemployed in the four categories divided by the number of employed.

[c] Totals may not be exact since the table is calculated by rounding weighted cases whose values are not integers.

TABLE 6.2
Models for the Analysis of the Averaged Effect of Business Cycle on Employment Status

Model	Fitted marginals	df	Likelihood ratio χ^2	p
1	(234567) (1)[a]	12,412[b]	15,245	.00
2	(234567) (14)	12,400	13,948	.00
3	(234567) (17) (16) (15) (13) (12)	12,352	7,328	.5
4	(234567) (17) (16) (15) (13) (12) (14)	12,340	5,895	.5
1 versus 2		12	1,297	.001
3 versus 4		12	1,433	.001

[a] 1 Employment status (dependent variable)
  2 Class segment
  3 Economic sector
  4 Business cycle
  5 Race
  6 Age
  7 Education
[b]The degrees of freedom are adjusted to take into account the number of cases constrained to be zero. See Chapter 3 for a discussion of this adjustment.

business cycle on unemployment controlling for the averaged two-way effects of personal characteristics, class, and capital sector. Also controlled are the following three-way interactions that are included in the final model from which the parameters were derived:

1. Employment status, class, and sector
2. Employment status, sector, and age
3. Employment status, race, and age
4. Employment status, race, and education
5. Employment status, class, and business cycle
6. Employment status, sector, and business cycle
7. Employment status, race, and business cycle.

These tau-parameters indicate that the propensity for unemployment increases dramatically over the business cycle. Cross-period odds ratios[6] calculated from these parameters and presented in Table 6.4 show the relative propensity of workers to be unemployed in one period of the business cycle rather than another. The chances for workers to be unemployed in the trough is 2.4 times greater than during the peak. As stark as it is, this

---

[6]See Appendix A for a discussion of how these odds ratios are calculated.

TABLE 6.3
Tau-Parameters for the Net Relationship of Employment Status and Business Cycle[a]

Employment status	Business-cycle period			
	Peak	Decline	Trough	Recovery
Temporary layoff	1.0075	1.0139	1.1530	.8490
Indefinite layoff	.6441	.8759	1.5675	1.1309
Firing	.8879	.8325	1.1282	1.1991
Quit	1.2806	1.1295	.7213	.9585
Employed	1.3627	1.2014	.6804	.8978

[a]Controlling for the other modeled relationships of employment status with class, sector, business cycle, race, age, and education.

difference is not surprising. Nor is it as important as the changing composition of unemployment over the business cycle.

The tau-parameters in Table 6.3 also estimate the relative differences in unemployment types for the different periods of the cycle. The parameters represent the relative distribution of workers by period to types of unemployment. It should be emphasized that these parameters present the relative, not absolute, propensity of types of unemployment within and across periods. In order to render the findings summarized by these parameters more intuitive, Table 6.5 was calculated. Although 6.1 shows the gross variation in unemployment type, Table 6.5, based on the net parameters, shows the same thing controlling for the other modeled effects just noted. Table 6.5 parallels Tables 4.4 and 5.5. It is calculated by fitting the observed distribution of Table 6.1 to the log-linear parameters of Table

Table 6.4
Cross-Period Odds Ratios Comparing Employment and Unemployment Likelihoods for Periods in the Business Cycle[a]

	Peak	Decline	Trough	Recovery
Peak	—	1.17	2.38	1.68
Decline	.85	—	2.04	1.44
Trough	.42	.49	—	.71
Recovery	.59	.69	1.41	—

[a]To obtain the relative likelihood of a worker's being employed rather than unemployed in period A in constrast to period B find period A's row and read across to the column of period B. To obtain the relative likelihood of a worker's being unemployed rather than employed in period A in contrast to period B, find period A's column and read down to the row of period B. See Appendix A for the method of calculating these odds ratios.

6.3. This produces a cross tabulation of cases of unemployment types by business cycle period net of the effect of the other modeled independent variables.

Column 1 of Table 6.5 shows the net absolute distribution of cases to employment status. On average (the panel marked "total") the most frequent form of unemployment is firings and the least frequent form is temporary layoff. Column 3 indicates that those on temporary layoff are 5.9% of the unemployed, those on indefinite layoff are 24%, those who were fired are 55.3%, and those who quit are 14.9%. There is substantial variation around that average in the relative proportions of the various types of unemployment from one period to the next in the business cycle, however. In absolute terms, firings remain the most frequent category for the unemployed in every period. The number of quits is greater, however, than the number of indefinite layoffs only when the economy is at the top of the cycle. At the peak, the percentage of unemployed on indefinite layoff are 16.8% while the percentage who quit are 22.5%. At the trough, the percentage of indefinite layoffs rises 88% to 31.5% of the total while the percentage of quits declines 130% to 9.8% of the total. In other words, when the unemployment rate is 3%, columns 3 and 4 of Table 6.5 show that indefinite layoffs are 43% less than on average while quits are 51% greater than average. In contrast, at the trough, when the unemployment rate has jumped to 7.4%, indefinite layoffs are 32% greater than on average whereas quits are 53% less than on average. Further comparisons may be made for all other employment status categories across the periods of the business cycle. For instance, temporary layoffs comprise 7.5% of the unemployed at the peak and decline, become 6.6% at the trough (because of the large increase in the proportion of indefinite layoffs), and decline to only 5.1% of the unemployed as the recovery sets in.

In sum, this first set of findings confirms the conventional knowledge that from peak to trough the trend is for involuntary unemployment to increase, especially due to indefinite layoffs, and for voluntary unemployment to decrease. This is only part of the picture: Besides the changing proportions in types of job separation over the cycle, another aspect is the change in the relative number of unemployed comprising those changed proportions. For instance, temporary layoffs are 28% greater than on average during the peak and decline and only 12% greater than the average distribution at the trough. Given this, columns 5 and 6 of Table 6.5 indicate that at the trough the figure 6.6% for temporary layoff represents a dramatic increase over the peak and decline in the relative propensity of temporary layoffs among the labor force. That is, the proportion of temporary layoffs relative to other forms of unemployment is less in the trough than in the peak and decline, but relative to the number in the labor force the proportion is greater in the trough. While

10.3% of the sample is in the labor force at the trough, 17.6% of the total number of layoffs occur during this period. Hence temporary layoffs are 72% overrepresented in this period despite comprising a smaller proportion of the unemployed. This discrepancy occurs because, as can be seen from column 6, indefinite layoffs become 103% overrepresented. A similar argument applies to firings, but in reverse. In the trough, firings are overrepresented by 46% relative to the labor force but are 6% less than average as a proportion of the unemployment in this period.

Taken together, the information from columns 3 and 4, on the one hand, and from columns 5 and 6, on the other, paint the following picture. First, these findings show that it is misleading to examine changes in the aggregate rate of unemployment over the business cycle without the added information that the relative propensity of forms of unemployment comprising that aggregate rate vary considerably over the cycle. Indefinite layoffs become a much more significant component of unemployment while quits decrease in importance. If the research stressing the voluntary or turnover aspects of unemployment is to be faulted, then the findings summarized in the preceding provide a good starting point.

In nonrecessionary times, firings and quits may be considered a "normal" market mechanism for adjusting the supply and demand for labor and, perhaps, less personally or socially costly than otherwise considered to be. Once the contingencies of the business cycle are introduced, however, it becomes clear that the degree of voluntary choice that may undergird the decision to quit in nonrecessionary times becomes greatly circumscribed in the recession. The relative propensity of quits decreases during the decline, plummets in a recession, and is slow to revive during the recovery. As a recession sets in, temporary layoffs and indefinite layoffs begin to replace firings as a form of labor-force adjustment. This is especially true for indefinite layoffs, which increase by 36% as a proportion of the unemployed. But in this period, as shown by column 6, the proportion of unemployed is less than the proportion of the labor force. At the trough, the total number of unemployed as a proportion of the labor force increases dramatically with all forms of involuntary unemployed climbing as a percentage of the labor force: Of the unemployed, 6.6% are in temporary layoff—less than in the peak and decline—but this 6.6% involves 93% more of the labor force ($1.72/.89$). In the recovery, temporary and indefinite layoffs decline both as a proportion of the unemployed and as a proportion of the labor force. Firings regain their prominence as a tool for labor force adjustments and quits return to their prerecession proportions.

Although these findings confirm the segmented impact of the business cycle on types of unemployment, they leave unanswered the important

TABLE 6.5
Net Distribution of Employment, Unemployment, and Labor Force by Business Cycle

Period	Number (1)	Percentage (2)	Percentage of unemployed (3)	Percentage deviation of (3) from average distribution (4)	Percentage of Total (5)	Percentage of total Unemployment–Percentage of total labor force (by category) (6)
Total						
Employed	217,165	95.24			100.00	
Unemployed[a]	10,847	4.76	100.00	—	100.00	1.00
Temporary layoff	645	.28	5.88	—	100.00	1.00
Indefinite layoff	2,602	1.14	23.95	—	100.00	1.00
Firing	5,988	2.63	55.25	—	100.00	1.00
Quit	1,611	.71	14.92	—	100.00	1.00
Labor force	228,012[c]	100.00			100.00	1.00
Unemployment ratio[b]	4.99					
Peak						
Employed	42,400	97.04			19.52	
Unemployed	1,294	2.96	100.00		11.93	-1.61
Temporary layoff	97	.22	7.50	+.28	15.04	-1.27
Indefinite layoff	217	.50	16.80	-.43	8.35	-2.29
Firing	689	1.58	53.22	-4.0	11.50	-1.67
Quit	291	.67	22.47	+.51	18.05	-1.06
Labor force	43,694	100.00			19.16	
Unemployment ratio	3.05					
Decline						
Employed	43,254	96.65			19.92	

Unemployed	1,499	3.35	100.00		13.82	−1.42
Temporary layoff	113	.25	7.54	+.28	17.51	−1.12
Indefinite layoff	342	.76	22.82	−.05	13.15	−1.49
Firing	747	1.67	49.84	−.11	12.48	−1.57
Quit	297	.67	19.80	+.33	18.42	−1.07
Labor force	44,753	100.00			19.63	
Unemployment ratio		3.47				
Trough						
Employed	21,681	92.65			9.98	
Unemployed	1,719	7.35	100.00		15.85	+1.54
Temporary layoff	114	.49	6.61	+.12	17.62	+1.72
Indefinite layoff	542	2.32	31.52	+.32	20.82	+2.03
Firing	896	3.83	52.13	−.06	14.96	+1.46
Quit	168	.72	9.75	−.53	10.41	+1.01
Labor force	23,400	100.00			10.26	
Unemployment ratio		7.93				
Recovery						
Employed	109,831	94.55			50.57	
Unemployed	6,335	5.45	100.00		58.40	+1.15
Temporary layoff	321	.28	5.07	−.16	49.82	−1.02
Indefinite layoff	1,501	1.29	23.70	−.01	57.68	+1.13
Firing	3,657	3.15	57.72	+.04	61.06	+1.20
Quit	856	.74	13.51	−.10	53.12	+1.04
Labor force	116,165	100.00			50.95	
Unemployment ratio		5.77				

[a] The unemployment rate is total number of workers unemployed through temporary layoffs, indefinite layoffs, firings, and quits divided by the total in the labor force.

[b] The unemployment ratio is the total number of unemployed in the four categories divided by the number of employed.

[c] Totals may not be exact since the table is calculated by rounding weighted cases whose values are not integers.

question of how this averaged impact of the business cycle itself varies over different economic sectors.[7] I now turn to the task of decomposing this averaged effect.

BUSINESS CYCLE, UNEMPLOYMENT, AND ECONOMIC SECTORS

This section first sets out the theoretical background about the sectoral dynamics underlying the business cycle. It then formulates a set of propositions based on the implications of this theory of the business cycle for unemployment. Finally, these propositions are tested by means of a log-linear analysis of the cyclical variation in unemployment by economic sector. The variables and model described in the previous section are employed again in this section.

Segmentation and Unemployment

The importance of institutional factors in the theory of the business cycle is an increasingly familiar theme in studies on the cyclical patterns of employment and unemployment. For instance, Sherman (1968) considers several features of concentrated industries—such as their cyclical patterns of output, prices, profits, and investment—that distinguish their cyclical behavior from that of competitive industries. Weisskopf (1978) discusses the variety of means open to the state to mitigate cyclical crises, the inflationary logic that induces the need for this intervention, and the requirement that labor be periodically disciplined through increased unemployment. This last factor prohibits the state from warding off a cyclical contraction too early even though is must eventually act to arrest the downward slide. Other researchers in the Marxist, segmentation, and industrial–organization traditions also emphasize the institutional relationships of market power that are relevant to the study of the business cycle.[8] Most directly relevant to the

---

[7]Also, these findings represent only one aspect of a more complex dynamic of unemployment that entails as well variation by demographic groups in labor-force participation rates resulting from their different patterns of entering, leaving, and reentering the labor force over the business cycle (see Clark and Summers, 1979).

[8]Job positions are categorized by classes (Wright, 1978, 1979), or as primary independent, primary subordinate, and secondary (Edwards, 1979; Edwards, Reich, and Gordon, 1975). Firms are divided into monopoly, old competitive, new competitive, and state (Averitt, 1968; Beck et al., 1978; Edwards, 1979; Hodson, 1978; O'Connor, 1973; Poulantzas, 1975).

(continued)

present research is the work of Sherman (1976) and that of Scherer (1980). Although the former author presents a Marxist version of economic cycles and the latter an industrial–organization version, the two approaches converge in their incorporation of institutional aspects of market power to explain the dynamics and outcomes of recession. Drawing on their research, I set out a theory of the relation of market power, business cycle, and unemployment.

Business Cycle, Unemployment, and Economic Sectors

COMPETITIVE SECTOR

The sectoral differences in unemployment over the business cycle reflect the general, static, characteristics of the sectors, and, in turn, determine the characteristics of the business cycle itself. In Chapter 5, I argued that differences in market power in competitive, oligopoly, and state sectors result in different rates and types of unemployment. There I found that despite the ambiguity in the literature concerning the nature and consequences of oligopoly structure, the pattern of unemployment differed substantially in the three sectors. Specifically, the findings confirmed the persistence of market

---

Labor economics and industrial organization literature have incorporated elements of their institutional heritage to account for anomalies neoclassical theory found difficult to explain. Various theorists postulate a consciously simplified two-sector model in which one sector is ruled by competitive market mechanisms for setting prices and quantities of factors and products and another sector in which such competitive mechanisms are more or less superseded by contracts, bilateral monopoly, administered prices, concentrated product markets, wage and price determination regulated by customs, firm specific human capital, etc. One common two-sector approach contrasts competitive and oligopoly firms with the latter characterized by concentrated product markets, administered pricing, large and stable profit margins, wage premiums, and output adjusting during downturns (Blair, 1974; Means, 1935; Shepherd, 1970; Weiss, 1977). Taking into account job as well as firm characteristics, Thurow (1975) formulates a two-sector model of wage and job competition mechanisms for clearing labor markets. Okun (1973, 1975) explains labor market rigidities, inflation, and relative wage differences over the business cycle by contrasting "auction" competitive factor and product markets with "career" labor markets and "customer-oriented" product markets.

Hall (1975) likewise assumes a two-sector model in his explanation of why workers do not respond to increased labor demand in the lower-paying sector even when unemployment is high. Due to various institutional factors, above-market wages persist in better-paying firms even during a recession. Thus workers who would otherwise respond to increased demand for labor in the lower-paying firms instead remain queued for positions in the higher-wage sector.

mechanisms in the competitive sector for setting prices and wages and for determining variation in output and employment.

Keynesian and the neoclassical theories of the business cycle differ on the extent to which endogenous forces maintain and restore equilibrium. But both agree that competitive mechanisms mitigate rather than exacerbate the business cycle. Although such a tendency may not exist throughout the entire economy, I argue that in the competitive sector, changes in aggregate demand will lead to short-run adjustments in output and employment. Once aggregate demand begins to contract, competitive firms that are price takers, will stabilize further declines in demand by lowering prices. Lowered prices will reduce nominal wages but as prices of outputs are lowered to stimulate demand, real buying power becomes restored, and the contraction of the economy reverses. I recognize, as Keynes argued, such restoration is neither automatic nor complete for the economy as a whole without some government intervention. But to the extent that competitive forces operate, I would expect that during the early phases of a recession, unemployment in the competitive sector would rise but only until price adjustments restore demand.

The cyclical variation in types of unemployment is less predictable than the variation in levels. Nevertheless, it is reasonable to expect that quits resulting in unemployment will decline as the recession deepens and alternative jobs become scarcer. Because of the initial short-run output adjustment in the competitive sector and the later (partial) restoration of demand through price adjustment, involuntary unemployment is expected to increase during the early stages of the decline and to begin to reverse before the recession bottoms out. Because competitive firms generally do not invest as highly as oligopoly firms in specific human capital (cf. Hall, 1975; Okun, 1973, 1975; Thurow, 1975), and since these enterprises generally employ a technology that enables the firm to hire workers on the basis of wage competition, competitive firms are expected to fire workers rather than lay them off with a guarantee of rehiring at their former wage rates.

OLIGOPOLY SECTOR

To explain oligopoly unemployment over the business cycle requires that the general association discussed in Chapter 5 among oligopoly market structure, administered prices, profit stability, wage premiums, output adjustments, and unemployment is sustained in a theoretically consistent manner over the business cycle. The general argument is that the classical model of macrodynamic analysis is not applicable to the oligopoly sector. The presence of an oligopoly sector with its capacity to "make" rather than

"take" its relations to labor and product markets produces in a recession not only a special set of consequences for the oligopoly sector but a peculiar (to classical theory) twist to the recession itself. As Sherman, (1976) claims, in the face of decreased aggregate demand, the oligopoly sector sustains "its prices and profit per unit at the expense of great decreases in production, and large-scale unemployment . . . [and that the economy as a whole] is thus more apt to produce high rates of unemployment in every decline [p. 164]."

That oligopolistic firms sustain their prices even in the midst of an economic slump has been a hotly contested proposition since Means (1935) first formulated his thesis of administered pricing. Nevertheless, a large body of empirical and theoretical research has now established the plausibility of the proposition that in recessions oligopoly market power creates greater unemployment, higher inflation, and a tendency for recessions to be deeper and less susceptible to reequilibrating market forces.[9] Such is the conclusion of Sherman (1976) and, with more reservations, of Scherer (1980) and Mueller (1974).

There are two aspects of the contemporary research on oligopoly market power that are directly relevant to the present discussion. The first is the general or static relationship of oligopoly price determination to market power, output adjustment, and unemployment. This has been reviewed in Chapter 5. The second is the relationship over the business cycle. Three aspects of this relationship are reviewed: (a) the cyclical rigidity of oligopoly prices; (b) the consequences for stagflation; and (c) the consequences for employment instability.

CYCLICAL RIGIDITY OF OLIGOPOLY PRICING

Research on the long-run dynamics of oligopoly pricing supports the notion that through price administration concentrated industries evidence price stability over the business cycle. Table 6.6 shows that in a recession, oligopoly prices either decline much less than competitive prices or increase. The only exception is for the 1973–1975 recession when competititve prices

---

[9] In the past few years some oliogopoly industries have become subject to more competitive pressures and, accordingly, have begun to return to competitive pricing policies in the product market. This is most evident in the automobile industry where, despite the introduction of some tariff restrictions on Japanese imports, numerous waves of rebates and other price-reducing inducements have been introduced to lure consumers (see The New York Times, Business Page, 12 February 1982). Since such price-adjusting procedures generally occurred in the oligopoly sector since 1978 (the last year analyzed here), the theoretical arguments made in the text remain valid.

increased slightly but oligopoly prices skyrocketed. Case studies of the oligopoly automobiles, oil, food, and steel industries reveal a similar "counter-cyclical pricing trend (see Akhdar, 1975; Blair, 1974; Edwards, 1975; Harrison, 1975; Means, 1962; Mueller, 1974; Robbins, 1974). Other research on oligopoly pricing over the business cycle presents mixed evidence on the countercyclical movement of prices in this sector.[10] Summarizing the literature, Scherer (1980:357) concludes that the "weight of the available statistical evidence on this topic suggests that concentrated industries do exhibit somewhat different pricing propensities over time than their more atomistic counterparts. They reduce prices and (perhaps more important) price–cost margins by less in response to a demand slump and increase them by less in the boom phase."

INFLATIONARY CONSEQUENCES
OF PRICE STABILITY

The second aspect of the relationship of market power to the business cycle is that oligopolistic pricing behavior contributes to recessionary inflation and the resiliency of the recession. Cagan (1975) for instance, found that concentration has a "negative partial effect on price changes 1967 to 1969, when inflation accelerated, and a positive effect in 1970–71, when inflation subsided. The effect turned negative again thereafter with the imposition of price controls in August 1971 and the resurgence of inflation in 1973 [p. 203]." Thus, I conclude with Scherer that price and wage behavior of oligopoly firms "Does sometimes create nontrivial dynamic instabilities with a net inflationary bias, but this view is held with less than overwhelming confidence [1980:363]." Administered pricing in the oligopoly sector produces countercyclical inflationary trends both by pricing policies that are not just "sticky downward" but actually increase in a recession and by wage

---

[10]This is the case for Weiss's research on concentration and price stability for a selection of years from 1953 to 1969. For the years 1953–1959, Weiss (1966b) found that prices rose more in concentrated industries but for 1959–1963, he found no statistically significant relationship between concentration and pricing. For 1967–1969, Weiss's (1970) research revealed a negative relationship between concentration and price rises. Despite these mixed findings, and the findings by Cagan (1975) that oligopoly pricing reflects lags in the transmission of prices rather than the administration of prices, the administered price theory has not been struck a fatal blow. That is because as Mueller (1974) argues, "Even if one accepts the . . . interpretation that industrial concentration supports a 'lagged' theory of seller-induced inflation [rather than a direct theory], the latter still undermines the traditional theory of demand–pull inflation and creates special problems for monetary and fiscal policy [p. 291].[11] Another critical view is offered by Stigler and Kindahl (1970). Consequently, the administered price hypothesis may be stated better as a theory of market power pricing across the business cycle.

TABLE 6.6
Competitive and Monopoly Contractions: Changes in Price Indexes from Cyclical Peak to Trough[a]

Cycle of peaks and troughs	Percentage change in competitive prices	Percentage change in monopoly prices
Nov. 1948–Oct. 1949	−7.8	−1.9
July 1953–Aug. 1954	−1.5	+1.9
July 1957–Apr. 1958	−0.3	+0.5
May 1960–Feb. 1961	−4.0	+0.1
Nov. 1969–Nov. 1970	−3.0	+5.9
Dec. 1973–May 1975	+1.8	+27.0

Sources: Price changes for 1948–1949, 1953–1954, and 1957–1958 from Robert Lanzillotti, Hearings before the Joint Economic Committee of the U.S. Congress, *Employment, Growth and Price Levels* (Washington, D.C.: U.S. Government Printing Office, 1959), p. 2238. Price changes for 1969–1970 from John Blair, "Market Power and Inflation," *Journal of Economic Issues* (June 1974). Price changes for 1960–1961 and 1973–1975 calculated by author from U.S. Department of Labor, *Wholesale Prices and Price Index* (Washington, D.C.: U.S. Government Printing Office, April 1961 and August 1975). Cycle peak and trough dates from Table 1.1.
[a]From Sherman (1976:165), Table 8.5.

policies that increase income among firms and workers with a relatively lower propensity to consume. This view is substantiated by Sherman (1976) as particularly relevant to the two periods of recession analyzed here. Table 6.7 shows that average profit rate increases with size of firm and that profit rates of larger firms are more stable, rising less in expansions, and declining less during contractions. The same conclusion is reached by Blair (1974:especially 466–474).

PRICE-STABILITY AND EMPLOYMENT INSTABILITY

The third aspect of the cyclical rigidity in oligopoly prices is the consequences for unemployment. During cyclical declines price stability results in output adjustment by oligopoly firms thereby producing a higher frequency of unemployment relative to the competitive sector. As Pasinetti (1974) argues, in the oligopoly sector "the traditional response mechanism is brought into use. To changes in demand, producers respond by changing production [as quoted in Kenyon, 1979:41]." Since prices are set in view of long-run profit margins[11] and since oligopoly firms hold a conspicuous

---

[11]Weintraub (1978), Eichner (1976), and Applebaum (1979) explain this organizational goal in terms of what Kalecki (1954) described as cost-determined pricing.

TABLE 6.7
Corporate Size and Profit Rate on Sales, 1970–1975[a]

Asset size (dollars)	Percentage change in expansion	Percentage change in contraction	Percentage average value of profit rate over whole cycle
0–$1 million	+87	−22	4
1–5 million	+36	−24	5
5–10 million	+22	−13	6
10–50 million	+27	−18	7
50–100 million	+29	−10	7
100–250 million	+12	−5	7
250–1 billion	−13	−8	8
over 1 billion	+22	−5	9
All	+25	−12	8

Source: Federal Trade Commission, *Quarterly Financial Reports of Manufacturing Corporations* (4th quarter 1970 through 2nd quarter 1975). Expansion from 4th quarter 1970 to 4th quarter 1973; contraction from 4th quarter 1973 to 2nd quarter 1975; cycle peak and trough dates from Table1.1.

Notes: Quarterly data, all U.S. manufacturing corporations. Average value set equal to 100 points. Expansion change measures rise in point standing from initial trough to cycle peak. Contraction change measures fall in point standing from cycle peak to final trough.

[a]From Sherman (1976:177), Table 8.7.

market position in relation to their competitors, recession-induced curtailment in the labor force is not mitigated by price adjustments aimed at sustaining production. Rather—with the caveat indicated in footnote 9— during a recession oligopoly firms maintain or even raise prices, sustain their target revenue and profits, and reduce output and employment.

EMPLOYMENT INSTABILITY
VERSUS ORGANIZATIONAL SLACK

The arguments just reviewed provide the theoretical basis for what Scherer (1980) calls the concentration–rigid-price–employment-instability hypothesis. It can be formulated as follows: because of oligopolistic market power, fixed technology in production, and mark-up or cost-plus pricing, the demand for labor is a direct function of the level of demand for products. In a recession, oligopoly firms will reduce employment rather than adjust the capital–labor ratio, change technology, or lower prices to sustain or recoup output.

The alternative hypothesis Scherer terms the concentration–organizational-slack hypothesis. This position claims that "concentrated

rigid-price industries accept more disguised unemployment during a recession than do atomistic, flexible-price industries." Since firms with market power are less likely to experience a liquidity crisis compelling cost reduction, "They can afford to maintain more organizational slack; or they may discount the future at a lower rate, placing more weight on avoiding future rehiring and retraining costs [pp. 364–365]."

HYPOTHESES

Although the two hypotheses just cited contain opposing expectations about the relative level of cyclical unemployment in the oligopoly sector, I suggest that these two views may be reconciled theoretically and empirically if cyclical variation in types of unemployment is introduced into the analysis. I expect, in accord with the employment–instability argument, that fluctuations in unemployment over the business cycle will be greater in the oligopoly sector than in the competitive sector. I argue that the form this increased relative frequency of unemployment will take, however, is better explained by the organizational-slack hypothesis, which suggests that firms will be reluctant to forfeit their sunk training costs by increasing unemployment in a recession. In particular, I expect that the relative frequency of involuntary unemployment will increase from the peak to the trough. But this increase will be especially true for layoffs that enable firms to output adjust without losing their investment in on-the-job training or threatening the stability of their work force. Through layoffs, employees remain stable but positions become unstable over the business cycle. Thus, the fear of future rehiring and retraining (an important element of the organizational-slack hypothesis) becomes reconciled to the concentration–employment instability theory if in fact oligopoly firms carry out their large labor force reductions by increasing the relative frequency of layoffs in a recession.

Concerning quits, I expect that their relative frequency will vary directly with the level of business activity. Concentrated firms offer wage premiums[12] to their workers who embody large amounts of specific human capital and on-the-job training (cf. Hall, 1975; Okun, 1973, 1975; Ross and Wachter, 1973). Thus, compared to competitive employees, I expect that oligopoly

---

[12]The source of these wage premiums is disputed. It is instructive for Marxist researchers that for the most part industrial organization literature is skeptical that an independent monopoly or oligopoly wage premium actually exists. Sources other than oligopoly profits and prices that are suggested as the cause of oligopoly wage premiums include unionization (Bowen, 1960), higher productivity growth (Weston and Lustgarten, 1974), and personal characteristics of workers that make them more productive (Weiss, 1966a).

employees will be even less likely to quit in a recession than during the peak or recovery.

SUMMARY

Drawing together the predictions for competitive and oligopoly sectors, I argue that oligopoly firms will experience a relatively greater increase in unemployment than the competitive sector during recessionary downturns. Quits in both sectors will decrease and involuntary unemployment increase. The increase in involuntary unemployment, however, will be less in the competitive, price-adjusting sector and will be more prone to be in the form of firings relative to the oligopoly sector. In contrast, the relative frequency of layoffs is expected to be greater in the oligopoly sector than in the competitive sector at the trough. Confirming these expectations will reconcile the employment-instability and organizational-slack hypotheses and will lend support indirectly to the institutional explanation of stagflation in which oligopoly output adjusting contributes to simultaneous high unemployment and rising prices.

CONSTRUCTION SECTOR

The construction sector, I have argued in Chapter 5, is expected to be similar to the oligopoly sector in unemployment types because it is generally concentrated in the product market on a regional level. Over and above the oligopolistic tendencies toward output adjustment, the rate and type of unemployment vary over the business cycle due to the high income elasticity of demand for housing and other construction. Consequently, the construction sector is expected to be highly mercurial in its employment levels over the business cycle. During recessions, quits are expected to become even lower than their normal rate whereas involuntary unemployment is expected to increase. Among types of involuntary unemployment, layoffs are expected to have a greater frequency relative to other sectors than are firings. Over and above the factor of unionism, which is controlled for by the class variable, layoffs are expected to be more predominant because of a number of factors explained in "contract theory [see Clark and Summers, 1979:46–51]." A mutual interest in employee stability is shared by construction firms and their workers. On the one hand, the firms desire to maintain a well-trained labor force; consequently wage rates are high to keep workers from quitting and to retain workers over periods of seasonal fluctuations in demand. This is especially important in this industry where workers are endowed with general, rather than specific human capital. On the other hand,

workers are willing to remain tied to a firm despite frequent and even long-term layoffs because this unemployment is compensated for by higher wage premiums during periods of employment and by job stability. Thus during a recession the unemployment level in the construction sector is expected to increase and to entail a relative increase in temporary and indefinite layoffs rather than firings.

STATE SECTOR

Cyclical variation in unemployment is expected to differ greatly in the state sector from that in the private, competitive, oligopoly, and construction sectors. Unlike the private sector, which is vulnerable to income elasticity of demand, the state sector actually experiences an increased demand for services during a recession. Even though revenue for the state may decrease through the recessionary erosion of the income or corporate tax base, the state does not face absolute constraints on spending since it can incur a deficit. Moreover, the state is at the center of the political struggle for economic resources and services. During a recession the population demand for such resources and services increases, making it not only possible but politically necessary for the state even to increase its employment relative to other sectors. Demand for hospital care, welfare and social services, education, unemployment compensation, and state-financed employment positions all increase during the decline and trough of a business cycle. Thus in a recession unemployment in the state sector should increase at a lower rate than in the private sector.[13]

Analysis: Unemployment, Business Cycle, and Economic Sector

The sectoral or market power theory of recession is a proposition about the interaction of the business cycle, sectors, and unemployment. The question is whether competitive sector and oligopoly sector differences in rate of employment vary over the business cycle. For reasons stated previously, the expectation is that the oligopoly sector will be more susceptible than the

---

[13] In the 1981–1982 recession, unlike what happened in the 1971 and 1975 recessions, there has been a more substantial cut in government employment, especially at the state level where tax-abatement laws have compounded the fiscal crisis. In this new dispensation, government hiring-freezes are common and much labor force reduction occurs through attrition. At the same time, specific job categories such as teachers, public transportation workers, fire fighters, and police, also incur direct job loss.

competitive sector to increased unemployment during declines in the business cycle. Analysis of the interaction effect of business cycle and economic sector on unemployment confirms this expectation. Moreover, it goes a step further by revealing the underlying sectoral composition of types of unemployment that produce the cyclical differences in aggregate unemployment levels.

Analyzing the interaction effect of business cycle and economic sector on unemployment requires that this interaction be included in the general model for explaining unemployment. Table 6.8 is an extension of Table 6.2. As such it differs from Table 3.2 in that five rather than seven industrial sectors and five rather than nine class segments are used in the determination of the model. Table 6.8 presents the base-line model (model 1) examined in Chapters 3–5 as well as a series of further models to test for the independent contribution of the four three-way interactions included in model 5, which is the basis for the analysis of this chapter.[14]

In Chapter 5, I found a sharp contrast in the unemployment pattern for competitive and oligopoly sectors controlling for the impact of the business

---

[14]Comparing the base line model to the series of models in which further three-way interactions are included, I find that only the interaction between employment status, class, and sector (model 5) is significant according to the criterion used up to this point, namely that the decrease in the likelihood-ratio χ^2 be at least four times greater than the associated reduction in degrees of freedom. None of the three interactions of employment status and business cycle with economic sector (model 3), class (model 2), or race (model 4) is significant according to the stated criterion. However, each of these three interactions is included along with the interaction of employment status, class, and sector in the final model for two reasons. The first is theoretical and the second empirical.

First, the literature on unemployment as well as the theory developed here suggests that such interactions occur. In particular, the arguments formulated in the preceding in reference to the sectoral variation in adjustments to declines in national income and in unemployment are premised on the empirical expectation that over the different periods of the business cycle, unemployment will vary differently in the oligopoly, competitive, and state sectors. Similarly, it is reasonable to expect that over and above the static differences in unemployment by class and race, rates and types of unemployment will vary for different classes and races in different ways across the business cycle.

The empirical rationale for including the three-way interactions is that the parameters estimating these interactions vary across cells in an interpretable way in view of the existing literature and the theoretical argument formulated here. Also, as footnote 5 indicates, the collapsed model with five class and sector categories picks up relatively more variation per cell than the fuller model with nine class categories and seven sector categories.

Consequently, the interactions of business cycle and employment status with sector, class, and race are included in the final model. However, the interaction with economic sector is accorded a higher status than the other two because this interaction meets the conventional statistical norm of significance along with the theoretical and empirical norms discussed previously. Thus, this interaction is examined with some confidence as a valid test of the theory of the differential impact of the business cycle on oligopoly prices, output, and unemployment.

TABLE 6.8
Models for the Analysis of Interactions of Employment Status and Business Cycle

Model	Fitted marginals	df	Likelihood ratio χ^2	p
1	(234567) (17) (16) (15) (14) (13) (12) (157) (156) (167) (136)[a]	12,232	5188	>.5
2	(234567) (17) (16) (15) (14) (13) (12) (157) (156) (167) (136) (124)	12,184	5119	>.5
3	(234567) (17) (16) (15) (14) (13) (12) (157) (156) (167) (136) (124) (134)	12,136	5021	>.5
4	(234567) (17) (16) (15) (14) (13) (12) (157) (156) (167) (136) (124) (134) (145)	12,124	5021	>.5
5	(234567) (17) (16) (15) (14) (13) (12) (157) (156) (167) (136) (124) (134) (145) (123)	12,063[b]	4725	>.5

Models compared	Ratio of change in χ^2 to change in df	Change in df	Change in ratio χ^2	p
1 versus 2	1.4	48	69	c.025
2 versus 3	1.6	48	79	<.001
3 versus 4	1.6	12	19	<.100
4 versus 5	4.9	61	296	<.001

[a]1 Employment status (dependent variable)
2 Class segment
3 Economic sector
4 Business cycle
5 Race
6 Age
7 Education
[b]The degrees of freedom are adjusted to take into account the number of cases constrained to be zero. See Chapter 3 for a discussion of this adjustment.

cycle, class, and personal characteristics. Although unemployment levels were similar in the two sectors, the relative frequency of types of unemployment comprising the similar rates were different. The proportion of firings and quits was greater and the proportion of layoffs was less in the competitive than in the oligopoly sector. I found, too, that the state sector evidenced the lowest unemployment rate relative to the other sectors whereas the construction sector had the greatest relative frequency of unemployment. These relationships comprise the average effect of economic sector. These relationships are replicated here where the averaged effect of economic sector is estimated with the five-sector model that includes the further interactions. This can be seen by comparing the tau-parameters generated from the model used in Chapter 5 (Table 5.3) with the parameters generated by the model used here (Table 6.3).

FINDINGS

One way to understand the findings from the analysis of the interaction effect of the business cycle, sector, and unemployment is in the form of log-linear parameters. To interpret this three-way interaction, two sets of parameters need to be considered simultaneously: the parameters representing the two-way affect of employment status and sector and the parameters representing the three-way interaction effect. These are presented in Table 6.9.[15]

An alternative mode of presentation serves to make the results more understandable. The two-way and three-way parameters of Table 6.9 are both geometrically transformed into generalized odds ratios (see Appendix A pp. 207–208). These odds ratios (Table 6.10) differ from the across-period odds ratios used previously to estimate the averaged effect of the business cycle. These latter odds ratios measure the relative chances of a member of the labor force being in a particular category of employment status and in particular period of the business cycle *relative to being in some other designated category* of either variable. In contrast, the generalized odds ratios for the two-way effect measure the relative chances of a member of the labor force being in a particular category of employment status and economic sector *relative to all the other categories*. The generalized odds ratio for the

---

[15]Given the two-way averaged effects, the three-way parameters indicate how, within each level or period of business cycle, the two-way relationship varies. A three-way effect greater than 1.0000 means that within the particular period of the business cycle the effect of sector or unemployment is greater than the averaged effect for the comparable relationship in the two-way table. A three-way parameter less than 1.0000 means that within that particular business cycle period, the effect of sector on unemployment is less than the averaged effect. Although all the information needed to interpret the findings is contained in these tables of tau-parameters presenting the results in this way is not intuitively understandable.

TABLE 6.9

Tau-Parameters for the Net Relationship of Employment Status, Sector, and Business Cycle[a]

Panel A: Employment status and economic sector				
	Sector			
Employment status	Competitive	Oligopoly	State	Construction	Farm, utility, nonprofit
---	---	---	---	---	---
Temporary layoff	.9091	1.2484	.6242	1.4004	.9857
Indefinite layoff	.9015	1.0810	.5167	2.2884	.9022
Firing	1.0692	.8524	1.0934	1.1229	.9050
Quit	1.2971	.9658	1.2876	.5757	.9959
Employed	.8803	.9124	2.0284	.4779	1.2464

Panel B: Employment status, economic sector, and business cycle

			Peak		
Temporary layoff	.9089	.7896	1.5899	.8423	1.0924
Indefinite layoff	.9377	.8654	1.0081	1.2839	.9712
Firing	1.0323	1.0660	.9193	.9200	1.0641
Quit	1.0614	1.1722	.8651	1.0343	.8979
Employed	1.0659	1.1582	.8531	.9499	.9895
			Decline		
Temporary layoff	1.0589	1.2767	.9168	1.1040	.7323
Indefinite layoff	1.1311	.9107	.8447	.9503	1.1966
Firing	.9515	.9713	10.965	.9874	1.0020
Quit	.9426	.9449	.9962	1.0337	1.0960
Employed	.9329	.9506	1.1628	.9519	1.0209
			Trough		
Temporary layoff	.9044	1.2034	.6312	1.1439	1.2053
Indefinite layoff	1.0554	1.1909	.9445	.8413	.9857
Firing	1.0865	.8964	1.0103	1.1004	.9309
Quit	.9564	.9229	1.3440	.8936	.9375
Employed	1.0005	.8519	1.1414	1.0654	.9746
			Recovery		
Temporary layoff	1.1488	.8243	1.0870	.9400	1.0372
Indefinite layoff	.8933	1.0655	1.2433	.9743	.8730
Firing	.9870	1.0775	.9820	1.0005	1.0076
Quit	1.0451	.9782	.8634	1.0467	1.0840
Employed	1.0052	1.0662	.8832	1.0381	1.0157

[a]Controlling for all other modeled relationships of employment status with class, sector, business cycle, race, age, and education.

TABLE 6.10
Generalized Odds Ratios for the Analysis of Employment Status and Sector over the Business Cycle

	Panel A: Generalized odds ratios:[a] Employment status and sector				
			Sector		
Employment status	Competitive	Oligopoly	State	Construction	Farm, utility nonprofit
Temporary layoff	.8617	1.4143	.4788	1.6925	.9777
Indefinite layoff	.8504	1.1294	.3564	3.6456	.8515
Firing	1.1102	.7792	1.1497	1.1985	.8555
Quit	1.5014	.9470	1.4843	.4220	.9936
Employed	.8194	.8666	3.0195	.3155	1.4108
	Panel B: Generalized odds ratios:[a] Employment status and sector over the business cycle				
			Peak		
Temporary layoff	.7423	.9778	.9881	1.2945	1.1224
Indefinite layoff	.7690	.9010	.3609	5.3868	.8135
Firing	1.1668	.8610	1.0080	1.0520	.9427
Quit	1.6479	1.2138	1.1835	.4449	.8397
Employed	.9053	1.0901	2.3558	.2911	1.3877
			Decline		
Temporary layoff	.9424	2.0715	.4180	1.9756	.6008
Indefinite layoff	1.0309	.9759	.2736	3.3663	1.1271
Firing	1.0273	.7445	1.3277	1.1749	.8582
Quit	1.3689	.8668	1.4755	.4444	1.1466
Employed	.7351	.8006	3.8218	.2921	1.4571
			Trough		
Temporary layoff	.7365	1.8888	.2333	2.0882	1.3089
Indefinite layoff	.9252	1.4839	.3260	2.7827	.8326
Firing	1.2439	.6567	1.1683	1.3917	.7649
Quit	1.4004	.8355	2.3557	.3540	.8983
Employed	.8200	.6745	3.7128	.3483	1.3553
			Recovery		
Temporary layoff	1.0703	1.0457	.5455	1.5365	1.0351
Indefinite layoff	.7130	1.2470	.5008	3.5003	.6886
Firing	1.0029	.8755	1.1175	1.1993	.8657
Quit	1.6085	.9150	1.1798	.4532	1.1271
Employed	.8261	.9578	2.4868	.3344	1.4456

[a]See Appendix A for an explanation of the formulas for calculating generalized odds ratios.

three-way effect measure, for each period of the business cycle, the relative propensity for a member of the labor force to be in a particular category of employment status and economic sector in contrast to all the others. Panel A of Table 6.10 presents the two-way generalized odds ratios. In this form, each numerical entry in panel B shows the propensity of workers to be distributed to categories of employment status and economic sector for each period. This is in contrast to the entries in panel A that show the relative distribution averaged over the business cycle and the other independent variables.

UNEMPLOYMENT, BUSINESS CYCLE, AND SECTOR

The relative variation by sector in the frequency of total unemployment supports the applicability of the rigid price–employment-instability hypothesis to the oligopoly sector. The findings indicate that the oligopoly sector is more mercurial in its employment pattern over the business cycle than is the competitive sector. They also show that the competitive sector tends to adjust to declines in national income by varying its employment less and recovering through price adjustments.

Although unemployment increases in both sectors as economic activity declines, the results in Table 6.10 and 6.11 reveal two important differences. The existence of these differences support the argument that variations between competitive and oligopoly sectors in their market power are consequential for sectoral unemployment patterns over the business cycle. First, the variation in the relative frequency of unemployment from peak to trough is greater in the oligopoly than in the competitive sector. Table 6.11 shows that unemployment varies by 48% from peak to trough in the oligopoly sector but only by 20.8% from peak to decline and 10.4% from peak to trough in the competitive sector. At the peak of the cycle, the frequency of unemployment is 1.26 times greater in the competitive than in the oligopoly sector but in the trough the relative frequency of unemployment is 1.28 times greater in the oligopoly sector.

Second, the point in the business cycle where the greatest frequency of unemployment occurs differs between the two sectors. For the competitive sector, the relative frequency of unemployment is greatest during the decline. For the oligopoly sector, the relative frequency of unemployment is greatest during the trough. Tables 6.10 and 6.11 show that in the competitive sector the relative frequency is 10.5% less than average during the decline but equal to average during the trough. In the oligopoly sector, unemployment is greatest at the trough. During the peak, unemployment is 25.8% less than the average rate; during the decline unemployment is 7.6% greater than average; and during the trough, unemployment is 22.2% greater than average. In both

TABLE 6.11
Percentage Cyclical Deviation of Unemployment Propensities by Sector

Competitive	Oligopoly	State	Construction	Farm, utility, nonprofit
		Peak		
+10.5	+25.8	−22.0	−7.7	−1.6
		Decline		
−10.3	−7.6	+26.0	−7.4	+3.3
		Trough		
+0.1	−22.2	+23.0	+10.4	−3.9
		Recovery		
+0.8	+10.5	−17.6	+6.0	+2.5

[a]These deviations are calculated from the generalized odds ratios in Table 6.10. Each entry is calculated as the percentage deviation from a sector's averaged employment–unemployment propensity of the sector's employment–unemployment propensity for a given period in the business cycle.

sectors, unemployment declines during the recovery. Thus in accord with the theory of the cycle under competitive conditions, the competitive sector appears to vary its employment less and to recover through price adjustment before the oligopoly sector recovers. In contrast, the oligopoly sector manifests a pattern of employment instability connected to its propensity for output rather than price adjusting during a recession. As the recession commences, unemployment increases; but in accord with the concentration–rigid-price–employment-instability hypothesis unemployment continues to rise even after competitive-sector unemployment has turned down. These two aspects of the relative difference between the two sectors (the degree of variation and the point in the cycle where unemployment is greatest) can be seen in Figure 6.1. The figure graphs for the competitive and oligopoly sectors the average propensity of unemployment along with its variation over the business cycle. The horizontal axis indicates the stage in the business cycle. The vertical axis, calculated from the generalized odds ratios of Table 6.10, graphs the relative propensity of unemployment.[16]

---

[16]The vertical axis of Figures 6.1 and 6.2 is the relative propensity of unemployment. The range of the scale is from negative to positive infinity with .0 representing the propensity of unemployment averaged across all sectors. The entries for the figures are derived from the generalized odds ratios for the rows marked "employed" in Table 6.10. These odds ratios vary from .0 to infinity with 1.0 representing the averaged propensity of employment across all sectors. In order to derive the scale in the figures from the odds ratios the following steps were

(continued)

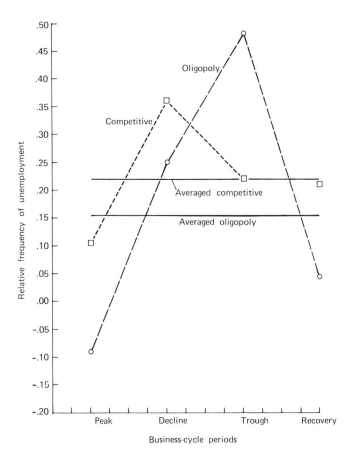

FIGURE 6.1. Unemployment in the competitive and oligopoly sectors over the business cycle.

taken. First, the inverse of the odds ratios less than 1.0 was taken in order transform the relative propensity of "employment" to the relative propensity of "unemployment." The resulting number (which is greater than 1.0) was reduced by 1.0 to create a scale that varied between .0 and infinity rather than between 1.0 and infinity. Second, in the case where the generalized odds for "employment" was greater than 1.0, the value was given a negative sign (in order to make the ratio represent the unemployment propensity) and then reduced by 1.0 to maintain .0 as the average propensity. In mathematical terms the two derivations are given, respectively, by Eqs. (1) and (2):

If $x < 1.0$

$$a = [(1/x) - 1].$$ (1)

If $x > 1.0$

$$a = -[x - 1]$$ (2)

where x is the generalized odds ratio for "employed" from the appropriate panel of Table 6.10 and a is the value scaled on Figs. 6.1 and 6.2.

The cyclical pattern of unemployment in the state sector supports the argument that this sector should evidence countercyclical adjustments. Although in absolute terms, unemployment is lower during the peak than in the trough, the generalized odds ratios indicate that relative to the cyclical pattern of the other sectors unemployment is less in the trough and greater in the peak. Compared to its average propensity, state sector unemployment is 22.2% greater in the peak while 26.6% less during the decline and 23% less during the trough (see Table 6.11). Figure 6.2 graphs this pattern for the state sector and compares it to the pattern for the competitive and oligopoly sectors. Over the entire business cycle the state sector has a much lower relative propensity of unemployment than any other sector. But during a recession the relative difference between the state and private competitive and oligopoly sectors is exaggerated further.

Finally, the construction sector, with its consistently higher frequency of unemployment, is found to be more susceptible to unemployment increases early in the cycle and to recover before the trough.

TYPES OF UNEMPLOYMENT, BUSINESS CYCLE, AND SECTOR

The second step in the analysis of the sectoral variation of unemployment over the business cycle is to examine the types of unemployment that constitute the variation in the general frequency of unemployment.

First, the findings support the prediction that in the competitive sector the relative frequency of quits decreases as the economy enters a recession whereas the relative frequency of involuntary unemployment increases. Within-period odds ratios[17] calculated from Table 6.9 indicate that during the decline when competitive unemployment is highest, the level of quits is 1.2 times lower than during the peak. In contrast, the frequency of temporary and indefinite layoffs is 1.3 times greater while the frequency of firings declines only slightly. At the trough, when the competitive sector has begun to recover, the frequency of layoffs decreases, the frequency of firings increases, and the frequency of quits remains close to the level during the decline. During the recovery the relative frequency of temporary layoffs rises but that of indefinite layoffs and quits declines; also the relative frequency of quits increases almost to the level of the peak.

In the oligopoly sector, a similar inverse relation between voluntary and involuntary unemployment holds over the business cycle. Quits are 1.5 times more likely to occur at the peak than at the trough. Temporary layoffs are 1.9 times more likely to occur, indefinite layoffs are 1.6 times more likely, and

---

[17]See Chapter 3 for the method of calculating these odds ratios.

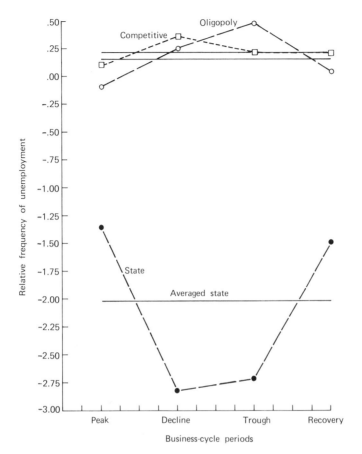

FIGURE 6.2. Unemployment in the competitive, oligopoly, and state sectors over the business cycle.

firings (the least likely form of involuntary unemployment) are 1.3 times more likely, however. Among types of involuntary unemployment, the component of the unemployment level that increases most in the oligopoly sector is layoffs. As expected when oligopoly unemployment increases through the recession, the proportion of layoffs jumps sharply. For instance, the propensity of temporary layoffs relative to the average distribution is 1.2 times greater than firings at the peak although 4.9 times greater than firings in the trough.

A further aspect of the cyclical behavior of unemployment types by sector is the difference in the patterns of temporary and indefinite layoffs over the cycle. During the decline, unemployment first increases through temporary

layoffs as evidenced by comparing the oligopoly sector generalized odds ratio (Table 6.10) for temporary layoffs at the peak (.9778) with that for the decline (2.0715). During the decline, indefinite layoffs begin to rise relative to other forms of unemployment in the oligopoly sector and reach their greatest propensity during the trough when temporary layoffs comprise a relatively smaller portion of the unemployment in this sector. During the recovery, the frequency of temporary layoffs declines, indefinite layoffs continue at a high level, and quits begin to return to their prerecession level. A similar pattern appears to occur in the construction sector if some adjustment is made for the generally high rate of indefinite layoffs. Such an adjustment is necessary since the seasonal vulnerability of this sector is accentuated by the use of data from March survey periods when the construction industry has not fully recovered from winter slowdowns.

The cyclical behavior of unemployment in the state sector is fundamentally different from that in the competitive and oligopoly sectors. First, the relative frequency of unemployment decreases—rather than increases—during the recession. That is, unemployment increases but not as much as in the other sectors. Second, reflecting this trend, unemployment due to quits increases relative to the other sectors as the recession sets in. This latter trend is consonant with the inverse relationship found for other sectors between unemployment quits entailing job loss. Specifically, compared to the sharp increment in unemployment in the other sectors, the state-sector unemployment propensity is 45% less in the trough than at the peak. Also the frequency of quits relative to firings and layoffs is greater during the decline and trough when unemployment is comparatively lower in the state sector. For instance, calculations of odds ratios based on Table 6.10 reveal that compared to the average pattern at the peak the frequency of quits is 1.2 times that for firings whereas at the bottom of the cycle, when unemployment is lower, the frequency of quits is 2.4 times greater than for firings.

Although these findings generally confirm the theoretical expectations about unemployment in the state sector some questions remain. Why, for instance, do firings increase despite the relative decrease of unemployment in the state sector? And why, despite the low sectoral unemployment rate, does the propensity of quits resulting in unemployment climb in the midst of a general recession? To answer these questions some speculations may be offered. The findings support the proposition that during a recession the state sector is less vulnerable both to decreases in revenue (even if they occur) and to decreased demand for its services. Relative to other sectors in a recession, increases in unemployment in the state were not as great as in other sectors. The cyclical rise in firings and quits as components of unemployment despite the general decreased relative frequency of unemployment is more difficult to explain.

One explanation for the firings may be that the state sector is itself segmented into more and less vulnerable sectors. Perhaps in a recession, local and state governments—which are more exclusively and immediately dependent on business-generated tax revenue—increase unemployment whereas the federal sector is more able to incur a deficit and more likely to be the focus of increased demand for medical, unemployment, and welfare services. Moreover, the state maintains a higher proportion of managerial and professional–technical positions than do other sectors. In general, these positions suffer much lower unemployment than working-class positions even during a recession. Consequently, the propensity to quit without a new job in hand, is not necessarily curtailed among the better-trained professional and technical employees of the state sector even during a recession. Such mobility remains possible for these employees during a recession since their major employment alternative is in the private nonprofit sector that does not suffer recessionary employment reductions as greatly as the competitive and oligopoly sectors.

DISCUSSION

Concerning the averaged effect of unemployment, the findings corroborate the well-established qualitative relationship between declines in national income and increased unemployment. Unemployment due to job loss is lowest at the peak of the business cycle, greatest at the trough, and at an intermediate level during the decline and recovery. More directly relevant to the specific purpose of the research is the finding that types of unemployment do not vary in an unidimensional way across the cycle. Quits vary in a countercyclical fashion whereas involuntary unemployment due to layoffs and firings vary directly with the business cycle. Especially significant is the finding that the most cyclically vulnerable type of unemployment is layoffs. Even though firings clearly increase in a recession the comparative odds ratio[18] calculated from the tau-parameters estimates that relative to the average pattern the chances of being unemployed through an indefinite layoff rather than a firing is 1.9 times greater in the trough than in the peak. Likewise, the increase in the likelihood of temporary layoffs surpasses that of firings in the decline when a full-fledged recession is not yet certain. Although not a large difference, the comparative odds ratio estimates that the ratio of temporary layoffs to firings is 7% greater in the decline than at the peak.

---

[18]See Appendix A for a discussion of the calculation of comparative odds ratios.

Second, the findings suggest that the use by the National Bureau of Economic Research of layoffs in manufacturing as a leading indicator of the business cycle may be misleading. The CPS rather than the Employment and Earnings series' definition of layoff may be more adequate for the task of predicting the business cycle. In the CPS, involuntary unemployment due to temporary layoffs, indefinite layoffs, and firings are separated. In the Employment and Earnings series published by the Department of Commerce from establishment data the concept of layoff includes in a single category (with the exception of firings for disciplinary reasons) all three forms of involuntary job loss. My findings show that temporary layoffs appear to be a leading indicator, whereas indefinite layoffs are a coincident or even lagging indicator. This can be seen from Table 6.12 where log-linear parameters are calculated for the net relationship of each of the 10 years from 1969–1978 and employment status. The general trend is for the relative propensity of temporary layoffs to increase before a recession (e.g., in 1970 and 1974), for the propensity of quits to decrease during the decline and in the recession (1970, 1974, 1975), and for the relative propensity of indefinite layoffs to be greatest during the trough (1975) and to persist into the recovery (1971, 1976).

Third, the analysis of the three-way interaction of employment status, business cycle and economic sector has produced two related sets of results: the first, concerning the cyclical variation by sector in overall unemployment and the second, concerning the cyclical variation by sector in types of unemployment. Again the theoretical expectations were confirmed, especially in regard to the differences between the competitive and oligopoly sector in unemployment types and levels over the business cycle. The fundamental conclusion of this part of the analysis is that in accord with the market-power–administered-pricing–output-adjusting hypothesis, the oligopoly sector responds to a recession with greater and more enduring labor cutbacks. Since these cutbacks are most likely to be in the form of layoffs, an important aspect of the competing concentration–organizational-slack theory is reconciled with the concentration–employment-instability hypothesis. The organizational-slack theory maintains that concentrated firms' size and profit margin both motivate and provide for an effort to keep workers attached to their positions during a recession. Due to the historical evolution of layoffs as a form of unemployment, these industries are able to combine employment instability with worker stability.

Fourth, the findings also shed light on the sectoral, market-power theory of the business cycle. A competitive economy, it is argued, should tend naturally to manifest countercyclical price adjustments in the product market that would encourage a recovery before a drastic recession sets in. Such price

TABLE 6.12
Log-Linear Tau-Parameters for the Net Relation between Employment Status and Years
1969 to 1978[a]

	Year				
Employment status	1969	1970	1971	1972	1973
Temporary layoff	.8825	.9973	.8810	.8604	.9471
Indefinite layoff	.5216	.8698	1.1326	.9556	.7838
Firing	.8927	.7831	1.0627	1.0569	.9038
Quit	1.2890	1.1323	.9402	1.1120	1.2751
Employed[b]	1.8751	1.2837	1.0031	1.0349	1.1689
	1974	1975	1976	1977	1978
Temporary layoff	1.2848	1.4449	.8664	1.0195	.9586
Indefinite layoff	.8858	1.6650	1.4511	1.1646	1.0423
Firing	.8268	1.0392	1.3107	1.1887	1.0394
Quit	1.0225	.7024	.7771	.8907	1.0339
Employed[b]	1.0393	.5694	.7809	.7955	.9313

[a]The parameters are based on model 11 in Table 3.2. It was necessary to collapse various categories of the other independent variables in order to obtain parameters for 10 years.
[b]The relative incidence of total unemployment for each year is simply the inverse of the parameter for the employed.

adjustment in both the product and labor markets would sustain the Phillips-curve tradeoff between unemployment and inflation. An economy with concentrated enclaves, however, is expected to be less responsive to competitive market mechanisms for reestablishing equilibrium, thereby extending the recession and introducing simultaneous inflation and unemployment. It is now often argued that this has been the pattern during the recessions of the 1970s. The analysis summarized in the preceding indicates that this theory of sectoral differences in the recession is credible. Much more research is needed on the complex interlocking arguments that undergird this theory in order to establish it convincingly. Nevertheless, the present research supports the proposition that the competitive sector responds by price adjustments in order to curtail the downturn whereas the oligopoly sector does not. Unemployment turns down at a greater rate in the competitive sector during a decline but by the trough has already begun to recover. In contrast, unemployment turns down in the oligopoly sector during the decline but continues to fall through the trough.

Finally, these findings also have an implication for two debates in the industrial-organization literature. The first concerns the applicability of the

Pigou effect. Pigou (1943) argues that during a recession real prices fall so that real buying power is maintained, stimulating a recovery without the massive economic dislocations of a severe recession. The alternative view, explains Scherer (1980:363) is that "the failure of monopolistic or oligopolistic prices to fall thwarts operation of the Pigou effect and thus chokes off one potential stimulant to economic recovery." Scherer goes on to point out that "with all but the most severe recessions" consumer decisions are not actually dictated by changes in real income. But since the 1975 recession was severe, the question remains what impact the "thwarted" Pigou effect might have played in extending its severity. Direct evidence on the employment instability of concentrated industries presented previously indirectly supports the proposition that rigid prices (that underlie this employment instability) both curtail the ability of the economy to recover spontaneously and contribute to stagflation.

Second, the findings are relevant to the problem of the persistence and depth of recessions. To the extent the evidence on cyclical employment instability in the oligopoly sector indirectly confirms the underlying rigid-price and profit-stability hypotheses, it also lends support to another proposition. That is, recessions are intractable in part because higher profits in this sector are not translated into demand-stimulating consumer or investment spending. If, on the one hand, the profits are paid out in the form of salaries and dividends, they tend to go to more wealthy individuals with a lower relative propensity to consume. If, on the other hand, these profits are retained for investment, the impact on increasing demand in the short run is minimized since these concentrated firms function below capacity during a recession. The result in either case is that the recession is prolonged.

Conclusions

The research presented in the preceding chapters has studied the structural contours of advanced capitalism within the framework of current research on unemployment and the sociology of labor markets. The fundamental proposition was that in the contemporary U. S. economy both employment and labor markets are segmented such that different forms of unemployment resulting from job separation (e.g., temporary layoffs, indefinite layoffs, firings, and quits) are systematically related to the segmentation in employment conditions. The research presented here formulated and tested theoretical arguments about how the structural determinants of vulnerability and power embedded in class, firm, and the business cycle systematically relate to fluctuations in the level of unemployment types. In so doing, it elucidated how in advanced capitalism vulnerability and power are distributed unevenly not only between capital and labor, but also within classes and economic sectors.

Log-linear techniques were used to analyze March Current Population Survey data for the period 1969–1978 for males in the labor force, ages 16 to 64. The findings verified that—controlling for the modeled effects of race, age, and education, as well as of the structural variables not considered in a particular analysis—class, sector, and business cycle make independent and significant contributions to the distribution of workers to unemployment. The argument is not that personal characteristics are unimportant in the

determination of unemployment outcomes. Indeed, the effects of race, age, and education are all significant, demonstrating that the effects of structural forces are played out in a complex web of labor market transactions linking persons in the household sector to jobs in the business sector. Nevertheless, despite a general recognition of this interaction of supply and demand in the determination of economic outcomes, too little attention has been devoted to studying the contribution of the diverse demand-side or structural determinants. Although the analysis of the structural determinants of unemployment reported here in no way represents the final work on the subject, the research does suggest a number of findings that shed some light on aspects of the demand side of the labor market that determine the shape of unemployment.

CLASS SEGMENTS AND UNEMPLOYMENT

Chapter 4 investigated the impact of class on the measured distribution of unemployment and unemployment types. The major conclusion was that class location of an employment position provides resources of bargaining power or sources of vulnerability that affect the employment status of an incumbent of that position. From this analysis were derived three important implications concerning the nature of unemployment, the structure of labor markets, and the theory of class struggle in advanced capitalism.

First, concerning the nature of unemployment, the analysis demonstrated that distinguishing types of unemployment and investigating how these types are distributed over the class structure helps to uncover the underlying structural differences among class positions in their vulnerability and power in the labor market. Three specific class trends in the distribution of persons to unemployment types were discerned. First, the findings show that positions endowed with power in the relations of authority (e.g., self-employment and managerial positions) are most capable of shielding their incumbents from unemployment. For the self-employed who own the means of production, such ownership grants the capacity to determine the unemployment of others while continuing their own status as active petty bourgeoisie or small employers as long as their enterprise continues in operation. What unemployment does occur can be interpreted as a rough maximum estimation of the potential for proletarianization of the self-employed as former incumbents of self-employment positions enter other locations in the class structure. In the case of the self-employed such as real estate agents and others who contract their labor, unemployment may be understood best as similar to that for employees in semi-autonomous

positions. But these conclusions about the meaning of unemployment among the self-employed remain speculative as the data allowed no way to distinguish between the self-employed who contract their labor and the self-employed who own the means of production as small employers.

It was expected that managerial positions, which also are defined by their location in the relations of authority, would enjoy lower unemployment likelihoods, because of their behavioral and ideological functions in carrying out details of economic ownership and possession. Behaviorally, the location of managerial positions in the hierarchical command structure of a firm results in managers being charged with determining economic policies including unemployment policy. Moreover, such managerial positions tend to be stable in that they are insulated, more than are other positions, from being eliminated because of the difficulty in dismantling and reconstructing a hierarchy of authority. Ideologically, the needs of an enterprise to preserve the self-motivation of its managers and to maintain the belief in the practical importance of the separation of mental and manual labor also shields managerial positions from unemployment. The findings confirmed these theoretical expectations as well as the expectation that the factors just described insulate higher-skill managerial positions from unemployment more than they insulate lower-skill managerial positions. However, the data show that—despite the general level of protection against unemployment and despite the general stability of managerial positions—managers (especially lower-skill ones) nonetheless are fired and are highly prone to quit without a job. This pattern of labor turnover within stable employment positions, rather than a pattern of instability of positions represented by layoffs, indicates that managerial unemployment (when it does occur) reflects the fact that managers remain susceptible to wage competition, evaluation of productivity, and other traditional labor-market pressures.

A second class trend concerns semi-autonomous positions. The findings confirmed that the semi-autonomous status of such positions (reflected in their insulation from direct and immediate evaluation of productivity, the application of professional standards of evaluation, and a high degree of job-specific training) curtails the level of unemployment, especially for the higher-skilled segment. Given this low propensity for unemployment, the findings on the types of unemployment indicate that higher-skill semi-autonomous positions have a pattern similar to that of managerial positions whereas lower-skill semi-autonomous positions have a pattern similar to that of the working class.

The third class trend concerns the pattern of unemployment facing the working class. As expected, the class position with the greatest vulnerability to market relations, the working class, evidences the greatest propensity to be

unemployed. But the effort to discern how such a propensity is distributed across fractions of the working class provided one of the most striking findings of the research: The popular belief that full wage-competition positions suffer the highest vulnerability to unemployment is not necessarily correct. It is true that working-class positions that are subject to competitive labor-market conditions receive lower wages and are subject to higher unemployment likelihoods than are non-working-class positions. But the findings reveal that the labor-market subordination of a full wage-competition segment is evidenced more in the types of unemployment (firings and quits without new jobs) than in the general level of unemployment. In fact, members of the strongest working-class segment, the union-bargaining segment, have the greatest unemployment propensity in the working class. But just as a lower propensity for the full wage-competition segment hides a more fundamental vulnerability to types of unemployment, the higher propensity for the union-bargaining segment reflects the presence rather than the absence of bargaining power. The very bargaining power that removes wages from competition for members of this segment limits the ability of their employers to adjust to decreased demand for output by lowering wages and, hence, prices for goods and services. As a result, the likelihood of unemployment is greater in this segment. Still, an examination of the types of unemployment comprising this higher propensity reveals that that same bargaining power that deters wage adjustments also increases the likelihood that the resulting unemployment will take the form of layoffs rather than firings.

In view of this and other findings, a second implication of the analysis challenges is the familiar notion that subordination in the labor market can be defined as the *exclusion* of members of a segment from participation in the workings of free competitive markets. Rather, the study of the class determinants of unemployment suggests that labor market subordination occurs precisely where competitive relations are most prominent. Because of the fundamental long-term ascendancy of capital embedded in the very nature of free and competitive labor markets, labor market vulnerability should be conceived as the presence rather than absence of such competitive dynamics. In turn, power in market relations should be viewed as the possession of resources which enable persons to exploit, circumvent, or otherwise shape competitive labor market relations in accord with their interests.

The third major implication of the analysis of class and unemployment concerns class struggle. The findings indicate that the development of a complex and variegated class structure is, at one and the same time, the development of capacities for struggle. In the case of unemployment,

differences in general levels and types of unemployment across the class structure reflect differences in the structural (embedded in the workplace) and organizational (purposefully constructed associations) capacities of classes to achieve favorable outcomes and ward off unfavorable ones. Instituting wage, employment, and unemployment differentials, for instance, augments control of the labor force by segmenting working-class interests. But, at the same time, such segmentation creates a more empowered segment which may eventually take a leading role in behalf of less empowered segments of the working class or become a standard to be emulated by them.

ECONOMIC SECTOR AND UNEMPLOYMENT

Chapter 5 studied the effect of a second structural determinant of unemployment, economic sector. It also investigated the interaction effect of economic sector and age by analyzing how age variation in unemployment differed by sector. While the discussion of class segment investigated the impact of job characteristics common to class positions across sectors, the treatment of economic sector examined the impact of firm characteristics common to employment positions across class segments. A number of conclusions may be derived from this research.

First, the analysis confirmed the general propositon that sectors differ significantly in their general unemployment propensity. The proportion of unemployed in the state, utility, and private nonprofit sectors is lower than in the competitive, oligopoly, construction, and farm sectors. Such differences were explained by the way in which the sectors differed in their vulnerability to declines in demand for their products, their vulnerability to traditional market mechanisms for adjusting to such declines in income, and their need to stabilize their labor forces.

A second set of findings, concerning the variation in types of unemployment across sectors, uncovered a more theoretically interesting conclusion. The concentration–employment instability hypothesis predicts that the output-adjusting oligopoly sector should have a higher general unemployment level than the competitive sector: Because the oligopoly sector meets a decline in demand by adjusting output rather than prices, oligopoly sector firms should evidence a greater fluctuation in employment. Yet the findings revealed that the overall unemployment propensities in the oligopoly and competitive sectors were virtually identical. A close scrutiny of the relative likelihoods of different types of unemployment, however, indicated

how the concentration–employment-instability hypothesis should be recast
so that it might retain its explanatory power. The analysis showed that the
likelihood of layoffs was greater in the oligopoly sector whereas the
likelihood of firings and quits was greater in the competitive sector. These
findings support the conclusion that firms facing competitive product markets
exhibit a more pronounced tendency to adjust to declines in product demand
by using free-market mechanisms of frictional or turnover forms of
unemployment (e.g., firings and quits) while firms participating in noncompetitive product markets have a greater tendency to adjust by using
layoffs. To the extent that such layoffs entail recall they represent a form of
unemployment in which an instability of positions coincides with a stability
of employment. As such, these results indicate one way to recast the
employment-instability hypothesis to account for the empirical finding that
the competitive and oligopoly sectors share similar unemployment propensities. Restated, the hypothesis becomes one about the relative incidence
of types of unemployment in a sector rather than about overall levels of
unemployment. The oligopoly sector is expected to evidence a greater
instability of positions and the competitive sector is expected to evidence a
greater instability of workers.

Finally, the analysis of the age–sector interaction effect on employment
status was examined in terms of its relation to the theory of internal labor
markets. In the oligopoly, construction, state, and utility sectors the presence
of age-based job and benefit ladders coincide with age-based insulation from
unemployment in general and from firings and quits in particular. In contrast,
the farm and competitive sectors provide a much weaker seniority-based
shelter from such turnover forms of unemployment. Thus, it appears that age-
based unemployment patterns constitute an important further dimension of
internal labor markets. Such patterns help establish a mutual interest
between employees and employers in job tenure and seniority and help elicit
compliance and creativity in the performance of work tasks.

BUSINESS CYCLE, UNEMPLOYMENT, AND ECONOMIC SECTOR

Chapter 6 investigated the averaged effect of the business cycle on
unemployment. It also analyzed how sectoral variation in unemployment
differs across periods of the business cycle. The business cycle, along with
class position and economic sector, is one further structural determinant of
vulnerability and power in a market economy. The findings indicated that
unemployment rises and falls in the expected directions over the business

cycle. But, as with the impact of class and economic sector, the impact of the business cycle on unemployment is such that types of unemployment are affected in different ways. The relative frequency of quits is directly related to the level of aggregate economic activity whereas involuntary unemployment, especially layoffs, is inversely related.

However, the more important analysis in the chapter studied how the vulnerability introduced by a recession is distributed in an uneven manner across economic sectors. The analysis of the interaction effect of business cycle, sector, and employment status revealed a striking variation among competitive, oligopoly, and state sectors in their relative frequencies of unemployment types over the business cycle. This analysis produced three major findings. First, the oligopoly sector fluctuates more in its unemployment likelihood over the business cycle than does the competitive sector. This finding was taken as support for the applicability of the rigid price–employment instability hypothesis to the oligopoly sector and the price-adjustment hypothesis to the competitive sector. Second, the point in the business cycle where the relative frequency of unemployment is greatest differs for the oligopoly and competitive sectors. In the competitive sector it occurs during the decline; in the oligopoly sector it occurs during the trough. This set of findings was interpreted as evidence for the concentration–rigid price–employment instability hypothesis. While the competitive sector appears to begin responding early to recessionary forces through price adjustments, the oligopoly sector manifests a tendency to continue increasing unemployment through the trough as would be expected from its output-rather than price-adjusting response to a recession. Third, the likelihood of unemployment in the state sector, relative to the competitive and oligopoly sectors, decreases during a recession. This pattern reflects the lower vulnerability of the state sector to declines in revenue during a recession, the ability to pursue deficit spending even when revenues are reduced substantially, and the increased demand for state services during a recession.

Taken together, these findings on the segmented structure of market vulnerability and power have implications for the depth and duration of the recession itself. Differences in cyclical vulnerability between the oligopoly and competitive sectors do more than merely reflect the lack of price adjustment in the concentrated sector: They also make a recession less responsive to natural tendencies toward reequilibrium, induce the conjunction of unemployment and inflation, and extend the recession until state intervention in the form of fiscal and monetary policy reverses the decline.

Thus, the research supports the concentration–employment instability hypothesis of how oligopoly responds to shifts of demand. Also, the findings indirectly support the hypothesis that market power contributes to recession-

ary inflation and constrains recovery. This second conclusion is consonant with other recent research on the coincidence of sustained recession, unemployment, and inflation that suggests that market relations no longer mediate transactions for a significant segment of the economy. Structural sources of vulnerability and power that affect economic sectors in different ways become translated into an increased general vulnerability of the economy to recession and once in a recession to the combined maladies of unemployment and inflation.

On the broadest level the aim of this research has been to explore the nature of unemployment and the segmented structure of advanced capitalism. It has done this by examining how different types of unemployment relate systematically to different classes, sectors, and periods of the business cycle. Combining insights derived from labor economics, industrial relations theory, and neo-Marxism, the research has demonstrated the importance of analyzing the structural determinants of unemployment as one avenue for deciphering the complex nature of contemporary capitalism. In doing so, the research has demonstrated a way to conceptualize unemployment that is more tractable than Marx's global notion of the industrial reserve army or conventional researchers' dependence on the aggregate measure. Finally, by examining how conditions of employment such as class, sector, and period in the business cycle affect the circumstances of unemployment, the research lends support to the relevant policy proposition that problems in the type and distribution of labor market outcomes derive in large part from the systematic workings of the economy itself and not simply from the personal capacities of individuals.

Appendix A
Technical Considerations:
Relation of Theory and Data,
Model Determination, and Odds Ratios

RELATION OF THEORY AND DATA

In this appendix, I review in a more technical way three methodological issues that were discussed in Chapter 3. The first concerns the appropriateness of using unadjusted Current Population Survey (CPS) unemployment data to measure the rate of job separation.[1] Although the CPS provides data on the *prevalence* of unemployment in the sample population, one aspect of the theory here focuses on the relative *incidence* of unemployment by class and sectors. The CPS survey provides cross-sectional data on the composition of the labor force in unemployment during the survey week. Because unemployment spells vary in duration the cross-sectional snapshot yields a picture of the employment status of the labor force rather than the number of occurrences of different types of unemployment. Since the theory contends that the variation in the relative incidence of types of unemployment captures aspects of class and sector vulnerability and power, this inadequacy of the data becomes especially significant. Equation (1) shows the relationship

[1] I am grateful to Aage Sørensen for his kind assistance in the development of the argument in this section.

between the measured proportion of unemployment and the rate of job separation:

$$P_1 = r_1/(r_2 + r_2),$$
(1)

where P_1 is the ratio of job separations to the labor force, r_1 is the true separation rate and r_2 is the true rate of reemployment.

The ratio of job separations to the labor force, P_1, is the dependent variable used in the analysis whereas r_1 is the true variable of interest for investigating arguments about job separation rates.

It is possible to transform data on P_1 into a measure of r_1 if the mean duration of unemployment spells is known, however. Solving Eq. (1) for this separation rate (r_1) we get

$$r_1 = \frac{P_1}{1 - P_1} \cdot r_2$$
(2)

$$r_1 = \frac{P_1}{1 - P_1} \cdot \frac{1}{d}$$
(3)

since the reemployment rate (r_2) is the inverse of the mean duration of job separation, assuming that the reemployment rate is constant and identical for all individuals.

Although the analysis presented in the preceding chapters does not adjust for this discontinuity between the measured prevalence and actual incidence of unemployment, the theory of job separation rates is adequately tested for two reasons. First, because log-linear analysis does not require that the mean duration of different types of unemployment be similar, only that the duration does not vary significantly across classes and sectors. Second, analysis of variance shows that in fact the duration only modestly varies across these segments.

First, the strongest case for the discontinuity between theory and data being inconsequential would be if the mean durations of different types of unemployment varied neither among themselves nor across classes and sectors. In this instance, the measured prevalence, although inaccurate in absolute numbers, would nevertheless approximate the relative incidence of unemployment across classes and sectors. This adjustment produces an approximation of the true incidence because the duration information provided by the CPS is censored, that is, the durations reported are not for completed spells of job separation.

The findings in Table A.1 show that the mean durations for the types of job separation vary greatly. They range from 3.48 weeks for workers on

TABLE A.1
Analysis of Variance of Duration of Unemployment by Unemployment Types

Unemployment type	Mean	Standard deviation	N^a
Temporary layoff	3.4794	5.4746	818
Indefinite layoff	13.1374	11.5313	3280
Firing	17.5439	19.0910	7582
Quit	12.4922	16.3263	2072
Total	14.8953	16.5719	13752

Significance: $p < .001$
[a]These numbers are approximately 1.25 times greater than the numbers reported elsewhere because they have not been deflated to adjust for nonrandomness in the sample. The significance tests are thus biased against rejecting the hypothesis that there are no differences in duration between categories.

temporary layoff to 17.54 weeks for workers who are fired. Even so, if the mean durations are constant across classes and sectors, the findings derived from the log-linear analysis remain unbiased. This is because log-linear parameters estimate the relative occurrence of events. For instance, the shorter duration of temporary layoffs and the longer duration of firings indicate that the actual incidence of the former is underestimated and the actual incidence of the latter is overestimated. But, as long as these biases are constant across classes and sectors, then the relative employment status frequencies summarized in the log-linear parameters approximate the true relative incidences.

To test whether differences in duration occur across classes and sectors, an analysis of variance was computed. For each type of unemployment the duration of unemployment was decomposed by classes and then by sectors. Where the F-test associated with a particular breakdown of unemployment type and segment is insignificant, it is correct to argue that the log-linear parameters are unbiased.

These results enable us to conclude cautiously that the bias in the parameters is generally weak and that the analysis conducted here is not seriously marred by the failure to weight unemployment by duration. Of the eight tests of significance reported in Table A.2—one for each of the four types of unemployment first across classes and then across sectors—five are insignificant at the .05 level and six at the .01 level.

Of the four tests of variation of duration over classes, two are strongly insignificant; one is marginally insignificant at the .05 level; and one is significant at the .05 but not at the .01 level. The marginally insignificant

TABLE A.2
Analysis of Variance of Duration of Unemployment by Unemployment Types by Class and by Sector

Class segment	Mean	Standard deviation	N^a
A. Temporary Layoffs by Class			
Self-employed	6.0982	5.2339	10
Higher-skill semi-autonomous	3.9805	4.2235	8
Lower-skill semi-autonomous	1.8456	1.2955	11
Higher-skill managerial	3.8880	4.2734	23
Lower-skill managerial	5.5640	8.6065	15
Union-bargaining working-class	3.3560	5.3134	527
Skill-bargaining working-class	3.5533	4.9201	28
Partial wage-competition working-class	3.4815	4.8690	80
Full wage-competition working-class	3.5435	6.6335	117
Total	3.4794	5.4813	818

Significance: $p = .6464$

B. Indefinite layoffs by Class			
Self-employed	12.0225	10.3070	29
Higher-skill semi-autonomous	14.4409	16.5214	41
Lower-skill semi-autonomous	15.6465	11.1398	45
Higher-skill managerial	12.1361	8.8108	83
Lower-skill managerial	13.5978	9.2788	73
Union-bargaining working-class	13.3267	11.9662	2088
Skill-bargaining working-class	14.1719	12.4135	115
Partial wage-competition working-class	12.7837	9.5468	437
Full wage-competition working class	11.9310	11.2583	369
Total	13.1374	11.5285	3280

Significance: $p = .2926$

C. Firings by Class			
Self-employed	14.6640	15.4559	94
Higher-skill semi-autonomous	19.6725	21.2742	246
Lower-skill semi-autonomous	20.4023	19.8449	156
Higher-skill managerial	21.2341	21.7922	263
Lower-skill managerial	18.2149	20.6295	414
Union-bargaining working-class	17.5843	18.9705	3410
Skill-bargaining working-class	16.3004	17.5342	245
Partial wage-competition working-class	17.0730	19.0349	932
Full wage-competition working-class	16.8085	18.4677	1824
Total	17.5439	19.0717	7582

Significance: $p = .0029$

D. Quits by Class			
Self-employed	12.6770	17.4970	61
Higher-skill semi-autonomous	15.9423	19.2182	54

(continued)

TABLE A.2 *(continued)*

Class segment	Mean	Standard deviation	N^a
D. Quits by Class (continued)			
Lower-skill semi-autonomous	11.6329	12.7278	58
Higher-skill managerial	12.1844	14.5243	79
Lower-skill managerial	11.1490	13.6342	137
Union-bargaining working-class	12.7902	17.2768	687
Skill-bargaining working-class	19.7271	19.7190	49
Partial wage-competition working-class	12.6982	16.3326	233
Full wage-competition working-class	11.7243	15.6108	715
Total	12.4922	16.2984	2072

Significance: $p = .0580$

	E. Temporary Layoffs by Sector		
Competitive	3.7058	5.8460	239
Construction	4.3586	7.2022	206
Farm	2.9294	3.0887	18
Oligopoly	2.8487	3.8745	332
State	3.5040	4.1700	14
Utility	1.4442	.7145	2
Private nonprofit	1.5700	1.0918	6
Total	3.4794	5.4565	818

Significance: $p = .0775$

	F. Indefinite Layoffs by Sector		
Competitive	12.0349	11.7074	734
Construction	13.0382	9.3600	1172
Farm	13.1556	6.1775	70
Oligopoly	13.8042	13.3776	1203
State	14.7860	12.2515	80
Utility	13.0285	2.6836	6
Private nonprofit	12.4195	10.9419	14
Total	13.1374	11.5198	3280

Significance: $p = .0511$

	G. Firings by Sector		
Competitive	17.4846	19.8027	2957
Construction	15.1237	15.2636	1769
Farm	12.6238	12.5598	226
Oligopoly	19.6458	21.0176	2040
State	19.7109	19.4101	424
Utility	14.6241	20.3223	25
Private Nonprofit	20.5911	20.3555	142
Total	17.5439	19.0003	7582

Significance: $p < .001$

(continued)

TABLE A.2 *(continued)*

Class segment		Mean	Standard deviation	N^a
H. Quits by Sector				
Competitive		11.2156	14.5539	1064
Construction		10.7237	13.1295	205
Farm		11.3439	16.3989	73
Oligopoly		13.8992	18.0914	513
State		18.6370	22.4643	158
Utility		31.8221	30.1294	4
Private Nonprofit		13.1580	14.9730	57
	Total	12.4922	16.1881	2072
Significance: $p < .001$				

^{a}See note a in Table A.1.

difference is for quits; the significant differences is for firings. Further one-way analyses of variance reported in Table A.3, however, show that for these two cases the significance is due to the effect of one category of class fractions. Comparing Table A.2D with Table A.3B, we find that when we omit the skill-bargaining working-class segment from the class-by-duration analysis for quits the variation in duration becomes more strongly insignificant. It is noteworthy that this working-class segment has the smallest number of quits and the largest standard deviation in duration. Similarly, comparing Table A.2C with Table A.3A, we discover that excluding the higher-skill managers (the class fraction with the largest standard deviation in duration) the variation by segment in duration of firings becomes insignificant.

Turning to the four tests of variation of duration over sector, Table A.2 shows that one is strongly insignificant, one is marginally insignificant at the .05 level, and two are significant. The marginally insignificant relationship in unemployment duration is for indefinite layoffs, whereas the significant relationships are for firings and quits. Omitting only the state sector in the table of duration for indefinite layoffs (compare Table A.2F with Table A.3C), the differences among sectors becomes more strongly insignificant. This is not the case, however, for the relationship of duration across sectors for firings and quits. Even excluding the farm sector in the table for firings (Table A.3D) and excluding the utility sector in the table for quits (Table A.3E) differences in duration among sectors does not become insignificant. It can be seen that differences in mean durations across sectors for these two

TABLE A.3
Analysis of Variance of Duration by Unemployment Types by Class and by Sector
(with Omitted Categories)

Class segment	Mean	Standard deviation	N^a
A. Firings by Class *(Excluding Higher-Skill Managers)*			
Self-employed	14.6640	15.4559	94
Higher-skill semi-autonomous	19.6725	21.2742	246
Lower-skill semi-autonomous	20.4023	19.8449	156
Lower-skill managerial	18.2149	20.6295	414
Union-bargaining working-class	17.5843	18.9705	3410
Skill-bargaining working-class	16.3004	17.5342	245
Partial wage-competition working-class	17.0730	19.0349	932
Full wage-competition working-class	19.8085	18.4677	1824
Total	17.4113	18.9670	7319
Significance $p = .0664$			
B. Quits by Class *(Excluding Skill-Bargaining Working-Class)*			
Self-employed	12.6770	17.4970	61
Higher-skill semi-autonomous	15.9423	19.2182	54
Lower-skill semi-autonomous	11.6329	12.7278	58
Higher-skill managerial	12.1844	14.5243	79
Lower-skill managerial	11.1490	13.6342	137
Union-bargaining working-class	12.7902	17.2768	687
Partial wage-competition working-class	12.6982	16.3326	233
Full wage-competition working class	11.7243	15.6108	715
Total	12.3166	16.2079	2023
Significance: $p = .6313$			
C. Indefinite Layoffs by Sector *(Excluding State Sector)*			
Competitive	12.0349	11.7074	734
Construction	13.0382	9.3600	1172
Farm	13.1556	6.1775	70
Oligopoly	13.8042	13.3776	1203
Utility	13.0285	2.6836	6
Private nonprofit	12.4195	10.9419	14
Total	13.0959	11.5010	3200
Significance: $p = .0540$			
D. Firings by Sector *(Excluding Farm Sector)*			
Competitive	17.4846	19.8027	2957
Construction	15.1237	15.2636	1769

(continued)

TABLE A.3 *(continued)*

Class segment		Mean	Standard deviation	N^a
D. Firings by Sector				
(Excluding Farm Sector)(continued)				
Oligopoly		19.6458	21.0176	2040
State		19.7109	19.4101	424
Utility		14.6241	20.3223	25
Private nonprofit		20.5911	20.3555	142
	Total	17.6950	19.1633	7356
Significance: $p < .001$				
E. Quits by Sector				
(Excluding Utility Sector)				
Competitive		11.2156	14.5539	1064
Construction		10.7237	13.1295	205
Farm		11.3439	16.3989	73
Oligopoly		13.8992	18.0914	513
State		18.6370	22.4643	158
Private nonprofit		13.1580	14.9730	57
	Total	12.4571	16.1615	2068
Significance: $p < .001$				

[a]See note *a* in Table A.1.

types of job separation are not great, however, especially among the competitive, oligopoly, and state sectors.

Although it is important for subsequent research directly to weight unemployment types by their duration in order to estimate the flow of job separation from classes and sectors,[2] we conclude that approximating such flows by CPS data does not seriously distort the log-linear analyses and that the data do allow for an appropriate test of the theory of job separation.

---

[2]It is possible to develop an appropriate weighting scheme to transform the CPS data on prevalence of unemployment types to estimate the flow of job separation without substantially altering the analysis. First, each case of unemployment is divided by its duration in weeks. If the duration is less than 50 weeks the case is divided by that number. If the duration is 50 weeks or longer, the case is divided by 50. The comparative category of the employed is weighted by dividing each employment case by 50 and then adding to the employment category each unemployment case divided by 50 minus the weeks in the current spell of unemployment. This produces a table with entries representing person-weeks in types of unemployment and employment. Inflating the table by a factor of 50 to return it to its original number of cases results in a distribution of the incidence of person-time in years in the various categories of employment status. This final table can then be analyzed by the same log-linear techniques employed in the present research.

DETERMINATION OF THE MODEL

In log-linear analysis, the object is to approximate closely the observed frequency distribution of cases in a multidimensional contingency table through the specification of a theoretically relevant model. The model produces an array of expected frequencies for each cell in the table and provides a measure of how well the modeled frequency distribution compares to the distribution of variables within the observed contingency table. A saturated model, which imposes all one-way and all possible bivariate and multivariate effects, simply reproduces the observed distribution. The usefulness of the technique, however, resides in its ability to derive expected frequency distributions from more parsimonious models. The technique contrasts these derived expected distributions with the observed distribution and calculates a likelihood-ratio χ^2 that summarizes the goodness of fit of the modeled with the observed distribution.

The logic of model building follows from the aim of determining the presence or absence of bivariate and multivariate relationships among the variables. The simplest baseline model includes constraints only for one-way univariate effects. Bivariate and multivariate interactions can then be added to the model in a hierarchical order until the disparity between the modeled, expected distribution and the observed distribution can be reduced no further. In the process of determining the most adequate model, a low likelihood-ratio χ^2 indicates the close approximation of the modeled to the observed distribution.

Also, two or more models of expected frequencies can be contrasted in order to test for the presence or absence of particular bivariate relationships between an independent and dependent variables, for instance, or of multivariate interactions where the bivariate (or highest-order) interaction varies over categories of a third or fourth variable. In testing models against each other a high likelihood-ratio χ^2 indicates a large degree of contrast between the two models and therefore the statistical significance of the added interactions.[3]

---

[3]It may seen that the large sample size should produce higher chi-square values in the first panel of Table 3.2. But two important considerations come into play. First, the table size of 40,320 cells offsets any inflation due to the large sample size. Second, precisely to reduce the likelihood that I would find significant differences between models that were simply artifacts of the sample size, I deflated the original sample by a factor of .75. If anything, therefore, given the number of cells and the .75 deflation of the sample, the chi-square values remain quite high. Moreover, for purposes of discerning significant differences between models, what matters is the change in chi-square relative to change in degrees of freedom, not the absolute level of the chi-square values themselves.

ODDS RATIOS

As stated in Chapter 3, the parameters derived from a fitted model can be used to estimate the relationships included in that model. The tau-parameters measure the propensity of cases to be distributed to a particular cell of an n-dimensional table relative to all the other cells. These tau-parameters, although meaningful in their own right, can be geometrically transformed to create various odd-ratio comparisons within and across dimensions of the table (cf. Daymont and Kaufman, 1979; Page, 1977). Four types of such odds ratios are used in presenting the analysis: within-category, cross-category, comparative, and generalized odds ratios. Within-category odds ratios calculate the odds of a worker within a single category of an independent variable being in one category of employment status versus another. Such within-category odds ratios are calculated according to the formula:

$$\left(\frac{T_{i_1j}}{T_{i_2j}}\right)^{J/J-1},$$

where T is the tau-parameter for the ith category of employment status in the jth category of the dependent variable. The quotient is raised to the $J/J-1$ power, where J is the number of categories in the independent variable.

Cross-category odds ratios calculate the odds of a worker in a single category of employment status being in one category versus another category of the independent variable. These cross-category odds ratios are calculated according to the formula:

$$\left(\frac{T_{ij_1}}{T_{ij_2}}\right)^{I/I-1},$$

where T is the tau-parameter for the ith category of employment status in a jth category of the independent variable. The quotient is raised to the $I/I-1$ power, where I is the number of categories in employment status.

Comparative odds ratios calculate the odds of a worker in one category of the independent variable versus another category of the same independent variable being in one category of employment status versus another. Comparative odds ratios are calculated according to the formula:

$$\left(\frac{T_{i_1j_1}}{T_{i_2j_1}}\right) \cdot \left(\frac{T_{i_2j_2}}{T_{i_1j_2}}\right),$$

where T is the tau-parameter for the ith category of employment status and the jth category of the independent variable.

Finally, generalized odds ratios are derived to facilitate the interpretation of three-way interactions. Whereas all the information needed to make such interpretations is contained in the two-way and three-way tau-parameters, the two sets of parameters are not easily related. If the parameters are used directly, the three-way parameters measure how, within each level of a third variable, the two-way relationship varies. A three-way effect greater than 1.0 means that within the particular level of the breakdown variable, the effect of the independent variable on employment status is greater than the effect averaged over the levels (i.e., in the two-way parameters). A three-way parameter less than 1.0 means that within the particular level, the effect is less than the averaged effect. By calculating generalized odds ratios, it is possible to discern more directly the variation over levels of the breakdown variable in the relationship between the other independent variable and the dependent variable. Because the three-way generalized odds ratios are calculated as a function of the two-way generalized odds ratios the three-way odds ratios have values that vary around the values of the comparable two-way odds ratios representing the averaged effect.

The two-way generalized odds ratio estimates the propensity for cases to be distributed to a particular cell relative to the distribution in *all other cells in the two-way table*. Two-way generalized odds ratios are calculated according to the formula:

$$T_{ij}^{IJ/(I-1)(J-1)},$$

where T_{ij} is the tau-parameter for the ith category of employment status and the jth category of independent variable. The tau-parameter is raised to the $IJ/(I-1)(J-1)$ power, where I is the number of categories of employment status and J is the number of categories of the independent variable.

Three-way generalized odds ratios are calculated from the appropriate two-way and three-way tau-parameters. These odds ratios measure for each level of a second, breakdown independent variable the relative propensity of cases to be in a particular cell of employment status and a first independent variable in contrast to *all other cells within the level of the breakdown variable*. Three-way generalized odds ratios are calculated according to the formula:

$$(T_{ij} \cdot T_{ijk})^{IJ/(I-1)(J-1)},$$

where T_{ij} is the two-way tau-parameter for the ith category of employment status and the jth category of the first independent variable and where T_{ijk} is

the three-way tau-parameter for the ith category of employment status, the jth category of the first independent variable, and the kth category of the breakdown variable. The product is raised to the $IJ/(I-1)(J-1)$ power, where I is the number of categories of employment status and J is the number of categories in the first independent variable.

Appendix B
Census Occupation Categories
Composing Class Segments

1960 Census code[a]	Number[b]	1960 Census code	Number	1960 Census code	Number	1960 Census code	Number
Self-employed		285	1.462	520	3.107	973	1.608
0	42.809	291	938.282	521	1.573	985	26.959
10	1.413	292	902.479	524	3.037		
12	1.460	301	5.424	525	2.153	Semi-autonomous	
13	13.621	310	4.438	530	1.363	higher-skill	
14	17.126	312	0.791	535	10.341	0	461.689
20	14.484	313	0.671	545	10.907	10	13.739
21	1.488	321	1.382	630	0.665	13	30.752
22	14.643	343	0.689	632	16.286	14	95.202
23	2.088	345	2.149	634	0.623	20	22.164
71	89.048	353	0.747	635	0.649	21	104.261
72	5.103	370	6.972	641	2.206	23	215.891
74	3.596	380	4.241	650	19.544	30	13.620
75	3.565	381	2.683	651	2.289	31	3.40
81	0.664	383	14.046	653	2.784	32	21.480
82	2.291	385	57.874	654	1.374	34	13.228
83	0.708	390	30.607	674	3.705	35	12.63
84	1.379	393	30.371	675	9.270	40	22.77
85	2.205	395	1.518	685	0.695	41	3.13
91	0.824	396	66.341	692	0.614	42	17.91
93	4.957	397	45.623	693	0.554	43	18.45
101	3.388	398	2.964	694	4.981	45	11.77
104	4.255	401	9.625	695	1.470	50	8.57
105	155.821	402	5.053	704	3.270	53	75.38
120	41.114	405	35.892	705	0.705	54	54.32
131	0.742	410	6.313	714	23.499	60	36.91
134	1.404	411	150.346	715	97.096	71	7.78
150	1.535	413	3.838	721	7.153	72	75.29
152	10.806	414	3.573	775	31.990	74	289.94
154	0.616	415	0.693	812	0.665	75	77.58
160	15.034	420	1.347	813	0.651	80	83.28
161	11.395	421	21.263	814	82.170	81	45.16
162	152.457	425	15.907	815	9.498	82	175.00
163	1.461	434	3.473	820	2.106	83	320.30
170	5.096	451	7.761	821	2.288	84	154.58
173	1.538	465	4.344	824	5.091	85	218.14
180	6.772	470	11.833	825	6.984	90	35.05
181	2.169	472	77.398	830	0.685	91	18.55
183	0.766	473	2.035	834	4.592	92	39.63
184	2.292	474	20.198	835	1.399	93	143.43
192	2.843	480	35.568	843	20.468	105	103.57
193	5.133	490	0.689	851	0.870	120	130.56
194	11.684	494	1.406	853	0.679	131	13.21
195	9.181	495	107.203	875	1.623	134	28.35
200	1459.724	503	0.645	890	0.684	135	7.06
248	3.423	504	0.824	905	5.604	140	30.93
249	0.645	505	10.516	962	12.941	145	6.31
251	4.519	510	30.490	964	15.774	152	1.45
262	10.432	514	9.126	970	30.770	160	59.14
265	2.134	515	10.746	971	2.073	162	104.55

1960 Census code	Number	1960 Census code	Number	1960 Census code	Number	1960 Census code	Number
165	33.078	248	225.155	524	19.809	450	126.809
170	33.216	262	40.888	525	155.911	451	12.881
172	61.576	265	48.124	530	226.358	461	11.278
173	21.916	270	244.278	545	103.382	470	108.718
174	19.865	280	24.913	602	4.345	495	293.423
175	2.140	285	146.010	603	13.701	514	41.522
183	542.815	291	1115.427	604	31.517	601	5.234
194	8.221	901	29.709	605	33.926	615	13.507
				610	12.453	814	71.225
Semi-autonomous lower-skill		Working class union bargaining		612	32.977	971	9.045
12	62.746	252	44.981	613	6.583		
70	1.948	323	297.136	614	18.622	Working class partial wage-competition	
101	10.111	340	247.541	620	20.992	314	71.210
102	6.367	352	4.640	621	5.719	343	358.004
103	41.603	353	14.660	630	32.922	350	409.937
104	24.807	401	87.654	631	500.634	354	66.337
111	16.349	402	5.562	634	1.338	444	21.872
130	9.961	403	35.069	635	6.006	641	185.976
150	7.156	404	17.214	640	67.383	650	520.674
151	0.743	405	189.741	643	352.102	704	103.777
154	136.901	411	800.183	653	200.051	705	31.254
161	41.414	413	68.818	670	69.316	714	144.378
163	33.117	414	165.627	671	13.458	962	11.679
164	39.911	415	161.398	672	11.427	973	178.163
171	67.247	421	463.387	675	169.674		
180	116.462	423	6.332	685	201.516	Working class full wage-competition	
181	35.385	425	331.204	690	15.011	302	23.843
182	240.719	431	7.262	691	9.206	303	1.976
184	94.635	435	18.408	692	51.615	305	32.327
185	74.164	452	89.725	693	263.814	310	118.279
190	169.804	453	395.501	694	157.755	312	119.728
191	284.232	454	56.901	701	42.703	313	26.684
192	89.343	460	24.214	703	31.444	320	18.439
193	29.766	465	539.094	712	75.498	324	54.661
195	787.809	471	177.643	713	47.021	325	177.471
260	105.134	475	33.970	715	1735.063	333	54.761
		480	1465.503	721	556.888	342	25.157
Managerial higher-skill		491	96.184	775	4344.793	345	7.977
249	44.650	492	37.432	831	27.939	351	1.385
251	2.860	493	13.337	841	130.163	360	21.952
253	48.039	502	38.256	850	175.784	370	1270.032
275	47.763	503	32.353	965	59.500	380	29.149
292	3114.896	504	0.930	985	2933.976	382	2.921
430	1501.477	505	27.609			383	26.133
		510	333.741	Working class skill bargaining		385	301.787
Managerial lower-skill		512	72.392	301	179.487	390	44.726
222	23.085	513	40.120	321	76.862	393	93.949
		520	195.298	410	53.836	395	16.413
		523	92.597	434	16.828		

(continued)

1960 Census code	Number	1960 Census code	Number	1970 Census code^c	Number	1970 Census code	Number
396	881.438	970	95.565	Self-employed		150	2.94
397	1070.801			1	237.200	151	0.67
398	81.861			2	71.208	152	9.60
420	25.874			3	7.056	153	2.07
424	9.371			4	1.816	161	21.65
472	819.783			6	0.820	163	18.38
473	92.703			11	16.700	173	5.59
474	79.019			12	14.713	174	2.80
490	6.995			13	13.482	180	15.7
494	24.245			14	8.784	181	66.34
515	5.775			21	6.158	183	29.38
521	2.006			22	1.647	184	14.59
535	33.871			23	22.337	185	6.67
632	559.192			25	2.286	190	107.94
642	22.672			31	548.327	191	0.74
651	2.184			32	1.711	192	8.75
652	29.777			33	4.496	194	9.30
654	2.607			36	1.584	195	7.0
673	14.388			42	1.268	203	31.18
674	84.326			44	1.350	205	37.9
695	31.681			45	1.389	212	7.25
720	20.759			51	15.748	216	46.96
801	11.951			52	0.217	220	5.8
803	0.724			53	0.787	221	5.61
804	18.038			55	0.671	222	0.64
810	156.532			56	14.788	225	3.8
812	46.207			61	60.979	230	472.91
813	50.533			62	289.510	231	10.1
815	109.820			63	59.288	233	8.1
821	1.463			64	74.631	235	1.5
823	1.333			65	439.702	240	2.7
824	92.029			71	23.402	247	3051.7
825	245.038			72	37.356	248	2295.0
830	76.817			73	0.659	260	18.4
832	37.752			75	4.154	261	10.1
834	716.569			76	4.754	262	3.9
835	203.450			80	0.777	264	61.0
842	7.684			81	0.596	265	285.3
843	34.642			83	1.349	266	125.4
851	321.624			85	2.234	270	282.8
852	3.902			86	36.067	271	39.9
853	361.238			90	5.194	281	20.6
854	38.316			91	18.451	282	268.7
860	6.361			92	1.008	283	146.1
874	8.770			93	17.289	284	101.3
875	81.658			95	1.788	285	11.9
890	181.912			100	2.351	303	0.3
902	712.723			101	0.592	305	21.9
960	78.730			141	2.526	310	5.3
964	185.165			145	55.938	312	0.8

1970 Census code	Number	1970 Census code	Number	1970 Census code	Number	1970 Census code	Number
313	2.778	473	421.742	645	2.396	964	10.924
314	2.087	475	1.513	650	0.577	Semi-autonomous	
315	3.356	480	13.333	651	13.964	higher-skill	
321	20.618	481	47.593	652	3.979		
323	0.725	482	60.059	653	0.878	1	2052.692
326	6.514	484	6.024	656	0.750	2	182.667
330	0.877	485	114.851	661	1.489	3	581.354
332	0.835	492	70.085	662	12.724	4	351.637
333	0.917	495	1.832	663	7.534	5	62.685
343	0.852	501	2.268	665	1.484	6	215.675
344	0.704	502	0.750	673	1.868	10	179.717
363	12.513	503	0.912	680	67.125	11	594.928
372	1.500	506	10.927	681	0.634	12	1133.618
374	0.842	510	394.149	690	21.212	13	652.255
375	0.761	512	34.946	692	0.851	14	762.506
376	4.568	515	3.614	694	38.459	15	66.289
381	1.843	516	14.193	695	3.539	20	17.806
394	6.699	520	23.499	701	1.362	21	52.645
401	11.998	522	146.464	703	12.457	22	144.095
402	15.838	530	6.334	705	112.950	23	513.322
403	18.439	534	85.365	706	0.719	30	51.731
404	0.927	535	11.734	711	1.479	31	679.530
405	0.880	543	27.301	714	75.970	34	28.652
410	148.640	545	2.241	715	525.994	35	16.560
412	41.230	546	3.688	740	5.500	44	124.563
413	62.413	550	3.977	752	67.408	45	410.957
415	760.851	551	10.914	753	17.058	51	77.778
420	83.426	552	2.208	754	18.996	52	22.173
421	33.988	560	28.193	755	173.929	53	74.928
422	18.060	561	5.886	761	130.683	54	8.622
424	3.808	563	40.410	762	8.561	61	2.056
425	17.139	575	19.880	763	1.719	62	74.479
426	25.841	601	7.110	764	12.164	63	11 726
430	131.457	602	8.418	770	0.782	64	272.562
433	1.028	603	2.348	780	29.233	65	630.403
435	3.253	604	0.817	785	4.799	71	1.521
436	88.782	612	3.170	801	4514.145	72	28.547
440	21.372	613	2.637	824	28.150	73	1.625
441	16.889	614	24.950	902	48.923	86	824.294
443	22.703	615	47.618	903	27.604	90	81.227
444	0.677	620	0.760	910	87.212	91	275.423
445	12.794	621	2.846	911	0.751	92	0.739
446	0.644	623	20.684	912	38.718	93	141.723
452	2.843	631	23.389	914	3.015	94	5.946
453	43.972	633	7.038	915	1.029	95	38.665
456	0.273	635	4.634	916	3.570	96	10.347
461	18.330	640	5.225	926	0.752	101	101.209
470	82.070	641	1.510	942	0.131	102	13.907
471	6.949	643	3.554	944	0.675	103	18.799
472	111.124	644	15.281	962	5.638	104	86.061

1970 Census code	Number	1970 Census code	Number	1970 Census code	Number	1970 Census code	Number
105	65.540	76	182.100	211	0.692	502	395.91
110	55.068	80	180.357	216	167.653	503	207.19
111	70.466	81	2.496	221	102.083	511	7.62
112	105.429	82	5.028	222	1076.473	512	24.46
113	61.811	83	83.512	224	94.054	514	143.03
114	79.616	84	5.250	225	578.945	515	125.49
115	53.458	85	162.523	230	772.391	516	6.35
116	45.393	100	431.620	231	846.416	520	101.96
120	57.862	141	133.076	247	7799.656	521	4.33
121	29.775	142	892.804	802	113.952	522	1399.73
122	59.389	143	19.871	821	109.706	523	75.88
123	109.509	144	2493.018			525	105.36
124	45.235	150	129.873	Working class union bargaining		530	486.28
125	37.702	151	274.341	226	128.372	533	63.67
126	97.794	153	690.092	331	941.050	535	608.48
130	46.485	154	41.468	334	135.848	536	23.88
132	16.830	155	44.931	361	790.266	540	63.84
133	19.154	161	258.063	384	14.205	545	696.34
134	11.827	162	688.103	385	64.042	550	336.93
135	89.738	163	235.758	392	132.946	551	115.11
140	127.243	171	119.437	402	229.452	552	1161.73
145	153.270	172	6.039	403	17.283	554	267.35
152	993.369	173	37.860	404	163.810	560	102.82
156	9.814	180	53.609	405	46.387	561	674.32
164	88.522	182	0.729	410	550.994	562	31.36
165	0.863	191	109.785	411	21.276	571	64.62
170	23.199	192	222.431	412	392.618	572	11.09
174	311.945	193	87.966	415	3485.801	575	206.37
175	11.633	194	110.198	416	53.200	601	158.54
181	33.343	213	78.239	421	296.636	602	2232.20
183	333.101	215	360.115	422	499.468	603	32.10
184	361.307			424	657.193	604	123.68
185	82.867	Managerial higher-skill		430	1992.402	610	1374.50
190	204.537	202	1443.711	431	111.398	611	93.43
195	232.317	203	46.335	433	409.530	612	673.15
		210	166.150	434	17.033	615	250.14
Semi-autonomous lower-skill		212	331.759	436	1147.356	621	348.88
24	38.008	220	548.872	442	52.571	622	266.51
25	155.895	223	312.524	446	88.651	624	48.34
26	2.428	233	1171.006	454	379.051	626	19.43
32	103.213	235	240.872	455	196.367	631	764.07
33	14.632	240	649.918	456	49.235	633	286.09
36	49.198	248	8748.945	461	1821.142	634	17.99
42	48.541	441	5252.668	462	45.229	640	689.01
43	26.388			471	482.204	641	361.22
55	420.021	Managerial lower-skill		481	3008.368	642	190.66
56	769.219	201	61.179	486	199.960	643	1016.69
74	9.257	205	306.369	491	54.878	644	536.34
75	75.726			495	117.717	650	221.88
						651	488.29

Column 1

1970 Census code	Number
652	436.740
653	203.163
656	454.182
661	91.518
666	311.752
680	2384.695
681	124.592
690	3807.542
692	935.377
694	2013.155
695	561.496
701	7.539
704	45.466
706	1385.345
710	44.514
712	203.036
713	198.925
715	6299.055
753	2912.551
760	180.784
780	937.705
785	1387.084
931	7.871
934	43.611
935	10.148
943	73.902
953	3.146
961	828.285

Working class skill bargaining

code	Number
326	298.820
363	85.400
413	214.385
423	19.841
426	91.818
440	45.111
444	4.757
445	121.298
452	489.127
453	102.268
470	608.530
474	19.284
475	223.132
482	467.174
483	62.478
510	1195.602
531	12.060
534	274.069
542	11.113

Column 2

1970 Census code	Number
543	51.883
635	126.674
763	17.445

Working class Partial wage-competition

code	Number
315	250.593
374	1497.060
381	1524.510
390	305.364
450	75.041
660	64.909
662	452.113
663	156.340
664	113.349
703	731.166
705	2193.052
714	495.855
751	3417.185
752	45.015
754	340.151
762	2619.208
764	648.362
770	821.553

Working class full wage-competition

code	Number
260	192.479
261	4.219
262	15.223
264	95.008
265	1352.948
266	178.987
270	580.642
271	268.055
281	1325.698
282	2439.101
283	2494.738
284	1331.882
285	341.925
301	145.894
303	76.045
305	631.954
310	519.662
311	6.454
312	255.575
313	112.530
314	187.499

Column 3

1970 Census code	Number
320	34.102
321	683.830
323	549.082
325	159.437
330	125.292
332	301.112
333	225.962
341	19.725
342	6.205
343	516.642
344	35.788
345	94.424
350	9.780
355	62.807
360	207.569
362	19.258
364	56.887
370	5.196
371	2.329
372	84.534
375	306.490
376	32.947
382	111.123
383	4.269
391	158.985
394	663.252
395	415.992
401	54.381
420	159.427
425	114.026
435	15.774
443	66.767
472	526.506
473	3143.177
480	228.939
484	223.301
485	379.491
492	671.954
501	16.283
504	2.486
505	7.440
506	123.354
546	14.740
563	135.667
605	54.335
613	4.713
614	162.614
620	88.415
623	1776.047
625	37.252

Column 4

1970 Census code	Number
630	69.937
636	1.118
645	126.029
665	41.338
670	87.273
671	48.626
672	224.734
673	55.515
674	323.470
711	115.874
740	172.972
750	374.150
755	925.665
761	273.896
822	2779.147
901	7.938
902	1188.372
903	4245.773
910	468.003
911	517.089
912	1500.330
913	632.262
914	255.962
915	342.862
916	439.667
921	2.118
922	123.248
923	4.455
924	0.551
925	553.784
926	51.303
932	83.659
944	0.776
950	126.426
952	11.486
954	31.848
960	43.952
962	1558.641
963	16.846
964	1748.045
965	188.141

(continued)

[a]Current Population Surveys for 1969 and 1970 used 1960 Census occupation co

[b]Numbers represent the counts from the weighted and deflated sample.

[c]Current Population Surveys for 1971-1978 used 1970 Census occupation codes

Appendix C
Census Industry Categories
Composing Economic Sectors

1960 Census code[a]	Number[b]	1960 Census code	Number	1960 Census code	Number	1960 Census code	Number
Competitive		658	164.980	269	168.184	257	0.73
17	8.015	659	985.330	276	173.597	258	0.70
18	30.098	666	208.243	286	252.211	259	1.31
156	86.845	676	308.967	287	84.799	267	0.62
206	199.037	678	83.013	289	17.290	268	2.86
207	364.242	679	35.210	296	285.089	269	93.36
208	103.248	686	37.271	306	273.537	296	2.31
209	400.065	687	102.194	307	250.216	318	1.34
346	65.233	689	407.775	308	159.097	319	1.44
347	70.553	696	8.933	309	130.544	349	1.45
348	42.781	806	97.400	316	265.294	359	0.62
349	405.685	807	753.366	317	37.296	387	1.49
356	46.426	808	595.856	318	227.921	398	10.90
359	293.833	809	355.023	319	130.211	409	5.63
367	54.125	816	124.055	326	5.032	426	0.74
396	270.116	826	319.308	329	38.808	429	0.74
398	548.647	828	240.528	386	283.903	506	10.41
436	36.529	829	2.994	387	204.184	507	153.02
437	107.740	836	18.124	389	155.608	508	1.88
438	28.922	838	213.082	406	60.526	516	0.68
459	11.978	839	84.397	407	115.204	517	11.58
507	139.943	846	181.523	408	66.750	518	3.70
508	112.183	848	59.984	409	766.427	526	16.76
509	992.333	849	176.192	416	224.861	536	5.19
516	102.435	896	255.203	419	26.798	538	0.74
517	182.841	897	125.353	426	215.438	567	72.84
519	12.871	898	88.339	429	178.409	568	9.6
526	50.339			506	664.100	569	8.9
536	115.644	Oligopoly		518	327.612	576	90.6
578	82.467	126	73.150	538	453.104	578	161.3
606	151.961	136	161.742	539	19.288	579	5.6
607	99.233	146	198.456	706	498.188	617	0.6
608	64.824	216	167.146	716	183.301	618	0.6
609	384.148	217	217.075	726	740.612	619	0.6
616	81.778	218	61.410	736	415.490	626	0.7
617	207.979	219	23.449	867	390.396	636	6.5
618	367.551	236	142.117	869	214.488	638	13.5
619	132.911	237	676.251			656	2.2
626	623.637	238	289.470	State		657	2.4
629	18.444	239	404.564	16	20.328	659	3.7
636	1276.682	246	121.915	17	42.239	678	14.8
637	15.346	247	459.124	18	4.059	679	0.6
638	755.818	248	869.997	196	548.931	687	1.4
639	62.536	249	0.737	206	0.813	689	2.8
646	160.234	256	176.892	207	0.686	706	16.2
647	84.415	257	300.642	208	0.675	716	0.6
648	270.033	258	1699.251	217	0.703	726	5.9
649	167.955	259	1397.209	246	0.648	736	35.0
656	1055.918	267	1136.259	247	1.427	807	6.3
657	707.654	268	832.005	248	42.333	808	1.7

1960 Census code	Number	1970 Census code ^{c}	Number	1970 Census code	Number	1970 Census code	Number
809	2.245	Competitive		617	195.116	889	715.301
828	2.905	27	48.700	618	214.621	897	413.575
836	0.667	28	141.595	619	344.281		
838	1.496	57	388.660	627	160.360	Oligopoly	
839	0.864	107	729.814	628	4474.289	47	422.767
846	1.542	108	1404.238	629	75.065	48	715.149
848	0.670	109	404.920	637	156.963	49	956.811
849	30.611	118	1500.607	638	296.707	119	585.551
867	70.912	307	312.472	639	2912.807	127	868.043
868	323.223	308	164.516	647	911.149	128	159.546
869	2.064	309	116.622	648	2619.366	137	88.707
876	2033.341	317	1187.696	649	372.987	138	442.833
879	27.749	318	173.502	657	629.959	139	2132.687
888	5.652	319	955.722	658	336.247	147	1309.753
896	0.708	327	230.592	667	1080.580	148	619.506
897	0.749	338	1128.360	668	726.585	149	801.386
898	14.087	339	2008.567	669	5187.926	157	406.394
906	721.107	388	73.026	677	732.925	158	1803.367
916	1122.772	389	324.545	678	291.735	159	324.607
926	418.494	397	81.367	679	464.294	167	520.487
936	971.998	398	30.589	687	199.111	168	1524.433
		408	569.019	688	335.514	169	2.667
Construction		409	445.836	689	170.322	177	365.883
196	4376.859	417	4327.922	697	1296.064	178	653.720
		418	455.374	698	32.903	179	1127.116
Farm		419	572.299	727	337.434	187	1093.590
16	2441.024	428	37.979	728	822.343	188	398.406
		429	245.014	729	332.385	189	666.377
Utility		447	415.644	737	191.095	197	3150.739
567	340.899	478	178.392	738	373.223	198	8.329
568	129.791	507	785.905	739	247.330	199	526.829
569	148.439	508	504.095	747	555.438	207	1423.152
576	24.391	509	224.440	748	1067.281	208	2894.586
579	4.874	527	1654.521	749	553.657	209	40.320
		528	341.976	757	1988.458	219	3700.008
Private Non-Profit		529	577.832	758	467.246	227	1872.387
868	340.486	537	449.296	759	927.814	228	833.040
876	545.821	538	0.824	769	483.208	229	184.705
879	403.030	539	2063.508	777	937.578	237	357.046
888	156.257	557	317.647	778	251.824	238	98.783
		558	556.229	779	650.529	239	433.171
		559	396.913	787	190.270	247	393.946
		567	326.588	788	410.623	248	343.984
		568	231.927	789	76.366	249	46.255
		569	447.079	797	2.031	257	5.314
		587	1054.170	798	456.611	258	565.933

(continued)

1960 Census code	Number	Competitive				Oligopoly	
		1970 Census code c	Number	1970 Census code	Number	1970 Census code	Number
		588	32.540	807	758.018	259	1135.743
		607	1199.931	808	200.797	268	1111.244
		608	821.662	809	881.231	269	714.030
		609	2507.175	888	1221.123	278	663.648

1970 Census code	Number	1970 Census code	Number	1970 Census code	Number	1970 Census code	Number
279	495.655	68	1941.001	447	13.009	777	1.285
287	813.676	69	15.071	448	7.609	778	5.082
288	170.997	107	0.847	467	290.873	779	2.594
289	809.469	109	1.417	468	90.771	788	1.250
297	514.993	127	2.572	469	15.470	807	9.251
298	18.212	138	0.765	477	409.289	808	3.709
299	189.262	139	1.596	478	706.864	809	183.866
328	985.844	147	1.672	479	35.484	828	2.446
329	544.156	158	0.840	508	0.714	829	0.855
337	659.371	167	2.656	527	0.330	838	1401.576
347	1270.861	168	0.751	558	0.866	839	130.206
348	313.847	178	0.657	559	0.818	848	369.808
349	237.795	179	0.870	567	0.635	849	4.131
357	454.790	189	0.653	587	0.790	857	5574.453
358	337.634	197	0.647	588	3.147	858	2607.941
359	287.738	207	0.866	607	1.544	859	87.340
367	249.725	208	3.660	608	0.868	867	180.945
368	332.549	219	0.654	609	3.109	868	0.833
369	94.705	227	3.946	618	0.691	869	51.810
377	671.903	228	221.150	627	31.762	877	1.519
378	95.868	258	80.887	628	46.771	878	421.512
379	919.526	259	16.490	629	0.757	879	36.872
387	789.315	268	2.769	638	0.416	888	3.134
407	2247.727	269	3.310	648	13.945	889	1.651
427	1156.194	278	0.704	649	0.828	897	195.238
448	2029.146	287	1.478	658	1.663	907	2224.139
449	147.468	307	0.779	669	16.167	917	3765.480
707	1608.965	308	0.287	677	2.701	927	1901.531
708	572.618	319	1.613	678	51.170	937	4455.148
709	604.843	328	1.170	679	0.794	Construction	
717	3007.831	338	1.518	688	0.645	67	6093.266
718	2312.053	339	46.504	697	23.810	68	2586.819
828	753.691	347	6.188	698	1.662	69	9268.746
829	375.059	359	0.781	707	14.415	77	752.417
837	60.573	367	8.070	708	47.571		
847	108.353	368	2.133	709	1.988	Farm	
848	333.679	377	1.478	717	19.694	17	7514.520
849	939.241	378	0.978	718	186.563	18	553.446
		379	0.877	727	0.735	19	559.894
State		387	2.274	728	2.639		
17	44.846	397	1.377	729	4.303	Utility	
18	11.596	398	8.433	737	3.923	467	1212.239
19	3.426	407	38.819	738	0.676	468	508.917
27	171.060	408	680.309	739	0.828	469	533.857
28	10.284	409	3.321	747	1.724	477	98.358
47	0.641	417	4.321	748	24.304	479	44.042
48	1.498	418	1.450	749	6.419		
49	2.123	419	53.381	757	3.342	Private Non-Profit	
57	0.731	427	46.537	758	0.524	838	1695.187
67	17.601	429	68.493	759	0.917		

(continued)

1970 Census code	Number
839	338.586
857	638.020
858	1248.133
859	13.855
867	220.663
868	3.541
869	54.341
877	1188.671
878	175.646
879	96.498
887	770.988

[a] Current Population Surveys for 1969 and 1970 used 1960 Census industry code

[b] Numbers represent the counts from the weighted and deflated sample.

[c] Current Population Surveys for 1971–1978 used 1970 Census industry codes.

References

Aiken, Michael, Louis A. Ferman, and Harold L. Sheppard
  1968   *Economic Failure, Alienation and Extremism.* Ann Arbor: University of Michigan
         Press.
Akhdar, Farouk
  1975   "Multinational firms and developing countries: A case study of the impact of the
         Arabian–American Oil Company (Aramco) on the development of the Saudi
         Arabian economy." Ph.D. dissertation, University of California, Riverside.
Alcaly, Roger E.
  1978   "An introduction to Marxian crisis theory." Pp. 15–22 in Union for Radical Political
         Economics (eds.), *U.S. Capitalism in Crisis.* New York: Union for Radical Political
         Economics.
Alexander, Arthur J.
  1974   "Income, experience, and the structure of internal labor markets." *Quarterly
         Journal of Economics* 88 (February): 63–85.
Althauser, Robert P., and Arne L. Kalleberg
  1981   "Firms, occupations, and the structure of labor markets: a conceptual analysis." Pp.
         119–149 in I. Berg (ed.), *Sociological Perspectives on Labor Markets.* New York:
         Academic Press.
Andrisani, Paul J.
  1973   "An empirical analysis of the dual market theory." Columbus: Ohio State
         University, Center for Human Resource Research.
Applebaum, Eileen
  1979   "The labor market." Pp. 100–119 in A. S. Eichner (ed.), *A guide to post-Keynesian
         economics.* White Plains, N.Y.: M.E. Sharpe.

Aronowitz, Stanley
1963   *Unionism and Relative Wages in the United States.* Chicago: University of Chicago Press.
1973   *False Promises: The Shaping of American Working-Class Consciousness.* New York: McGraw-Hill.
Averitt, Robert T.
1968   *The Dual Economy.* New York: W.W. Norton.
Baron, James N., and William T. Bielby
1980   "Bringing the firms back in." *American Sociological Review* 45 (October): 737–765.
Beck, E.M.
1980   "Labor unionism and racial inequality: A time-series analysis of the post-World War II period." *American Journal of Sociology* 85: 791–814.
Beck, E.M., Patrick M. Horan, and Charles M. Tolbert II
1978   "Stratification in a dual economy: A sectoral model of earnings determination." *American Sociological Review* 43 (October): 704–720.
Becker, Gary S.
1962   "Investment in Human Capital: a theoretical analysis." *Journal of Political Economy* 70 (Supplement, October): 9–49.
Berg, Ivar, Robert Bibb, T. Aldrich Finegan, and Michael Swafford
1981   "Toward model specification in the structural unemployment thesis: Issues and prospects." Pp. 347–367 in I. Berg (ed.), *Sociological Perspectives on Labor Markets.* New York: Academic Press.
Best, Fred
1981   "Short-time compensation and work sharing: Redistributing the hardships of unemployment." Unpublished paper, California Employment Development Department.
Bishop, Y.M.M., S.E. Fienberg, and P.W. Holland
1975   *Discrete Multivariate Analysis.* Cambridge: MIT Press.
Blair, John M.
1974   "Market power and inflation: A short-term target return model." *Journal of Economic Issues* 8: 453–478.
Bluestone, Barry
1970
        "The tripartite economy: Labor markets and the working poor." *Poverty and Human Resources Abstracts* (March–April): 14–35.
Bluestone, Barry, Peter Jordan, and Mark Sullivan
1981   *Aircraft Industry Dynamics: An Analysis of Competition, Capital and Labor.* Boston: Auburn House.
Bluestone, Barry, William Murphy, and Mary Stevenson
1973   "Low wages and the working poor." Ann Arbor: Institute of Labor and Industrial Relations, University of Michigan–Wayne State University. Mimeo.
Bluestone, Barry, and Mary Huff Stevenson
1980   "Industrial transformation and the evolution of dual labor markets: The case of retail trade in the United States." Unpublished paper, Boston College, Social Welfare Research Institute.
Boddy, Raford, and James Crotty
1975   "Class conflict and micro-policy." *Review of Radical Political Economics* 7, 1: 1–19.

Bolle, Michael
    1981   "The impact of shorter work time on unemployment. The case of West Germany and some implications for the U.S. labor market." Unpublished paper. Institute for Research on Poverty. University of Wisconsin, Madison.
Bowen, William G.
    1960   *Wage Behavior in the Postwar Period.* Princeton: Princeton University Industrial Relations Section.
Braverman, Harry
    1974   *Labor and Monopoly Capital.* New York: Monthly Review Press.
Brenner, M. Harvey
    1976   "Estimating the social costs of national economic policy: Implications for mental and physical health and criminal aggression." Volume 1—Employment, Paper No. 5 of Achieving the Goals of the Employment Act of 1946, Thirtieth Anniversary Review. Washington, D.C.: U.S. Government Printing Office.
Buchele, Robert
    1976   "Jobs and workers: A labor market segmentation perspective on the work experience of middle-aged men." Unpublished paper submitted to the Secretary of Labor's Conference on the National Longitudinal Survey of the Pre-Retirement Years, Boston.
Burawoy, Michael
    1978   "Toward a Marxist theory of the labor process: Braverman and beyond." *Politics and Society* 8: 247–312.
    1979   *Manufacturing Consent: Changes in the Labor Process Under Monopoly Capitalism.* Chicago: The University of Chicago Press.
Burns, Arthur F., and Wesley C. Mitchell
    1946   *Measuring Business Cycles.* New York: National Bureau of Economic Research.
Cagan, Phillip
    1975   "Inflation and market structure, 1967–1973." *Explorations in Economic Research* 2: 203–216.
Cain, Glen G.
    1966   *Married Women in the Labor Force.* Chicago: University of Chicago Press.
    1976   "The challenge of segmented labor market theory to orthodox theory." *Journal of Economic Literature* 14 (December): 1215–1257.
Castells, Manuel
    1980   *The Economic Crisis and American Society.* Princeton: Princeton University Press.
Clark, Kim B., and Richard B. Freeman
    1980   "How elastic is the demand for labor?" *Review of Economics and Statistics* 62: 509–520.
Clark, Kim B., and Lawrence H. Summers
    1979   "Labor market dynamics and unemployment: A reconsideration." *Brookings Papers on Economic Activity* 1:13–60.
Cohn, Richard M.
    1977   "The consequences of unemployment on evaluations of self." Unpublished Ph.D dissertation, University of Michigan.
Commons, John R.
    1918–   *The History of Labor in the United States.* New York: Macmillan.
    1935
Corcoran, Mary, and Martha S. Hill

1979   "The incidence and consequences of short- and long-run unemployment." Pp. 1–64
        in G.J. Duncan and J.N. Morgan (eds.), *Five Thousand Families—Patterns of
        Economic Progress,* Vol. VII. Ann Arbor: Institute for Social Research.
1980   "Persistence in unemployment among adult men." Pp. 39–71 in G.J. Duncan and
        J.N. Morgan (eds.), *Five Thousand Families—Patterns of Economic Progress,* Vol.
        VIII. Ann Arbor: Institute for Social Research.
Cornfield, Daniel B.
1980   "Layoffs: An inquiry into the social causes of separations from the firm." Ph.D.
        dissertation, University of Chicago.
1981   "Industrial social organization and layoffs in American manufacturing industry." Pp.
        219–248 in Ivar Berg (ed.), *Sociological Perspectives on Labor Markets.* New
        York: Academic Press.
Daymont, Thomas N., and Robert L. Kaufman
1977   "Interpreting parameters in log-linear models: An application to industrial variation
        in racial discrimination." *Center for Demography and Ecology Working Paper* 77–
        25, University of Wisconsin, Madison.
1979   "Measuring industrial variation in racial discrimination using log-linear models."
        Social Science Research 8: 41–62.
Dobb, Maurice
1945   *Political Economy and Capitalism.* New York: International Publishers.
Doeringer, Peter B., and Michael J. Piore
1971
        Internal Labor Markets and Manpower Analysis. Lexington, Mass.: Heath
        Lexington Books.
1975   "Unemployment and the 'dual labor market.' " *Public Interest* 38 (Winter): 67–
        79.
Doeringer, Peter B., Michael J. Piore, Penny H. Feldman, David M. Gordon, and
Michael Reich
1972   "Low income labor markets and urban manpower programs: A critical assessment."
        Research and Development Findings, No. 12. Washington, D.C.: U.S. Department
        of Labor, Manpower Administration.
Dornbusch, Rudiger, and Stanley Fischer
1978   *Macro-Economics.* New York: McGraw-Hill.
Edwards, Richard C.
1972   "Alienation and inequality: Social relations in the capitalist firm." Unpublished
        Ph.D. dissertation. Harvard University.
1975   "The impact of industrial concentration on the economic crisis." Pp. 213–222 in
        David Mermelstein (ed.), *The Economic Crisis Reader.* New York: Basic Books.
1979   *Contested Terrain: The Transformation of the Workplace in the Twentieth
        Century.* New York: Basic Books.
Edwards, Richard C., Michael Reich, and David M. Gordon
1975   *Labor Market Segmentation.* Lexington, Mass.: D.C. Heath.
Eichner, Alfred S.
1973   "A theory of the determination of mark-up under oligopoly." *The Economic Journal*
        83: 294.
1976   *The Megacorp and Oligopoly.* Cambridge: Cambridge University Press.
Federal Trade Commission
1970–   *Quarterly Financial Reports of Manufacturing Corporations* (4th quarter 1970
1975   through 2nd quarter 1975). Washington D.C.: U.S. Government Printing Office.
Feinberg, Robert M.

1979   "Market structure and employment instability." *Review of Economics and Statistics*
        59: 497–505.
Feldstein, Martin S.
1973   "Lowering the permanent rate of unemployment." A Study Prepared for the Use of
        the Joint Economic Committee, 93 Congress, 1st Session.
1975   "The importance of temporary layoffs: An empirical analysis." *Brookings Papers on
        Economic Activity* 3: 725–744.
1976   "Temporary layoffs in the theory of unemployment. *Journal of Political Economy*
        84: 937–958.
Fellner, William
1951   "The capital–output ratio" in *Money, Trade, and Economic Growth*: Essays in
        Honor of John Henry Williams. New York: Macmillan.
Ferman, Louis A.
1964   "Sociological perspectives in unemployment research." Pp. 504–514 in A. Shosak
        and W. Comberg (eds.), *Blue Collar World: Studies of the American Worker*. New
        York: Prentice-Hall.
Fienberg, Stephen E.
1977
        The Analysis of Cross-Classified Categorical Data. Cambridge: MIT Press.
Freeman, Richard B., and James L. Medoff
1979   "New estimates of private sector unionism in the United States." *Industrial and
        Labor Relations Review* 32: 143–174.
Galbraith, John K.
1967   *The New Industrial State*. Boston: Houghton Mifflin.
Glyn, Andrew and Bob Sutcliffe
1972   *British Capitalism, Workers, and the Profit Squeeze*. Baltimore: Penguin Books.
Goodman, Leo A.
1972   "A modified multiple regression approach to the analysis of dichotomous variables."
        American Sociological Review 37 (February): 28–46.
Gordon, David M.
1971   "Class, productivity and the ghetto: A study of labor market stratification."
        Unpublished Ph.D. dissertation. Harvard University.
1972   *Theories of Poverty and Underemployment*. Lexington, Mass.: D.C. Heath.
1978   "Up and down the long roller coaster." Pp. 22–35 in Union for Radical Political
        Economics (eds.), *U.S. Capitalism in Crisis*. New York: Union for Radical Political
        Economics.
1980   "Stages of accumulation and long economic cycles." Pp. 9–45 in Terrence Hopkins
        and Immanuel Wsllerstein (eds.), *Processes of the World System*. Beverly Hills,
        Calif.: Sage Publications.
Gordon, David M., Richard Edwards, and Michael Reich
1982   *Segmented Work, Divided Workers: The Historical Transformation of Labor in
        the United States*. Cambridge: Cambridge University Press.
Granovetter, Mark
1981   "Toward a sociological theory of income differences." Pp. 11–47 in I. Berg (ed.),
        Sociological Perspectives on Labor Markets. New York: Academic Press.
Hall, Robert E.
1970a   "Recent increases in unemployment." *Brookings Papers on Economic Activity* 1:
        147–150.
1970b   "Why is the unemployment rate so high at full employment? *Brookings Papers on
        Economic Activity* 3: 369–402.

1972   "Turnover in the labor force." *Brookings Papers on Economic Activity* 3:709–
        756.
1975   "The rigidity of the wages and the persistence of the unemployment." *Brookings
        Papers on Economic Activity* 2: 301–335.
Hamermesh, Daniel S.
1976   "Econometric studies of labor demand and their application to policy analysis."
        Journal of Human Resources 11: 507–525.
Harrison, Bennett
1972a   *Education, Training, and the Urban Ghetto.* Baltimore: The Johns Hopkins
        University Press.

1972b   "Education and underemployment in the urban ghetto." *American Economic
        Review.* 62: 796–812.
1975   "Inflation by oligopoly: Two case histories." *The Nation* (August 30).
Hauser, Robert M., and David L. Featherman.
1977   *The Process of Stratification: Trends and Analysis.* New York: Academic Press.
1978   *Opportunity and Change.* New York: Academic Press.
Haveman, Robert H., and Frederick L. Golladay
1976   *The Economic Impacts of Tax-Transfer Policy.* New York: Academic Press.
Hicks, J.R.
1950   *The Trade Cycle.* New York: Oxford University Press.
Hobson, John A.
1922   *Economics of Unemployment.* London: G. Allen and Unwin.
1930   *Rationalisation and Unemployment.* London: G. Allen and Unwin.
Hodson, Randy
1978   "Labor in the monopoly, competitive, and state sectors of production." *Politics and
        Society* 8: 429–480.
1980   "The social impact of industrial structure on working conditions." Unpublished
        Ph.D. dissertation, University of Wisconsin, Madison.
Hodson, Randy, Paul G. Schervish, Robin Stryker, and Glenn Yago
1980   "Defining the class structure: Fractions and social categories." Presented at the 75th
        annual convention of the American Sociological Association, New York, September
        1980.
Jacobs, Paul
1965   "A view from the other side: Unemployment as part of identity." Pp. 45–63 in W.G.
        Bowen and F.H. Harbinson (eds.), *Unemployment in a Prosperous Economy.*
        Princeton: The Industrial Relations Sections, Woodrow Wilson School of Public and
        International Affairs.
Kalecki, Michal
1943   *Studies in Economic Dynamics.* Winchester, Mass.: Allen and Unwin.
1954   *Theory of Economic Dynamics, An Essay on Cyclical and Long-Run Changes in
        Capitalist Economy.* New York: Reinhart.
Kalleberg, Arne L. and Larry Griffin
1980   "Class, occupation, and inequality in job rewards." *American Journal of Sociology*
        85: 731–768.
Kalleberg, Arne L., and Aage B. Sørensen
1979   "The sociology of labor markets." *Annual Review of Sociology* 5: 351–379.
Kalleberg, Arne L., Michael Wallace, and Robert P. Althauser

1981   "Economic segmentation, worker power, and income inequality." *American Journal of Sociology* 87: 651–683.
Kaufman, Robert L.
1981   "Racial discrimination and segmented labor markets." Ph.D. dissertation, University of Wisconsin, Madison.
Kaufman, Robert L., Randy Hodson, and Neil D. Fligstein
1981   "Defrocking dualism: A new approach to defining industrial structure." *Social Science Research* 1: 225–255.
Kenyon, Peter
1979   "Pricing." Pp. 34–45 in A. S. Eichner (ed.), *A Guide to Post-Keynesian Economics*. White Plains, N.Y.: M.E. Sharpe.
Kerr, Clark
1950   "Labor markets: Their character and consequences." *American Economic Review* 40: 278–291.
1954   "The Balkanization of labor markets." Pp. 92–110 in E. Wright Bakke, P.M. Hauser, G.L. Palmer, C.A. Myers, D. Yoder, and C. Kerr (eds), *Labor Mobility and Economic Opportunity*. Cambridge: MIT Press.
Keynes, John Maynard
1936   *The General Theory of Employment, Interest, and Money*. New York: Harcourt, Brace and World.
Killingsworth, Charles C.
1974   "Unemployment: A fresh perspective." Pp. 97–102 in L.G. Reynolds, S.H. Masters, and C. Moser (eds.), *Readings in Labor Economics and Labor Relations*. Englewood Cliffs: Prentice-Hall. A prepared statement before the Joint Committee, August 6, 1971, U.S. Congress.
Killingsworth, Charles C. and Christopher T. King
1977   "Tax cuts and employment policy." Pp. 1–33 in R. Taggart (ed.), *Job Creation: What Works?* Salt Lake City: Olympus.
Komarovsky, Mirra
1940   *The Unemployed Man and His Family*. New York: Dryden Press.
Kondratieff, Nikolai D.
1935   "The long wages in economic life." *Review of Economic Statistics* 17:105–115.
Lanzillotti, Robert
1959   "Testimony before the Joint Economic Committee of the U.S. Congress." *Employment, Growth and Price Levels* 2:2237–2262. Washington, D.C.: U.S. Government Printing Office.
Leigh, Duane E.
1978   *An Analysis of the Determinants of Occupational Upgrading*. New York: Academic Press.
Levitan, Sar A., and Robert Taggart III
1974   Employment and Earnings Inadequacy. Baltimore: Johns Hopkins University Press.
Lewis, H. Gregg
1963   *Unionism and Relative Wages in the United States*. Chicago: University of Chicago Press.
Liebow, Elliot
1967   *Tally's Corner*. Boston: Little, Brown.
Lillien, David M.

1977   *Politics and Markets.* New York: Basic Books.
Lindblom, Charles E.
1977   *Politics and Markets.* New York: Basic Books.
Lippman, S., and J.J. McCall
1976   "The economics of job search: A survey." *Economic Inquiry* 14: 155–189.
Lowell, Ruth Fabricant
1973   "The dual labor market in New York City." Paper presented at Human Resources Administration's Welfare Conference, New York, December 1.
Marston, Stephen T.
1975   "The impact of unemployment insurance on job search." *Brookings Papers on Economic Activity* 1: 13–48.
Marx, Karl
1967   *Capital.* Frederick Engels (ed.). Trans. Samuel Moore and Edward Aveling. New York: International Publishers.
Means, Gardiner C.
1935   "Industrial prices and their relative inflexibility" U.S. Senate Document 13, 74th Congress, 1st Session, Washington, D.C.
1962   *Steel Prices and Administered Inflation.* New York: Harper.
Medoff, James L.
1979   "Layoffs and alternatives under trade unions in U.S. manufacturing." *American Economic Review* 69:380–95
Mincer, Jacob
1962   "On-the-job training: Costs, returns, and some implications." *Journal of Political Economy* 70,5 (Part 2: Supplement): 50–79.
1963   "Labor force participation of married women." Pp. 63–97 in *Aspects of Labor Economics,* National Bureau of Economic Research, New York.
Moore, Geoffrey H.
1980   *Business Cycles, Inflation, and Forecasting.* Cambridge, Mass.: National Bureau of Economic Research.
Morgan, Dan
1979   *Merchants of Grain.* New York: Viking.
MRPIS: Multi-Regional Policy Impact Simulation
1981   *Literature Review,* Social Welfare Research Institute, Boston College.
Mueller, Willard F.
1972   "Monopoly and the inflation–unemployment dilemma: Trustbusting or administrative 'controls'?" *Antitrust Law and Economics Review* 5, 4: 15–34.
1974   "Industrial concentration: An important inflationary force." Pp. 280–306 in H.J. Goldschmid, H.M. Mann, J.F. Weston (eds.), *Industrial Concentration: The New Learning.* Boston: Little, Brown.
NACLA (North American Congress on Latin America)
1975   "The reserve army of labor" and other essays. NACLA's *Latin America and Empire Report* IX, 5: 2–15.
Niemi, Bess
1975   "Geographic immobility and labor force mobility: A study of female unemployment." Pp. 61–89 in C.B. Lloyd (ed.), *Sex, Discrimination, and the Division of Labor.* New York: Columbia University Press.
Nadiri, Ishaq, and Sherwin Rosen
1973   *A Disequilibrium Model of the Demand for Factors of Production.* New York: National Bureau of Economic Research.
Norris, G. M.
1978   "Unemployment, subemployment and personal characteristics." *The Sociological*

Review Part 1, 26: 89–108; Part 2, 26, 2: 327–348

O'Connor, James
1973   *The Fiscal Crisis of the State.* New York: St. Martin's.

Oi, Walter
1962   "Labor as a quasi-fixed factor." *Journal of Political Economy* 70: 538–555.

Okun, Arthur M.
1962   "Potential GNP: Its measurement and significance." *Proceedings of the Business and Economic Statistics Section,* American Statistical Association: 98–104.
1973   "Upward mobility in a high-pressure economy." *Brookings Papers on Economic Activity* 1: 207–252.
1975   "Inflation: Its mechanics and welfare costs." *Brookings Papers on Economic Activity* 1: 351–390.
1975   "Conflicting national goals." Pp. 59–84 in E. Ginzberg (ed.), *Jobs for Americans.* Englewood Cliffs: Prentice-Hall.

Osterman, Paul
1975   "An empirical study of labor market segmentation." *Industrial and Labor Relations Review* 28: 508–523.
1980   *Getting Started: The Youth Labor Market.* Cambridge: MIT Press.

Page, William F.
1977   "Interpretation of Goodman's log-linear model effects: An odds ratio approach." *Sociological Methods and Research* 5: 419–435.

Parsons, Donald O.
1972   "Specific human capital: An application to quit rates and layoff rates." *Journal of Political Economy* 80: 1120–1143.

Pasinetti, Luigi
1974   *Growth and Income Distribution.* Cambridge: Cambridge University Press.

Perlman, Selig
1928   *A Theory of the Labor Movement.* New York: Macmillan.

Perry, George L.
1972   "Unemployment flows in the U.S. labor market." *Brookings Papers on Economic Activity* 2: 245–278.

Pigou, Arthur C.
1943   "The classical stationary state." *Economic Journal* 53: 343–351.

Piore, Michael J.
1970   "Jobs and training." Pp. 53–83 in S. Beer and R. Barringer (eds.), *The State and the Poor.* Cambridge, Mass.: Winthrop.
1971   "The dual labor market: Theory and implications." Pp. 90–94 in D.M. Gordon (ed.), *Problems in Political Economy: An Urban Perspective.* Lexington, Mass.: D.C. Heath.
1972–   "Notes for a theory of labor market stratification." The Center for Educational
1975   Policy Research, Havard Graduate School of Education. Cambridge, Mass. October 1972. Mimeo. Also in R.C. Edwards, M. Reich, and D.M. Gordon (eds.) *Labor Market Segmentation.* Lexington: D.C. Heath. 1975.

Poulantzas, Nicos
1975   *Classes in Contemporary Capitalism.* London: New Left Books.

Przeworski, Adam
1977   "The process of class formation from Karl Kautsky's *The Class Struggle* to recent debates." *Politics and Society* 7: 343–403.

Rees, Albert
1966   "Labor economics: Effects of more knowledge—information networks in labor markets." *American Economic Review* 56: 559–566.

1973   *The Economics of Work and Pay*. New York: Harper and Row.
Reich, Michael
1973   "Racial discrimination and the white income distribution." Unpublished Ph.D. dissertation, Harvard University.
1980   "The persistence of racial inequality in urban areas and industries, 1950–1970." *American Economic Review* 70: 1229–1231.
Reich, Michael, David M. Gordon, and Richard C. Edwards
1973   "A theory of labor market segmentation." *American Economic Review* 63: 359–365.
Robinns, William
1974   *The American Food Scandal*. New York: Morrow.
Robinson, Joan
1969   *The Economics of Imperfect Competition*. New York: St. Martin's.
[1933]
Robinson, Joan, and John Eatwell
1974   *An Introduction to Modern Economics*. J.R. Crutchfield (ed.) New York: McGraw-Hill.
Rosenberg, Samuel
1975   "The dual labor market: Its existence and consequences." Unpublished Ph.D. thesis, University of California, Berkeley.
1980   "Male occupational standing and the dual labor market." *Industrial Relations* 19:34–49.
Ross, Stephen A., and Michael Wachter
1973   "Wage determination, inflation, and the industrial structure." *American Economic Review* 63: 675–692.
Samuelson, Paul
1939   "Interactions between the multiplier analysis and the principle of acceleration." *Review of Economic Statistics* 21: 75–78.
Scherer, F.M.
1980   *Industrial Market Structure and Economic Performance*, 2nd ed. Chicago: Rand McNally.
Schervish, Paul G.
1977   "A theory of the social relations of unemployment." *The Peninsular Papers* 2, 2:1–14.
1981   "The structure of employment and unemployment." Pp. 153–186 in I. Berg (ed.), *Sociological Perspectives on Labor Markets*. New York: Academic Press.
Shaikh, Anwar
1978   "An introduction to the history of crisis theories." Pp. 219–240 in *Union for Radical Political Economics, U.S. Capitalism in Crisis*. New York: distributed by Monthly Review Press.
Shepherd, William
1970   *Market Power and Economic Welfare*. New York: Random House.
Sherman, Howard J.
1968   *Profits in the United States: An Introduction to a Study of Economic Concentration and Business Cycles*. Ithaca: Cornell University Press.
1976   *Stagflation: A Radical Theory of Unemployment and Inflation*. New York: Harper and Row.
1979   "A Marxist theory of the business cycle." *Review of Radical Political Economics* 11: 1–23.
Sørensen, Aage B.

1977   "The structure of inequality and the process of attainment." *American Sociological Review* 42:965–978.

1979   "A model and a metric of the analysis of intragenerational status attainment process." *American Journal of Sociology* 85: 361–384.

Sørensen, Aage B., and Arne L. Kalleberg

1981   "An outline of a theory for the matching of persons to jobs." Pp. 49–74 in I. Berg (ed.), *Sociological Perspectives on Labor Markets*. New York: Academic Press.

Stafford, Frank

1968   "Concentration and labor earnings: Comment." *American Economic Review* 58: 174–181.

Stevens, Gillian

1977   "Women's intergenerational occupational mobility: A new perspective." M.A. thesis, Carleton University.

Stigler, George J.

1961   "The economics of information." *Journal of Political Economy* 69: 213–225.

1962   "Information in the labor market." *Journal of Political Economy* 50, 5 (Part 2: Supplement, October): 94–105.

Stigler, George J., and James K. Kindahl

1970   *The Behavior of Industrial Prices*. New York: Columbia University Press.

Stolzenberg, Ross M.

1975   "Occupations, labor markets and the process of wage attainment." *American Sociological Review* 40: 645–665.

Sweezy, Paul

1958   *Theory of Capitalist Development*. New York: Monthly Review Press.
[1942]

Thurow, Lester C.

1975   *Generating Inequality*. New York: Basic Books.

1978   "For wage subsidies to help fight unemployment." *The New York Times* 10 January.

1980   *The Zero-Sum Society*. New York: Basic Books.

Tiffany, Donald W., James R. Cowan, and Phyllis M. Tiffany

1970   *The Unemployed: A Social Psychological Portrait*. Englewood Cliffs: Prentice-Hall.

U.S. Department of Commerce

        Business Conditions Digest. Washington, D.C.: U.S. Government Printing Office.

U.S. Department of Labor

1961   *Wholesale Prices and Price Index* (April). Washington, D.C.: U.S. Government Printing Office.

1975   *Wholesale Prices and Price Index* (August). Washington, D.C.: U.S. Government Printing Office.

U.S. Department of Labor, Bureau of Employment Security

1965   *Dictionary of Occupational Titles* Volumes 1 and 2. Washington, D.C.: U.S. Government Printing Office.

von Hayek, Friedrich A.

1933   *Monetary Theory and the Trade Cycle*. New York: Harcourt Brace Jovanovich.

Wachtel, Howard M., and Charles Betsey

1972   "Employment at low wages." *Review of Economics and Statistics* 54 (May): 121–129.

Wachter, Michael L.

1974   "Primary and secondary labor markets: A critique of the dual approach." *Brookings Papers on Economic Activity* 3: 637–680.
Wallace, Michael, and Arne L. Kalleberg
1981   "Economic organization of firms and labor market consequences: toward a specification of dual economy theory." Pp. 77–117 in I. Berg (ed.), *Sociological Perspectives on Labor Markets*. New York: Academic Press.
1982   "Industrial transformation and decline of craft: The decomposition of skill in the printing industry, 1931–1978." *American Sociological Review* 47: 307–324.
Watts, Harold W., and Albert Rees (eds.)
1977   *The New Jersey Income Maintenance Experiment: Volume II, Labor Supply Response*. New York: Academic Press.
Weintraub, Sidney
1978   *Capitalism's Inflation and Unemployment Crisis*. Reading, Mass.: Addison-Welsey.
Weisbrod, Burton, A.
1977   "The private non-profit sector: what is it? *Institute for Research on Poverty Discussion Paper* 416–477, University of Wisconsin, Madison.
Weisbrod, Burton, A., and Stephen H. Long
1977   "The size of the voluntary nonprofit sector: Concepts and measures." Research Papers, Sponsored by the Commission on Private Philanthropy and Public Needs. Volume I: *History, Trends, and Current Magnitudes*. Department of the Treasury 339–364.
Weiss, Leonard W.
1963   "Factors in changing concentration." *Review of Economics and Statistics* 45: 70–77.
1966a   "Concentration and labor earnings." *American Economic Review* 56: 96–117.
1966b   "Business pricing policies and inflation reconsidered." *Journal of Political Economy* 74: 177–187.
1968   "Concentration and labor earnings: A reply." *American Economic Review* 58: 181–184.
1970   "The role of concentration in recent inflation." Appendix to testimony of Richard W. McLaren in the 1970 Midyear Review of the State of the Economy, Hearings Before the Joint Economic Committee, 91st Congress, 2nd Session, part 1.
1977   "Stigler, Kindahl, and Means on administered prices." *American Economic Review* 67: 610–619.
Weisskopf, Thomas E.
1978   "Marxist perspectives on cyclical crises." Pp. 241–260 in Union for Radical Political Economics (eds.), *U.S. Capitalism in Crisis*. New York: Union for Radical Political Economics.
1981   "The current economic crisis in historical perspective." *Socialist Review* 11: 9–53.
Weston, J. Fred, and Steven H. Lustgarten
1974   "Concentration and wage–price changes." Pp. 307–332 in H.J. Goldschmid, H.M. Mann, and J.F. Weston (eds.), *Industrial Concentration: The New Learning*. Boston: Little, Brown.
White, Harrison C.
1970   *Chains of Opportunity: System Models of Mobility in Organizations*. Cambridge: Harvard University Press.
Wilcock, Richard C., and Walter H. Granke
1974   *Unwanted Workers*. Toronto: The Free Press.

Wright, Erik Olin
  1978   *Class, Crisis and the State*. London: New Left Books.
  1979   *Class Structure and Income Determination*. New York: Academic Press.
  1980   "Class and occupation." *Politics and Society* 9:177–214.
Wright, Erik Olin, and Luca Perrone
  1977   "Marxist class categories and income inequality." *American Sociological Review*
          42: 32–55.
Yaffe, David
  1973   "The crisis of profitability: A critique of the Glyn–Sutcliffe thesis." *New Left Review*
          80: 45–62.
Zwerdling, Daniel
  1979   "The food monopolies." Pp. 41–50 in J.H. Skolnick and E. Currie (eds.), *Crisis in*
  [1974] *American Institutions*. Boston: Little, Brown.

Subject Index

A

Administered pricing
  and employment instability, 116, 118,
    119, 122–124, 130, 146–147,
    169–172, 179–182, 186–188
  and inflation, 168–169, 186–188
  and oligoply behavior, 42–43, 118–119,
    122–124, 164n, 166–171, 179–182,
    186–188
  and recession, 167, 179–182
Age, 6–7, 70, 75, 140–144, 147, 194

B

Business cycle
  definition, 43–44, 149–150
  independent contribution, 154–155, 158t
  indicators of, 186–187
  interaction with economic sector, 7,
    43–44, 45, 75, 148–149, 164–185,
    186–188, 195–196
  operationalization of, 150

relation to unemployment, 4–7, 45, 149,
    151–164, 164–182, 185, 194–195
  relation to unemployment types, 154,
    159–164, 171–172, 182–185, 186–188
  source of vulnerability and power, 4–7,
    34–35, 36–39, 164–172, 186–188,
    195–196
  as structural determinant, 5–7, 36–37,
    43–44, 75, 148–153, 155, 194
  theory, 151–153, 164–171
Business sector, 11–14, 45

C

Capitalism, 15, 17–18, 36–44, 113,
    151–153, 186–188, 192–193
Chronic immobility, 21–22
Class fraction, *see* Class segment
Class segment, *see also* specific class
    segment
  in advanced capitalism, 39–41, 79–80,
    110

237

QUANTITATIVE STUDIES IN SOCIAL RELATIONS

Michael D. Ornstein, ENTRY INTO THE AMERICAN LABOR FORCE

Carl A. Bennett and Arthur A. Lumsdaine (Eds.), EVALUATION AND EX-
PERIMENT: *Some Critical Issues in Assessing Social Programs*

*H. M. Blalock, A. Aganbegian, F. M. Borodkin, Raymond Boudon, and Vit-
torio Capecchi (Eds.),* QUANTITATIVE SOCIOLOGY: *International Perspectives on Mathematical and Statistical Modeling*

N. J. Demerath, III, Otto Larsen, and Karl F. Schuessler (Eds.), SOCIAL
POLICY AND SOCIOLOGY

Henry W. Riecken and Robert F. Boruch (Eds.), SOCIAL EXPERIMENTA-
TION: *A Method for Planning and Evaluating Social Intervention*

Arthur S. Goldberger and Otis Dudley Duncan (Eds.), STRUCTURAL
EQUATION MODELS IN THE SOCIAL SCIENCES

Robert B. Tapp, RELIGION AMONG THE UNITARIAN UNIVERSAL-
ISTS: *Converts in the Stepfathers' House*

Kent S. Miller and Ralph Mason Dreger (Eds.), COMPARATIVE STUDIES
OF BLACKS AND WHITES IN THE UNITED STATES

Douglas T. Hall and Benjamin Schneider, ORGANIZATIONAL CLIMATES
AND CAREERS: *The Work Lives of Priests*

Robert L. Crain and Carol S. Weisman, DISCRIMINATION, PERSON-
ALITY, AND ACHIEVEMENT: *A Survey of Northern Blacks*

Roger N. Shepard, A. Kimball Romney, and Sara Beth Nerlove (Eds.),
MULTIDIMENSIONAL SCALING: *Theory and Applications in the Behavioral Sciences,* Volume I — Theory; Volume II — Applications

Peter H. Rossi and Walter Williams (Eds.), EVALUATING SOCIAL PRO-
GRAMS: *Theory, Practice, and Politics*

B2